WINNING THE FUTURE

WINNING THE FUTURE

ROBERT ARNOLD RUSSEL

Carroll & Graf Publishers, inc.
New York

First Carroll & Graf edition 1986

Carroll & Graf Publishers, Inc.
260 Fifth Avenue
New York, NY 10001

Library of Congress Cataloging-in-Publication Data

Russel, Robert Arnold, 1927–
  Winning the future.

  1. Finance, Personal.   I. Title.
HG179.R823 1986   332.024   86-1014
ISBN 0-88184-191-9

Manufactured in the United States of America

TABLE OF CONTENTS

TO FERNAND BRAUDEL

Even before his death in 1985, it was recognized that Fernand Braudel, the French economic historian, ws one of the great minds of our time. He challenged historians to look to the details of everyday life, the account books of shopkeepers and merchants, for clues to the forces which ruled history. He demonstrated to his aristocratic colleagues how strongly history was governed by economic forces, how little by popes and princes. He helped academic specialists understand the broad sweep of European history, and the surrounding civilizations which Europe so forcefully influenced. He explained the mechanisms of the economy with scientific clarity: the functioning of markets and fairs, of long-distance trade, of banks, warehouses and exchanges, and of the mountain of paper upon which trade and wealth is based.

His last great work, the three volume history of the commercial age in the West, completed in the summer of 1979 and translated into English in the early eighties, demonstrated all these qualities. But he left us one last challenge. In the concluding pages of the final volume, he directed his successors to study the great tidal movements of growth and slowdown, not merely to chart their course, but to find the underlying causes of these centuries-long secular trends.

"Is it really possible to believe that human history obeys all-commanding rhythms which ordinary logic cannot explain?" he asked at the end of his career. "I am inclined to answer yes" was his reply. "I believe in these tidal movements which seem to govern the physical and economic history of the world, even if the [events] which trigger them off . . . remain a mystery.''

And if our present difficulties are more than the downward slope of a Kondriatieff cycle, he asked, if we are indeed embarking upon a much longer slide, then are not the day-to-day remedies proposed to meet the crisis completely illusory?

If he were starting anew, Braudel said he would seek to unravel the ''long sequence of secular cycles in the past,'' in the name of history and with the goal of understanding the economic maelstrom in which we find ourselves. This book is undertaken in that spirit. It is dedicated to the living tradition of Fernand Braudel.

Robert Arnold Russel
Toronto, March 1986

PART ONE

ABOUT ECONOMIC REVOLUTIONS

Chapter 1
THE ECONOMY AS NATURAL FORCE

This is a book about the economy. It proposes that

1. The economy is a dynamic, natural force;
2. It progresses through predetermined stages initiated by well-defined periods called economic revolutions;
3. These stages are marked by radical restructuring of our values, institutions, and means of creating wealth;
4. These stages are cumulative; the older economic systems are not replaced, they are modified and enriched as the new system starts to drive the economy;
5. Understanding this process provides a new basis for forecasting, goal setting, and strategy development.

There has to be a good reason to change our formal economic systems. The reason is, we have no choice. The classic system no longer describes the way the economy operates, it does not predict what the economy will do next, it does not conform to the currently held values of the majority of people, and it does not prescribe effective action. While most of us occupy our lives working with and consuming information, it is concerned exclusively with the production, distribution and consumption of physical things. While we are concerned with quality, it knows only quantity. It served its time, but that time is past. Now it must be replaced or transformed.

I am all in favor of evolutionary change. Much of the problem with the present formal system arises because it abandoned the economic wisdom and intangible values of the past. Yet its contributions are enormous. I propose that we put it in perspective, restore what has been lost, and add new dimensions which will allow us to measure and trade those intangibles with which we are so preoccupied.

The formal economic system I envision will evaluate and reward more if not all dimensions of our lives, activities, and resources, including our environment, human capital, cultural achievements, and unique ethnic or regional qualities. It will be developmental in nature, seeking growth in favor of immediate returns, and sharing the risks as well as the rewards of entrepreneurial creation. It will be expansionist, seeking the improvement of the global economy.

This formal economic system can only evolve to the extent that we understand and agree on the nature and direction of the turbulent changes taking place in the natural economy. This means studying economic revolution, those periods when the natural economy and the formal system undergo a major restructuring.

I believe that a study of economic revolution can provide us with clues not only to the nature of the changes currently taking place, but also to the society we will become when this revolution plays itself out. I believe it will provide a timetable of these changes. Its most important contribution will be a growing awareness that we are undergoing not a senseless buffeting but a meaningful transformation to a richer and more prosperous stage in our evolution.

Such an understanding could inform the political process. We could see where our cities will go, and our schools. We could understand what will happen to our factories and our jobs. We could plan our collective investments, the restructuring of our institutions, and the kind of government needed to carry these things out.

On the economic level, this understanding can be enormously productive. There is so much latent demand, so many new ventures proposed, so much that needs to be done, and yet so little skill within the business community to evaluate innovative proposals. As the businessman discerns what businesses to build, the kind of human capital to be invested, and the structures required to maximize growth, then all our opportunities will expand.

Personally, this enriched vision of the new economy can guide our careers, show us where to place our loyalties, how to advise and prepare our children, how and where to build our homes, and above all how to invest in our own human capital.

This understanding will not be carried on the back of a few slogans or catchwords. It will require a change in perspective in the way we see the world and our place in it. I believe it can come through an understanding of the nature of economic revolution, that great fifty-year shift in values and opportunities presently underway. The deeper that understanding, the richer can be the vision of things to come. So take a deep breath, open your mind to the sweep of civilizations, and follow me into the past.

Classic civilizations, such as the Egyptian, Chinese, Islamic, Greek and Roman, all reached the commercial stage in their development before their brilliance dimmed. Two centures ago the West passed beyond its own brilliant commercial economy into an Industrial Age, the first civilization in human history to break this barrier. Now a further transformation is restructuring Western civilization into something profoundly different from and categorically more advanced than the Industrial Age we are rapidly leaving behind.

This transformation is characterized by postmechanical (or high) technology, automation of work, digitization of information and proliferation of networks, commercialization of services (many of which had been offered "free" by government in the previous age), and globalization of values.

These changes are seen by some as catastrophic, depriving them of much that fortune has given them and all they have worked to earn. Others more open to change see it as a joyous period of great opportunity in which the fish jump right into the boat. If we have already forgotten the emotion aroused in 1969 by the first human step on the moon, we may still have choked up in 1983 as paraplegic Nan Davis, aided by a computer bypassing the break in her spine, took five steps to the podium to receive her college degree."What hath God wrought?" indeed. It is we who have done these things: exuberant human spirits writing miracles on tiny silicon chips as our ancestors once wrote books.

With the proliferation of knowledge come larger overviews. As details pile up, we decipher the mechanics of the universe and the periodic pattern of the elements. We decode the evolution of the species and the workings of genes. We determine how continents form, why the volcano erupts, what makes the earth quake. We discover the global links and rhythms of the ecology. If these forces are yet too large to control, we have learned to admire and use them, and to predict their happenings.

Quite recently, we discovered how deserts are formed: Farmers mine the soil, then abandon it to herdsmen whose flocks graze it to death. Without soil and roots, the water table sinks. The wind dries. We see the swollen bellies and taut faces of starving children by satellite. Now that we understand this natural process, what must we do to reverse it?

All our Industrial Age efforts to help the undeveloped have

failed. Caught in the grip of feudal leaders, they sleep on the edge of famine. They resist change in the name of one or another God. Then, one by one they awaken. They steal, claw, scratch their way to prosperity. What we could not give them, they take. They fake, pirate, and counterfeit our secrets, selling them back to us, often considerably improved. And then they are us, and we are them, and a new West is born from the union. The miracle is, the more they take and the more of our work they appropriate, the larger our civilization grows, and the richer we all become. Growth, it seems, can neither be taught nor fostered, but it can be learned. The way we stole, pirated, pillaged, and learned it from the Arabs a thousand years ago.

If growth can be learned but cannot be taught, it must be a process we don't yet understand—we who have more economists than philosophers. Or is it a mystery, as baffling as the coming of eclipses and comets and the eruptions of volcanoes once were, as remarkable and ineffable as the touch of heavenly grace or the spirit of Christmas? Or is it an unborn science whose centuries-long macrowaves will one day be as easily measurable as micro-waves are today? If we can believe in and trust the ecology as a dynamic, natural, life-giving planetary force, why not the economy?

The way to know the economy, like any living thing, is to study its life cycle. It seems to grow in fits and starts, as in the Industrial Revolution. Everybody has heard about the Industrial Revolution. But what about economic revolutions in general? That's quite another thing.

ABOUT ECONOMIC REVOLUTIONS

This is a book about economic revolutions. It is about three glorious revolutions in the West that have taken us from following an ox across someone else's fields and put us in our own car, heading to a comfortable apartment or home. It is about the global economic revolution we are undergoing now, which, among other things, brings us the world each day on a magic screen, and about the one to come, which could take us to the stars.

An economic revolution is a rapid reshaping of the way we organize our work. Behind it is a technological breakthrough permitting a great improvement in our productive capacity. Operating in harmony, these two factors change the way we live our lives.

Each revolution adds a new level of wealth-making to the previous system, thereby creating a richer world and offering a wider choice of roles through which we can seek fulfillment.

Each revolution develops a new set of values, breaking through the straitjacket of the old, disturbing those who cling to traditional beliefs, and provoking, if not war, at the very least a profound reaction. As the ritual expression of this struggle, each revolution is accompanied or soon followed by a golden age of culture in which the clash of values is played out for all to share. This revolutionary culture is so precious to us that we keep it alive and celebrate it continuously.

Just as each revolution permits the creation of a promising new economy, it also dethrones and restructures the old, which has become overtaxed and overregulated, corrupt and collusive, growthless and unproductive. For those in the vanguard, as for those of the old guard, there is clarity and singleness of purpose. They are for it or against it. For the rest of us it is a Pandora's box full of contradiction and conflict, where confusion alternates with searching, nostalgia with cynicism, hope with despair. Finally, the revolution nears its end. The new growth system spreads throughout the economy. Hope is transformed into opportunity, direction, purpose, and meaning.

While each revolution puts a characteristic stamp on all human activity, they all tend toward a common shape and duration. An economic revolution normally last two generations, perhaps fifty years in all, and usually has two distinct phases: the first tentative and disturbed as the old system breaks down; the second bold and purposeful as the new is installed. Ordinarily, but not necessarily, these two periods are directly connected in time. They may be separated by as much as a century.

In some cases, structural change takes place by osmosis, permeating national borders without any dramatic period of struggle and triumph. In others, the forces of the old regime are so powerful they must be violently overthrown. Whatever its merits, political revolution often leads either to an idealistic, impractical regime maintained by terror and repression, or as in America, to a tradition of violence and a fascination with arms.

Once an economic revolution is successfully completed, confidence and prosperity ensues for generation after generation. Venice coasted for five hundred years on the strength of its achievements in the thirteenth century. Florence, Portugal, Holland, Britain, and France soared for centuries. Germany and Japan, which came to their revolutions late, now lead the world in growth. Whichever course America follows, its economic might, energy, and influence will not soon dissipate.

A revolution's prosperity endures because of the depth of change it provokes in society's institutions. Everything is renewed and reinvigorated in the general leap to a higher level of economic activity. Government is renewed. Commerce is refreshed. Churches find new purpose and new support. Universities clamor with new life. New businesses are formed and rise like bubbles in champagne. The arts, creativity, invention flourish. Perhaps most important, that institution which harnesses human energy and turns it into wealth, the corporation, is reborn.

ABOUT CORPORATIONS

This is also a book about corporations. The first formal acts of incorporation created the towns and guilds and universities that awakened us from the centuries of economic darkness and set us on the adventure of growth. Throughout the first half of our millennium, while knight, bishop, and king fought for control of the chessboard, the corporation grew richer and stronger. It was the instrument for building the new world and remaking the old in the centuries since Columbus. Now an era is beginning in which the corporation may assume spiritual as well as economic leadership of our postindustrial, post-Christian, Northern civilization.

Each revolution adds a layer of organization and technology to the system that preceded it. To the feudal administrator of church and manor, the Small-Business Revolution brought the incorporation of town and guild, as many were freed from the fields by the productive new technologies of horse, harness, and plow. The Commercial Revolution added the wealth and diversity of the merchant-banking house, based on marine technology, and letters of credit, and pen and ink, all borrowed from the East. The Industrial Revolution brought the factory and skyscraper, served by the steam railroad and internal combustion engine, the telephone and typewriter.

In the reaction following the Industrial Revolution in Britain, the corporation, the instrument of change, was blamed for fouling the air and creating poverty and slums, although these had many causes. As the Industrial Revolution ended in America, muckrakers and reformers set out to prove that the wealth-making corporations were evil conspiracies out to cheat the people and exploit their workers, myths still sustained by a trickle of revelations from a vigilant press, Nader's Raiders, and "60 Minutes."

In the cynical phase of corporate America following World War II, one spoke of the rat race and the gray flannel trap, of Parkinson's Law and "cover your ass," of shortsighted managers more concerned with golden parachutes than stockholders, and hiding behind a barrage of flak. Meanwhile, across the Pacific, Japanese employees gathered each day before work to sing company songs. "Perhaps it's some sort of publicity stunt," we said to ourselves. "They must be pretty unsophisticated, to be sucked in like that!"

Not all corporations are equally demoralized. New-age firms like Apple Computer, McDonald's, and Disney enjoy a great esprit de corporation. Top to bottom, most IBM employees believe in the changes they are bringing about. The owner-crews of People Express flash real smiles at the passengers of their airline. The team who put on Expo 67 in Montreal slaved with the pride of the leading edge, like the engineers at NASA Control or Jet Propulsion Lab when their probes send snapshots back from the other side of space.

Was it like that when the railroads were building? Or at Edison's lab? Or at Burbage's theater when Shakespeare, Marlowe, and Johnson were making plays? Or in the Amsterdam shipyards of the seventeenth century when the Dutch were inventing the production line? Or in the Cistercian monasteries back in the twelfth century when they were teaching the West to farm? Or when the masons were making cathedral stone soar halfway to heaven?

Will the Information Revolution bring us firms we can believe in? Corporations so rich in value, so geared to change that we are proud to give them our custom and labor? Organizations that will harness our energies and bring know-how to the world? Institutions that will provide fulfillment as our ultimate right? Is this what the future holds?

DIVINING THE FUTURE

This is also a book about the future. During each revolution we look to both past and future for clues about the strange forces pushing us onto some new course. Historians concerned with the meaning of change take us back to times of previous tumult—the fall of the Roman Empire or the horrendous fourteenth century—to analyze the details until they yield their patterns, warnings and promises.

In this revolution, we are attempting to turn the study of the future from an intuitive art into a profession or even a science. After a slow start in the sixties, forecasting took off with journals and world congresses, techniques and tools, newsletters and specialists. Even the government became involved: To avoid the side effects of industrial technology, Congress mandated that all new legislation must have a foresight section, while the White House established the Office of Technological Assessment to ensure that future roses would come without thorns. (If such farseeing legislation had existed at the time of James Watt or Henry Ford, we might have been spared the air pollution and accidental deaths their industries brought in their wake. But then we might still be spending much of our time bumping along in a buggy, overlooking a horse's ass.)

Quite clearly, if long term plans are to be laid and great sums committed to them during a time of radical change, then some considerable effort must be made to envision the impact of a new system and the changing circumstances of the world into which it will be introduced. Business plans for new ventures would be otherwise incomplete and less than convincing.

Telephone planners regularly look twenty-five years ahead, the expected lifetime of new equipment and plant. The Pentagon's think tanks routinely prepare Delphi forecasts, round robins of expert opinion leading to a consensus about the future. The government is fond of cross-impact matrix analyses, which carefully weigh the effect of each of a series of future developments on all of the others. Analysts write endless scenarios, like science fiction essays, to explore the different ways the future might unfold.

This is far from an exercise in futility. Some aspects of the future are reasonably predictable. We know a great deal about tomorrow's population distribution. Tomorrow's decision-makers are already in school or entering the work force. We already have a good idea what they know and think. We know how many of them there will be. We can make useful assumptions about what they will require from and bring to the upcoming marketplace.

The dominant technology of the Information Revolution is electronics, which has been following predictable patterns of growth for years. We know how many more components we can fit on a microchip each year and how much information can be stored in tomorrow's optical memories. We can tell how much software the next generation of computers can handle, and can make some hard estimates of what it will be able to do.

To help all this along is a body of statistical techniques that permit the measurement and ever more accurate projection of current trends. There is also a rapidly expanding community of experienced corporate managers who can estimate the quality of a forecast by evaluating its components and comparing its assumptions and conclusions to a growing body of literature.

Unfortunately the tendency is to evaluate the seriousness of these professional forecasts by the number of pages or volumes, or the cost of the study, which can easily match the cost of a comfortable home. In fact, despite their sophisticated techniques and ponderous size, they are only as good as the futurist in charge. There are, however, some talented futurists leading these teams, and their track records improve with experience.

Forecasting is weakest in estimating the nature and speed of structural change. There is nothing to warn the blotting-paper manufacturer that his thirty-year estimates and capital requirements are about to be rendered meaningless by the ball-point pen. There is nothing to tell the company pension manager that tomorrow there may be no clerks at all in the office to contribute to the plan, and little to guide the architect of the headquarters building off in the rolling hills about the size of the employee parking lot.

Inspired by the surprise of the oil shock, new attention is being paid to the work of René Thom on "catastrophic" (his word for "sudden structural") change. He has shown that once conditions are ripe, there often occurs a sudden reversal of opinion which would be quite unimaginable before the fact. Who could have foreseen that journalists would have so quickly turned in their typewriters and taken so willingly to videodisplay terminals in the newsroom? Certainly not the journalists themselves, so many of whom went on record forecasting a difficult and painful transition.

Paralleling these developments is our compulsive if stumbling struggle to leap into space: Sputnik in 1957, yesterday's moondances, today's spaceprobes and shuttles, and tomorrow's space stations. Played out on our living room screens, with all its drama and tragedy, it does far more to unite our world and proclaim our civilization than politicians do to divide and diminish it.

The cumulative effect of these developments on our collective psyche over the past thirty years has been immense. In the fifties, we could think of reality as some fixed condition that we might at least partially grasp (''So that's the way it is!''). But as the future loomed ever larger in our awareness and we shared a richer view of where we were heading, we began to think of reality as a process of becoming. And if we believe in a richer future, then we can invest our energy in getting us there, and that gives meaning to our lives.

The missing link in the process is a theory of change, an understanding of the mechanics of growth. This would transform the study of the future from a consensual art with its bag of professional tricks into a true discipline, in harmony with all we have learned about history, culture, economics, technology, and the evolution of the human spirit.

This then is a book about growth and structural change. It examines yesterday's economic revolutions with a futurist's eye for patterns—looking specifically for structural changes in the thousand years of our economic childhood and adolescence; analyzing the preconditions for economic metamorphoses; identifying the slithery instruments of transformation; and seeking out signs of decay in the old systems and the nature of the birth of the new. In this way, we begin to place ourselves in the perspective of social evolution and to map our strategies for collective and personal growth.

There is more original material in this book than is usually thrust on the reader. First, there is a ''revolutionary'' model of the way economies grow, describing the revolutions and ages we have been through and the ones still to come. Once the order of their coming is established, we look at the shape and characteristics of the revolutions themselves: how they affect our old institutions and create typical new ones. We examine various kinds of slither which permit sudden structural changes to occur; and then we characterize the search for new values that fuels the transformation with psychic energy.

Each economic revolution happens over and over in different places at different times. It often begins in an obscure region, then spreads across the West. The next section examines some *revolutions past,* locates them in place and time, and describes the new wealth-making structures and technologies upon which they are based.

The *present revolution,* up to its midpoint in the late seventies, is then reexamined in the light of what we have learned. This enables us to put in perspective events since the Second World War and to seek the sense of so much that appeared so destructive at the time.

The *future* of the present revolution takes us into the next century, shows us a new Northern civilization based on a marriage of East and West, and promises to launch the next millennium on a harmonious and prosperous course. If the historic pattern holds, however, this new economy will, like its predecessors, eventually become oppressive and stifling. And so the story of paradise lost and paradise regained is replayed in the twenty-first century as the Space Revolution unfolds with its new technologies and new forms of organization.

The book concludes with *strategic responses* to a world in the final throes of economic revolution. Operating on a global scale, this revolution demands responses that are both collective and individual. What should be the role of the government in the Information Age? What kind of institutions, corporations, and financial houses will best serve our interests and theirs? What challenges face the new class of information processors, from high-tech engineers and biologists to programmers and media creators? What opportunities open for the entrepreneurs and growth-makers who must build the new economy?

In the twenties, Oswald Spengler stunned the world with his vision of the decline of the West. The decay which began with the Industrial Revolution, he predicted, would sadly conclude in the closing years of this century. Spengler was wrong. The West is in a state of expansion; its value system is growing to encompass that of the East; the elitist ideas of the Commercial Age are yielding to powerful and popular global dreams; and the nineties—the last decade of the century, of the millennium, and of the revolution—open a golden age.

Chapter 2
THE SHAPE OF
THE ECONOMY

AN EVOLUTIONARY MODEL

A model serves several purposes. It helps us understand the changes we're going through as well as the process of change. It helps us appreciate the forces at work, see what's coming, and find our most useful place. It helps us make business, investment and political decisions. Beyond that, it helps us understand other civilizations at different stages of evolution (higher or lower)—and to enjoy our own more deeply by giving us an orderly structure on which to hang our cultural treasures and innovations.

An economic model of our society is so essential that we cannot function without it. Unfortunately, because of our nationalistic educational systems, the models with which we begin our working lives are unsystematic and overspecialized, filled with holes and charged with social and economic prejudices, political distortions, and hypocritical sententiousness. Like the Polish cavalry faced with Hitler's Wermacht, we have been instilled with the wrong values, given the wrong training and equipment, and sent off to fight a war we do not understand.

The need for a new model is widely felt. The success of the proto-models inherent in *The Third Wave* and *Megatrends* is apparent in everyday conversation, and makes gurus of their authors. There are now shelves of books on the Japanese model of economic organization, plus a stream of amorphous models exemplified by *The Search for Excellence*. Business, institutions, and goverment are poised to restructure. The question is, To what? If it begins by describing structure, our model must end by disclosing goals.

The new model must explain the process of change: how the old system is transformed; how dead trees fall; how the new system slips through the cracks of the old and expands and grows; how values change and goals are formed. It must instruct us when to be patient and when to be bold, when to seek advice and when to keep our own counsel, and even more difficult, how to cope with the disorder which is as essential to growth as predators are to the natural world.

The new model must inform our view of the future, tell us where we are going, show us where we are on the curve. It must help us evaluate the forecasts with which we are bombarded, the systems we are offered, the plans being urged upon us. It must help us decide what we may expect to accomplish, what we count on in our planning, or what may leapfrog or bypass us en route.

THE BASIC ECONOMY

In the premonetary West of feudal times, beginning around the year 800 with Charlemagne and stretching into the next millennium, the economy was at its simplest: There was a small ruling hierarchy supported by an enormous underclass of unpaid serfs. Monks, priests, warlords, and knights ruled the West, establishing the basic social order and emotional patterns of authority and trust, faith and fear, and honor and loyalty that still prevail today.

FEUDAL ECONOMY
8TH TO 12TH CENTURIES

ADMINIS-
TRATION

The ruling class, let's call it "the administration," for that is what it will become, provided protection and salvation to the people. In exchange, they were rewarded with food and service. It's a one-stage economy.

There's a lively debate underway about how the West's economic awakening occurred. The traditionalists say it started gradually with the introduction of agricultural technology from the East around the tenth century. The harness, horse, and plow, along with the three-field crop rotation, made farming doubly or triply productive. And the Asian broadax and draining techniques allowed new land to be opened and farmers to leave the feudal manor and go into business for themselves.

With the development of agriculture, it is argued, the town could come into being. Assured of a supply of food, townsfolk could specialize in crafts and services. Trade could open up between towns and regions by selling the surpluses and specialties of the one to the other. An act of incorporation from the king freed the town from the jurisdiction of the feudal warlord and allowed townspeople to pursue their economic interests.

Jane Jacobs, the urban economist, rejects the traditional view. First came the cities, she says, with city people growing their own food, and then came country agriculture. Whichever came first, historians have established that in the eleventh and twelfth centuries there was an explosion of towns across Europe, and a wave of serfs left the manor to set up their own farms. With farmers producing food for sale, fiber for cloth, leather for parchment and harness, horses to ride, wood for construction and warmth, and manpower as well, the towns could grow and flourish and trade, while the farmers had money to spend on what the town offered for sale. It was a glorious time, some say Europe's golden age.

Within a relatively brief period, Europe was colonized by refugees from the manors. Forests were taken down and marshy riverbeds and seacoasts reclaimed, while a thousand towns sprang up, with walls and bridges, squares and markets, halls and homes for the newly free. New institutions appeared: schools, hospitals, universities. Old institutions, such as manors and monasteries, were reformed. How this happened is important for us to learn.

At each of our economic revolutions, a new class, using a new technology and abandoning the old rules, breaks away from the old system and launches a new cycle of growth. At first unhappy with the upstarts, the old establishment soon coopts the revolution by adapting the new techniques to their own affairs. In this way the revolutionary approach spreads across the whole society.

Soon after the Small-Business Revolution, the feudal administrators discovered their interests in the new economic order and surrendered some of their perquisites and prerogatives to the new economic classes. They still managed, however, to maintain control at the top of the political and economic hierarchy.

The guildmasters and merchants became the burghers who ran the towns. Battles for political control broke out between the new burghers and the old nobility, now firmly ensconced in the new economy. The pope and the king also wanted their say in the way the West was run. Administration was becoming a more sophisticated and hierarchical process than in the old feudal regime. Where there had been the simplest of systems, now there were whole new orders of knighthood set to defend the faith, new kinds of courtiers, and a new class of officers to carry out their will. The Church erupted with specialized orders of friars and monks, this to preach, that to nurse, this to administer, these for the inquisition. Sheriffs and bailiffs, lawyers and judges, mayors and guildmasters peopled the new hierarchy. In this newly created corporate world, there was much to decide, much to enforce. One served many masters and obeyed many rules.

By the twelfth century, the structure of this new, small-business economy was in place. Its ability to free up labor and produce wealth was enormous, and it was reflected in the cathedrals, towns, and castles, many of which are still standing to amaze and attract the tourist, and in the Crusades, whose aftershocks still trouble the Middle East.

This is a model of the new economy:

SMALL-BUSINESS ECONOMY
10TH TO 12TH CENTURIES

SMALL
BUSINESS

ADMINIS-
TRATION

By the fourteenth century, the exuberant small-business economy had become strangled by a thicket of rules and customs.
Europe was colonized, and there was no more land on which to
expand. The limitations on the spread of small business soon were
reached, and no longer could the journeyman's dream of a shop of
his own be fulfilled. Decades before the plague arrived to control
the population in midcentury, growth had ceased and the miseries
had begun. Cathedrals were left unfinished. Extended city walls
enclosed empty land. Grass grew in the streets. Wars became
endemic.

In Venice, fat with income, ships, loot and colonies from the
Crusades, one of history's great breakthroughs occurred, the Commercial Revolution. With the detested and overcivilized Arabs
driven at last from the Mediterranean sea, long-distance trade was
discovered to be the new road to wealth, and the Venetians, along
with their archrivals the Genoans, felt none of the religious constraints which limited small businessmen to modest ventures.

Meanwhile, inland at Lucca and Florence, far from the sea,
several noble families, rich with rents from their vast estates and
with profits from their commercial ventures in town, established
merchant-banking houses. They traded over the Alps at the fairs of
Europe, lent money to kings in exchange for monopolies, and
manufactured wool cloth so fine it graced the shoulders of princes
of Church and realm.

It took many failures before the instruments of credit, exchange
and bookkeeping borrowed from the Arabs were perfected, before
the organization of a European network of factors could be established and stabilized—but the merchant princes persevered. Their
techniques gradually spread, on the wings of print and on the oars
of galleys to Portugal and Spain, to Bruges and Amsterdam, until
all of Europe had adopted their ways.

Once again, administration was transformed. Where there had
been princedoms and duchies, now there were nation states with
commercial empires extending around the globe. There was now
an elaborate court and judiciary, governors and planters and civil
servants, navies and armies, tax collectors, parliamentarians, and
inspectors. There was even a theory, by Machiavelli, to guide it.

The small business class, still partly organized in guilds but now
highly specialized, soon extended to include a merchant marine,
publicans, painters, writers, artists and performers in the newly
commercialized arts, hawkers, slavers, and colonists. And there
were shopkeepers galore, handling the merchandise pouring in
from the corners of the world.

Now the economy looked like this:

COMMERCIAL ECONOMY
13TH TO 18TH CENTURIES

COMMERCIAL

SMALL
BUSINESS

ADMINIS-
TRATION

It took many centuries before Europe had adopted the commercial system and commercialized its arts and institutions. By that time it had turned into something else. In the years leading up to the French Revolution (the political revolution of 1789), a struggle developed between the merchant-bankers, in company with their colleagues of the new commercial class, and the state, embodied in the glorious person of the king. Rules and regulations codified what would be manufactured, who would transport it, what the colonies could buy and sell, the length of a piece of ribbon, the number of threads in a piece of lace. Taxes to pay for all this bureaucracy,—and for the standing armies and navies that maintained and expanded the empire, as well as for the splendors of the state—choked off all growth and angered the creators of wealth beyond endurance.

Out of these dreary constraints emerged a new way of producing wealth, the factory, and a new technology, steam-driven machines. Industrialization took shape with revolutionary speed in England at the end of the eighteenth century, and in America, Japan, and Germany at the end of the nineteenth, while the rest of the world struggled to catch up well into the twentieth.

Now there were four economic classes. There were the administrators, who quickly industrialized their bureaucracies, with millions of human cogs in their vast machines, run by thousands of "big wheels" at the top: a finely mechanized system of utterly standardized and thoroughly replaceable parts. Next there were the small businessmen: inventors, promoters, scientists, salesmen, designers, prospectors, entertainers, and all those others whose creativity and independent spirit kept them apart from the bureaucracy. They had come a long way from the masons and craftsmen and guildsmen, the millers, smiths, scribners, and other small businessmen of the Small-Business Revolution. They could not be compared, however, to the merchants and industralists, who together ran the economy, established great trusts, built steamships and railroads, stretched submarine cables across oceans, lit skyscrapers and cities, and broadcast to the remotest farms.

Now the economy was shaped like this:

INDUSTRIAL ECONOMY
19TH AND 20TH CENTURIES

INDUSTRIAL

COMMERCIAL

SMALL BUSINESS

ADMINIS-TRATION

Most of us can remember the unhappy days following the oil shocks when industry ground to a halt. But even in the sixties, when big business seemed to be prospering, the economy was in serious trouble and the end of the age was approaching. More and more taxes were needed to keep the system running—income taxes, corporation, purchase, and inheritance taxes, state and civic taxes. Rules grew so complex that lawyers and accountants were required to transact the smallest business. Once again, everything was regulated, and an enormous bureaucracy was required to think up new regulations and keep track of the old. People who should have been creating wealth were filling out forms. Large corporations couldn't innovate. Enormous research departments labored to produce mouse-sized modifications. Small inventors discovered that distributors' doors were closed to all but the established. Products got worse with each new model. The air was so foul with industrial pollution it rotted the buildings. Water became undrinkable; processed food, unsafe to eat. Hospital deaths rose with each new piece of medical equipment. School graduates couldn't read. Workers sabotaged their work. Mental homes filled with people who thought they were machines. Each advance of the industrial system seemed to push civilization back another step.

While the gears of the old smokestack industrial system were seizing up, an explosion of knowledge-based technologies, a new form of organization, and a new spirit of enterprise began breaking down national borders, creating a marketplace for intangibles, and replacing the rigid old hierarchies with dynamic networks. Electrons and digital bits, photons of light, quarks of energy, genes and biological molecules became the alphabets of the Information Revolution and the building blocks of systems of Faustian power.

While high-tech entrepreneurs dazzle the marketplace, administrators are beginning to informationize, small businessmen to computerize, the world of commerce to digitize, industrialists to robotize. When the economy is fully automated and globalized, a generation from now, it will look like this:

INFORMATION ECONOMY
20TH AND 21ST CENTURIES

INFORMATION

INDUSTRIAL

COMMERCIAL

SMALL BUSINESS

ADMINIS-TRATION

Does the Information Age follow the pattern of the ages that went before? Will some new economic age, based on new technology and new organization, replace the age we are presently putting in place? How long will this take to happen? The model says yes, yes, and soon.

Within three generations of its establishment as the spiritual force of humanity, the information economy will become corrupt, rigid, overregulated and overtaxed, and worst of all, growthless. To imagine the international bureaucracy of 2060, think of a world ruled by Greenpeace. Those without valid credentials, swelling the underground economy and scheming to reinstate nationalism, will dream of escape from the oppressive global institutions of the now stagnant information economy. On earth there will be nowhere to hide. The one way to go is out.

The Space Revolution (2060–2100 A.D.) will seem a long time coming. Building and launching viable space colonies, space factories, and space powerplants can't be done by "two guys in a garage," the high-tech entrepreneurs behind the Information Revolution. But a hundred years of improvements since Sputnik, coupled with the growing need to bring new energy and materials into earth's depleting system, will hasten the development of new technology, of the monastic form of organization and the soaring spirit of the Space Revolution.

As has always happened before, the Space Revolution will create a new class of entrepreneurs, and the "Opening to Infinity" will transform, unburden, reinvigorate the administrators, the small businessmen, the commercial community, the industrialists, and the informationists, all of whom will find vast new markets for their talents, wares, and services.

SPACE ECONOMY
21ST TO 25TH CENTURIES

Such will be the variety of opportunity, richness of challenge, and possibility for growth that the Space Age could last for five hundred years. Every generation or so, there will be a new economic breakthrough, a new technology, a new form of organization. But these minirevolutions will now come so quickly and will be so easily assimilated that they no longer constitute a transformation of our Northern civilization, which will have spread across and unified the world.

And after that? There is at least one further revolution yet to come: the discovery of organized life in space (or perhaps their discovery of us). If the Opening, or Space Revolution of the twenty-first century is the repeat of the Small-Business Revolution of the eleventh century, then the Universal Revolution of the twenty-sixth century could be a replay of our Commercial Revolution with the discovery of New Worlds and the explosion of trade.

Having identified and briefly described our economic ages, we can see that a revolution is not a replacement of one system by another, but a cumulative addition whereby a new type of economic acitivity breaks through the rigidities of the old system and gradually assumes a dominant position; it recasts our older institutions in its image, and creates a host of characteristic institutions of its own. With each revolution, the economy becomes increasingly rich and complex. And yet, because the whole economy starts over again as it renews and restructures itself, it is at its simplest during and immediately after a revolution, in the springtime of its life cycle. It appears inscrutably complex to those who are locked in the old way of seeing, and marvelously simple to those in tune with the change.

This, then, is the general pattern of economic growth, and revolution, like metamorphosis, like puberty, marriage, and parenthood, is the rather frightening and always surprising instrument. It is time to explore its characteristics.

Chapter 3
REVOLUTION

Revolution is by no means the only or even the most common road to economic transformation. Change comes to most of the world through gradual assimilation of revolutionary developments from more adventurous regions. Defeat in war clears the deck for a peaceful yet powerful restructuring of the economy. But when a new economic order first appears in our civilization, it is installed through an economic revolution—that is, a sudden increase in the pace of innovation, lasting about two generations and creating a profound reordering and restructuring of our institutions and our means of creating wealth.

Sometimes the revolution is late in arriving, coming long after the previous age has decayed into a thicket of regulations and taxes when barriers to entry have risen to prevent further growth. Young people are alienated from the system, and there is widespread social malaise. All of this is the very opposite of the way the age had begun, with its excitement, challenge, and opportunities, its new ways of making money and circumventing the problems of the age before. Our own Information Revolution, delayed by the Depression and World War II, was long overdue by the time it got underway in the fifties, and perhaps more troubled than usual as a result.

Sometimes the revolution comes hot on the heels of its predecessor, like a new wave of energy, carrying on the renewal begun by previous generations. The Commercial Revolution in Italy seemed to flow easily out of the Small-Business Revolution (although it had a most protracted and painful birth beyond the Alps) and Britain's Industrial Revolution seemed at first like a quiet continuation of her Commercial Revolution.

Even though an economic revolution may begin quietly with a wave of invention in some out-of-the-way part of the world, it soon grows into a powerful force, generating opposition from the old guard, who see their investments threatened, their values questioned, their control weakened. The fierce determination of the establishment to hold on to the best of the old—and to power—while accepting only the most useful of the new, creates a struggle that lasts at least two generations (until the old guard dies off or retires) and which may persist for centuries. Whatever the revolution's duration, a characteristic element of the struggle is slither: temporary institutions, such as inflation, piracy, terrorism, youth revolt and romanticism, which work to push out the old economic system and install the new.

An economic revolution is a two-phase event, each of which lasts a generation or about twenty-five years. In the first phase, a group of outsiders develops a new way of generating wealth, quite outside the rules and traditions of society, to which they owe little allegiance. Society is preoccupied with the problems of the old economic system, which are proving particularly intractable and are the cause of much social unrest. During this "accidental" phase of the revolution, scant attention is paid to the new forms of organization and novel technologies, some of which are very successful. This phase of the revolution is so perilous, trackless, and unprecedented that many pioneers fall like Icarus after flying too close to the sun. The first phase ends as large profits and continued rapid growth are realized by the surviving pioneers. Big investors move in, saturating the market and creating a capital glut.

The second, or "purposeful," phase begins as more ambitious projects soak up the surplus investment from phase one. The new forms of organization become more sophisticated, the technology more suited to society's needs. A much clearer image is forming of the new economy. As the revolution's reputation builds, operations on a greatly enlarged scale become both practical and hugely profitable. As these projects mature, their threat to the establishment grows, and a reaction sets in. Social ostracism and restrictive legislation combine with professional management to slow the pace of innovation and maximize short-term profits. Economic growth stabilizes while innovation moves from the economic to the social plane.

The two phases of the revolution are closely related not only in time (they usually happen in immediate sequence), but also in spirit, with the second phase completing the work of the first.

The first phase of the Small-Business Revolution saw the development of farms and towns; the second phase consolidated the first with the development of guilds and immense land-clearing projects. The first phase of the Commercial Revolution developed instruments of long-distance trade; the second created banks and the domestic production system. The first phase of the Industrial Revolution created factories and machines; the second, railroads and the industrial system.

Usually the revolution breaks out in some closely confined part ot the world (Venice, the British Midlands, Silicon Valley). The region soon leaps ahead of its rivals, who attempt to take the best of the new approach without sacrificing their old values and ways. This struggle may last for a century or more, and then suddenly, one after the other, the nations of the world grasp the spirit of innovation and leapfrog their predecessors.

This leapfrog process can be most clearly seen in the Industrial Revolution. It first took flight in the British Midlands in the 1780s with the development of the factory system and the use of steam-driven machinery, and took half a century to establish itself and set its mark on the age. As phase two arrived in Britain, in the early nineteenth century, other countries borrowed the factory system and later the railroads, and slowly put them to use. But they didn't really take off on an innovative spurt of their own until much later. Then, about 1870, Germany, America and Japan suddenly grasped the creative principle. Invention tumbled after invention, their economies surged ahead, and all three quickly leapfrogged the faltering British growth rate. By 1914 Germany and America were larger in economic terms, while in 1905 a partially industrialized Japan trounced a humbled Russia and became the first Asian nation to defeat a European power.

This leapfrog phase of the Industrial Revolution was, if anything, more radical and surprising than the first, bringing with it gasoline and electricity, the automobile and the plane, the telegraph and the telephone, phonograph records and movies, and the international firm. Britain, exhausted by its efforts and redolent with wealth from its colonies, benefited least.

An economic revolution has little in common with its better known political counterparts, such as the French or Russian Revolutions, which are more likely to arise from the power of the old to prevent change, and the frustration of innovation. Thus these revolutions become a substitute for economic revolution, and they usually result in economic regression because they destroy rather than add to the economic fabric.

Because of the force of arms, the political revolution itself is quickly over, then it is usually followed by a reign of terror, which lasts until the strong man who establishes order disappears. Such a process took twenty-five years in France, (from 1789 to Napoleon's banishment in 1815) and thirty-seven years in Russia (from 1917 down to Stalin's death in 1954).

Such revolutions seriously impede the pace of useful economic innovation by placing its primary responsibility in the hands of the state rather than in those of entrepreneurs.

With the notable exception of the American Revolution, wars of liberation from foreign masters have not been notably successful in establishing vibrant economies. America shared the economic vigor and inventiveness that grew out of Britain's Glorious Revolution, which established the Commercial Revolution; it also shared a common language. Perhaps this is why it was able to foster innovation and economic growth, and to surpass its former masters on both counts, with the arrival of its own Commercial and Industrial Revolutions in the 1870s.

Is it possible to compare the transformative power of the two kinds of revolutions? Crane Brinton, the Harvard historian who wrote the classic *The Anatomy of Revolution*, argues that the economic revolutions are more powerful than their political counterpart. In his view, "the social and economic changes since 1945 add up to a more significant set of changes than those of the Great Revolution of 1785–1815." If that is stretching the comparison through too many centuries, he also states his belief that the Industrial Revolution had a much greater effect than the concurrent political revolution in France.

Because of their immense power of transformation, their liberation of creative forces, and their enormous enriching effect, it is surprising that there has been no overall study of economic revolutions. Business could use such a study to map out markets, structures and techniques, and it is directly in the interests of government to learn the rules which control economic growth. (But since government's ranks are traditionally drawn from the establishment and the socially concerned, it is far better at controlling the wealth-makers than creating the circumstances under which they flourish.)

Even more important for governments than economic growth is the effect economic revolutions have on a nation's institutions, including government itself. These we will examine next.

Chapter 4
REVOLUTIONARY INSTITUTIONS

The spirit of each age is expressed through its institutions. Some institutions are magic rituals, such as handshakes and signatures, prayers and marriages, or ranks and titles, and these change very slowly. The more tangible variety, those embodied in stone and employing large numbers of people, such as schools, churches, banks, hospitals, palaces, or asylums, generally undergo some re-structuring with each change of economic regime. In addition to transforming its institutional heritage, each age creates new and characteristic institutions of its own. This monument building is its principal business; the age lasts until this work is completed, and then draws to a close.

There is a third group of institutions wholly specific to the revolutionary period, which facilitate the transformation process and then go into hibernation once the revolution is completed and the new age has begun. Some of the West's most fascinating institutions are in this group. They break roughly into three types: institutions associated with economic and social collapse; those which deal with economic change (''slither''); and those associated with the search for new values. They can all be clearly seen in the prolonged transition from the Small-Business Era (still largely feudal), to the Commercial Age. They are all at work during the Industrial Revolution, and we appear not to be spared any of the steps as we turn from (and against) the Industrial Age to build the information economy.

INSTITUTIONS OF THE COLLAPSE

ESCALATION OF WARFARE

One of the first institutions of the collapse of an established economic system is an escalated form of warfare, which provides society an opportunity to field-test the new technology. During the Commercial Revolution, the new crossbow or gunpowder and musket let a common soldier slay a nobleman from a distance, much to the nobility's frustration and disgust. Napoleon's highly organized and ruthless warfare (described by von Clausewitz at the time as total war) coincided with the first Industrial Revolution, just as the armored train and machine gun of the American Civil and the Franco-Prussian Wars sped its second incarnation. Hitler's Wermacht and rocket bombs, British radar, and American nuclear weapons, and guided missiles announced the Information Revolution. War escalates with each great restructuring, leaving the scars of terror and despair in the pysche of its survivors, along with a rich legacy of field-tested technology and technique.

Nations which have undergone their economic revolution and mastered the technologies of the new economy are apt to try them out on their neighbors or traditional enemies. Japan attacked Russia once her industrial technology was mastered; Germany went after France and then Britain to demonstrate her industrial efficiency, extending demonstrations of her new chemical might to poison gas. Thus all-out war is one of the traditional companions of economic revolution.

Total war, however, can be much more than a proving ground for new technology. American economist Mancur Olson argues that suitably devastating military defeats can lead to massive spurts of economic growth. This is because long periods of economic stability preceding war permit collusive arrangements to develop among powerful corporations, interest groups and government. These cozy arrangements reduce competition, limit entry and innovation, promote regulation, and drag the economy down. Defeat in war usually wipes out these establishment deals and their accompanying regulatory institutions, and gives the loser a fresh start. Defeated countries gain a headstart on the victors and may soon win the peace, as was demonstrated by Germany and Japan after World War II, and by Holland in the Commercial Revolution.

Once prosperity returns, Olson argues in *The Rise and Decline of Nations*, so do corporate collusion and government regulation, bringing the spurt to an end. Hence our expectations that the German and the Japanese economic miracles will slow down. Britain, the victor in both World Wars, was able to maintain its historic institutions and coalitions, and as a result, "suffers from an institutional sclerosis that slows its adaptation to changing circumstances and technologies."

These coalitions, Olson believes, operate by lobbying government. "Lobbying increases the complexity of regulation and the scope of government by creating special provisions and exceptions. . . . The more elaborate the regulation, the greater the need for specialists to deal with these regulations, such as lawyers, accountants, or other consultants."

Since Olson suspects other processes may be at work in economic renewal, he takes pains to insist that no country should "seek a revolution or even provoke a war in which it would be defeated" in order to clean house and reinstate growth, as a Peter Sellers movie once suggested. And if the process can be controlled, Olson keeps the secret.

OVERREGULATION AND TAXATION

Northcote Parkinson's Law first appeared in the late fifties in an article for The Economist. Published soon after in book form, the piece received instant attention, rapid fame and subsequent immortality—unusual for an economic study. It is ironical that even as its wisdom becomes part of our folklore, the law might be repealed.

As an economic historian, Parkinson had noted the steady decline in men and ships in Britain's Royal Navy between 1914 and 1928, and the steady increase in dockyard and Admiralty officials required to administer them. He established the general expansion of the bureaucracy at 5.5 percent per annum regardless of the amount of work (if any) to be done.

Reviewing the situation in the 1970s, Parkinson noted that the rate of growth in the bureaucracies had escalated from 5.5 to 9.3 percent per annum. "Whereas 1914 represented the culmination of an arms race, where 4366 officials could administer what was then the largest navy in the world, 1967 represents the point at which we became practically powerless, by which time over 33,000 civil servants are barely sufficient to administer the navy we no longer possess," he wrote with mock dismay.

Parkinson's Law states that "work expands so as to fill the time available for its completion." Because he described the situation without any reference to its causes, he suggested this was a natural, unchanging law, and that we should have the good grace to laugh at things we cannot change. As we will later see, information technology and popular pressure could soon make Parkinson's Law obsolete, but its apparent immutability in the first half of the current revolution was the source of much cynicism and despair.

Every end of era suffers from Parkinson's Law. Government work increases because regulation is needed to restrain the excesses of business and to oversee the regulatory system, which is forever growing more complex to accommodate the special privileges of the establishment. Taxation rises to pay for it. Soon the burden drives its citizens to desperate acts, and the business community out of the competitive marketplace. Innovation passes to virgin territory, or as Mancur Olson says, to centers emerging from a crisis sufficiently terrible to decimate the establishment and its special privileges.

CYNICISM AND VALUE COLLAPSE

When economic growth stops, officials grow corrupt. Leadership tends toward graft and patronage under a mask of hypocrisy. Transfer payments are made from the public coffers to the establishment in exchange for modest bribes. Everything has its price. So it was in the Italy of the Borgias, in Grant's America, in Louis XVI's France, in George III's Britain, in the twin papacies of the schism. Machiavelli's *The Prince* confirmed the fears of the cynical world: Political success in a dying economy is incompatible with public morality, and truth should only be used if it happens to serve the state.

As cynicism spreads, workers are mocked for doing their best. Quality, honesty, and service are sacrificed for quick profits. Managers "cover their asses," as office jargon would have it, and avoid all risk. Theft and waste become endemic, while the corporation advances through connections, bribes, takeovers, and stock-market manipulations. Change a few words and this picture of a contemporary industrial corporation, such as a supplier to the US military, could as easily apply to the fourteenth-century Church, an eighteenth-century court, or a twentieth-century government department.

VILIFICATION

When corruption is rife, scolding the dying age becomes institutionalized. In feudal times this was the role of Irish priests. As the Commercial Revolution spread throughout Europe, Martin Luther excoriated the venality of the Church. Voltaire urged his readers to "Écrasez l'Infame" ("Kill the Bastards") and end the Commercial Age. The main castigator from the British Industrial Revolution was Thomas Carlyle, who painted the spiritual degeneracy of his predecessors in vivid hues. In *Heroes and Hero Worship* he asks:

> What century since the end of the Roman world, which was also a time of scepticism and universal decadence, so abounds with quacks as that Eighteenth? Consider them, with their tumid sentimental vapouring about virtue and benevolence. It seems to me, you lay your finger on the heart of the world's maladies, when you call it a Sceptical World. An insincere world; a godless untruth of a world!

So much for the enlightenment, the most brilliant century in Western history! Forgotten was Voltaire and the French encyclopedists; Johnson and the British publishing explosion; Bach, Handel, and Mozart, and the musical ascendency; Wedgwood, Watteau, and Hogarth, and the flourishing of the visual arts; Kant and Goethe, and the flowering of German thought; Newton and Priestley, and the scientific revolution; Rousseau and Burke, Jefferson and Franklin, and the political revolution; Watt, Boulton, Arkwright, Cartwright, and the Industrial Revolution. The previous age was simply dismissed in the great Victorian quest for muscular Christianity and spiritual truth.

The Information Revolution is as ripe with invective against the dying Industrial Age as any in the past. Ralph Nader, as pure of heart as Galahad, sought out the corporate dragons in their darkest lairs. Worker priest Ivan Illich demonstrated that even our best-intentioned institutions had flip-flopped into sources of evil: Schools destroyed our minds, hospitals killed, roads silted up with grid-locked traffic. Harvard Professors Alpert and Leary advised drugs as education: "Turn on, tune in, drop out!" We were reliving the dying years of the *ancien régime* of prerevolutionary France, when the Marquis de Sade could demonstrate in book after book that virtue was deadly folly, and vice the only road to wealth, honor, and fame.

TERRORISM AND ANARCHY

In the fifties it was the Beat Generation in America. England provided the outraged cries of its Angry Young Men. Paris con-tributed the refined anarchy of existentialism, the New Wave and the Theatre of the Absurd. In the sixties, this frustrated anger heated up with Black Panthers, Watts rioter/looters, violent student agitators from Berkeley to Tokyo, and the Paris of the sixty-eighters with their paving-stone barricades. Political kidnappings, hijackings, and kneecappings outraged the seventies. The old re-gime was well attended with impatient gravediggers, with wolves and jackals hungry for establishment flesh.

CRIME

With unemployment institutionalized, crime becomes the princi-pal career of the disinherited. As it was at the end of the Feudal, Small-Business, and Commercial Ages, so it is once again as the gears of the Industrial Age seize up. No one's home is safe. Brighter streetlights help muggers choose better victims. Crowds provide purse-snatchers a safe escape. Jails overflow. Witnesses refuse to testify. Juries won't prosecute. Judges won't sentence. Citizens take up arms and look to their own defense.

SLITHER

Restructuring is rarely a formal or systematic process. No leader suddenly decrees that henceforth we will abandon the old and operate by new economic rules. The establishment will not surrender the values to which it is dedicated, no matter how empty they have become or how hard it is pressed. Old money is honored, new money derided, no matter how decadent the former, how virile and creative the latter. For change to take place, slither is required: temporary, slippery institutions that allow the old to be eased aside and the new to take its place.

Typically, slither includes such infamous lubricants as inflation, dispossession, brain drain, underground economy, smuggling, piracy, espionage, deregulation, and bypass. Like seventeen-year locusts, most agents of slither lie dormant beneath the ground for years, then emerge for a season, do their necessary work, and then disappear, unlamented, until needed again. Nor are these instruments of change confined to those parts of the world struggling through an economic revolution: Neighboring nations or city states unwilling to take the economic plunge are as subject to the social side effects, cultural repercussions, fads and fashions accompanying the economic revolution as the leaders undergoing the change.

INFLATION

The foremost agent of slither is inflation. It usually appears at the beginning of the era of change and lasts until the end of the first phase. The bank discount rate made its first moves up from stability in Britain in August 1954, about the time computers and automation first appeared. Within a year, other nations caught this British affliction.

About the time the British bank discount rate made its first flutter upward, Sir Henry Phelps Brown, the distinguished British labor economist, published a pair of articles on historical inflation in Britain, in the journal *Economica*. He noted an inexplicable jump in prices from 1520 to 1640 and another from 1750 to 1820. There was no classical explanation that he could find:

For a century or more, it seems, prices will obey one all-powerful law: it changes, and a new law prevails; a war that would have cast the trend up to new heights in one dispensation is powerless to deflect it in another. Do we yet know what are the factors that set this stamp on an age; and why, after they have held so long through such shakings, they give way quickly and completely to others?"

American financial journalist David Warsh noted the coincidence of Sir Henry's price jumps and the Commercial (or as he called it, Capitalist) and Industrial Revolutions. Through further research, Warsh was able to find a third such period between 1100 and 1200, which he called the Commercial Revolution (the Small-Business Revolution actually arrived in Britain at this time). Since Warsh's purpose was to explain the inflation just starting its desperate zoom in the mid-1970s, he was able to add a fourth inflation/revolution example to his argument.

The price inflation of the early stage of the Commercial Revolution was well known to economic historians for its severity: "In England the general price level rose five times between 1530 and 1640, wheat prices six times," writes Christopher Hill. But on the continent, inflation was even worse, and so England had a ready market for its comparatively low-priced cloth, and prospered accordingly. In 1967 Hill observed in his *Reformation to Industrial Revolution*:

Historians today are more cautious than they were thirty years ago of attributing too much to the sixteenth-century inflation, and still more cautious of giving the influx of American silver as its sole cause. Prices were already rising before any American metals arrived in Europe . . . The effects of the price revolution differed from country to country. In England it stimulated (or was accompanied by) a considerable industrial development. In Spain it first stimulated an industrial boom, then led to (or was accompanied by) industrial decline. In France it seems to have had no very marked effects on industry. We cannot use the price revolution as a deus ex machina: its effect was probably only to accelerate economic changes which were going to take place anyway.

As Warsh pointed out, a similar inflation slithered through the

British small business revolution at the end of the twelfth century. According to Maurice Postan in *The Medieval Economy and Society*, "Prices of all agricultural products rose sharply and suddenly in the closing years of the twelfth and opening years of the thirteenth centuries." A similar, and longer-lasting inflation hit the price of land.

Inflation, like predation in nature, permits the weak to be cut back and the strong and agile to move forward. Businessmen operating on borrowed money are forgiven part of their debt since they repay in inflated coin. Inflation also permits government to steal from its pensioners and bondholders and increase its share of national wealth through higher taxes on ostensibly higher incomes.

DISPOSSESSION

Economic revolutions provide the rich and clever the opportunity to rob the slow and poor. During both the Commercial and Industrial Revolutions, landowners fenced in and took claim to the common fields traditionally used by cottagers to grow food and pasture cattle. Similarly in the 1980s, the banks, after persuading otherwise viable farmers to go over their heads into debt, move in and take possession of their farms. From an economic point of view, this form of rationalization is as necessary as predation in nature, but the cost in human suffering cannot be ignored. Karl Polanyi, the great-hearted economic historian of the Industrial Revolution *(The Great Transformation)* is particularly indignant about this kind of slither:

> Enclosures have appropriately been called a revolution of the rich against the poor. The lords and nobles were upsetting the social order, breaking down ancient law and custom, sometimes by means of violence, often by pressure and intimidation. They were literally robbing the poor of their share in the common, tearing down the houses which, by the hitherto unbreakable force of custom, the poor had long regarded as theirs and their heirs'. The fabric of society was being disrupted; desolate villages and ruins of human dwellings testified to the fierceness with which the revolutions raged, endangering the defenses of the country, wasting its towns, decimat-

ing its population, turning its overburdened soil into dust, harassing its people and turning them from decent husbandmen into a mob of beggars and thieves.

Historians have long noted the secondary effect of dispossession by enclosure: deprived of their stake in the commons, the rural poor were forced onto the labor market, driving wages down. Again Karl Polanyi takes exception to this cruel form of progress:

> As long as domestic industry was supplemented by the facilities and amenities of a garden plot, a scrap of land, or grazing rights, the dependence of the labourer on money earnings was not absolute; the potato plot . . . a cow or even an ass in the commons made all the difference; and family earnings acted as a kind of unemployment insurance. The rationalization of agriculture inevitably uprooted the labourer and undermined his social security.

Dispossession from the land is not the only form forced restructuring takes. Downsizing is another version, deskilling another, disenfranchisement a fourth, patronage a fifth.

"Downsizing" is 1980s jargon for the culling of middle managers. Industrial firms grew fat and prosperous in the well-protected dying days of the Industrial Era. Suddenly faced with sleek foreign competition, office hierarchies had to be flattened, management and staff released. Settlements were generous, and outplaced managers often transferred their new wealth and managerial skills to the small-business sector, making franchised service operations the fastest growing segment of the economy. Here, at least, the pain was minimized.

As "intelligence" is built into machines, skilled operators are reduced to machine tenders. Their obsolete skills no longer command a premium. Whole professions disappear. Elevator operators, comptometer operators, and punch-card data-entry operators found themselves with unmarketable skills. This deskilling was particularly hard on the female work force, which was just establishing a beachhead in the office as the ground was washed away.

Disenfranchisement of union labor happens in several ways. First, as automation develops, the need for workers declines. Then, as competition for world markets globalizes, generous labor settlements which threaten corporate, industry, and even national survival are repudiated, and new contracts offer less than before.

The new, high-tech industries, built on a collaborative rather than confrontational model, have avoided unionization, in part by refusing to hire retrained industrial workers with their deep-seated hostiliy to employers. By the end of the Information Revolution, it is predicted, industrial workers will have declined from a third to a twentieth of the work force.

Patronage is a reward for faithful service or a warehouse for hacks, depending on who's talking. During economic revolutions, however, this form of slither brings new blood to offices filled with tired time-servers. In Germany's Commercial Revolution, Martin Luther expressed his outrage at the Church's practice of simony, selling offices for what usually amounted to a year's revenues in advance. Whatever its disadvantages, it refreshed not only the coffers of the organization but also the office. François I of France, who reigned as the Commercial Revolution swept north of the Alps, borrowed from the Church the idea of the sale of offices from the Church, and applied it to his civil service; successful businessmen were thus allowed to enter areas dominated by an enfeebled nobility. In the general hypocrisy surrounding public service, the great French king is generally disparaged rather than credited for inventing this instrument of renewal.

BRAIN DRAIN

Typically, the brain drain precedes an economic revolution; it is one of the symptoms of a dying and intolerant society that it blames its troubles on a narrow group, which it persecutes. This group leaves for a more tolerant society. Tolerance is a characteristic of societies just beginning an economic revolution and both eager and able to profit from the brains and special skills of its new arrivals.

The religious intolerance of Spain toward the Moors and the Jews deprived it of talents that could have consolidated its coming Golden Age. While Colbert and Louis XIV were trying to build their economy by political ends, they chased the protestant Huguenots from the north of France mainly to England, where they helped set the stage for the Industrial Revolution. Lack of support for scientists and intellectuals in postwar socialist Britain sent many to North America, where they helped launch the Information Revolution on its wealth-creating course.

GRAY MARKET

Estimates of the underground economy vary widely, and the most conservative are not necessarily the most reliable.Some put this form of slither as high as 50 percent in some parts of the world. It is tolerated because it provides unemployment relief at no apparent cost to the government, and its practitioners disappear from the embarrassing statistics of the unemployed. In California, the underground economy surrounds the flood of illegal workers who provide low-cost services and a competitive alternative to sending work offshore.

As taxes grow and government efficiency falls, barter, unreported income, tax evasion, and smuggling become acts of protest. Arbitrary laws against drugs and sex create tax-free leisure markets in the service sector, where protest and pleasure are combined. Christopher Hill, again in *Restoration to Industrial Revolution,* describes the underground economy during the last phase of the British Commercial Revolution (1680–1720):

> In the eighteenth century smuggling was almost a national sport, with popular sympathies on the side of the smugglers against custom officers. The severe laws against wool export were ineffective: in 1696 penalties had to be reduced in order to encourage prosecution of smugglers. Before and after the Union of 1707, smuggling and Jacobites throve together in Scotland. In England Sir Robert Walpole himself engaged in smuggling even when he was Secretary of War. In 1733, illicit trade with France and Holland was estimated at one-third of the legitimate trade. Liverpool's slave trade could not have existed without beads smuggled in from Holland, and much illegal sugar came from the French West Indies. At the end of our period scarcely one-third of the tea consumed in England seems to have been imported legally; and a great deal of English wool was smuggled into France. In America smuggling was almost a patriotic duty. Adam Smith thought that the chief French and English merchants were engaged in smuggling, and himself sympathized with the smuggler, who "would have been, in every respect, an excellent citizen had not the laws of his country made that a crime which nature never meant to be so."

PIRACY, COUNTERFEIT

No temporary institutions illustrate better the slither required for
a successful restructuring of the economy than piracy, counterfeit,
fakes, and tax havens, the systematic countervention of national
laws of property.

Piracy once referred to professional buccaneering, frequently
practiced or supported by a nation against its rivals. The city states
of Pisa and Genoa practiced it in the early days of their Commercial Revolution. Small Mediterranean and Caribbean ports lived
off it. During the first phase of her Commercial Revolution,
England formally backed a fleet of pirates who ravaged the Spanish Main, helping to spread the wealth stolen from the Incas and
the Aztecs by the Spanish conquistadores. At least where piracy is
public policy, there is no hypocrisy, and the state gets its share of
the proceeds.

In the Information Age, piracy has newer dimensions. In countries which make culture a vehicle of national purpose, keeping it
pure of commercial greed, broadcast piracy becomes an act of
popular liberation. Radio Caroline, operating from a ship moored
in international waters off the British coast, brought rock and roll
to the youth of England at a time when the BBC, armed with
monopoly, was dedicated to uplift. Fortunately, piracy triumphed;
Britain became the popular music center of the world, and its
employment, tourism, balance of payments, and the global quo-
tient of joy benefited immeasurably.

In a similar vein, music and movie piracy have broken the
American cultural hegemony established after World War I. The
American system for worldwide entertainment distribution was
under attack for secrecy, high-handedness, corruption, and theft
from its creative and performing artists. Both tape recorder and
video cassette player became accidental instruments of policy,
because they allowed much of the money usually siphoned back to
America to stay in the exploited land. As a result, the world now
enjoys stronger domestic movie- and music-makers, a richer output, a more global cultural marketplace, and the transfer of the
movie screen from the sticky-floored cinema to the relative comfort of home.

Such are the rewards of global success with information products (including fashion, which is chosen less for its warmth and
protection than for the statement it makes) that world centers grow

fat at the expense of the regions. Pacific-rim knockoffs of Paris perfumes and watches, New York designer jeans, California movies and records, home computers and software, chips, calculators, and games helped bring that part of the world into the Western orbit. The growth of new production centers, new customers, new industries—in brief, this major expansion of the free-world economy—is , based largely on piracy, counterfeit, and smuggling. This form of slither has obviously received a bad press; it should perhaps be called, in honor of Adam Smith, the invisible sleight-of-hand behind Western economic growth.

It has not been clearly established that piracy damages the interests of the successful copyright, trademark, or patent holder. The opposite case can be made. Through imitation, the pirate helps position the original product on top of the market, greatly increasing its sales. Since only the most successful products are illicitly copied, piracy is not only an independent proof of quality, but an instrument of their further success. Piracy may well be the most effective piece of slither in the revolutionary arsenal.

ESPIONAGE

Another instrument of slither with a bad press is espionage. Those who "globalize" military secrets are habitually mistreated, dishonored, and sometimes even shot. Yet, by creating a balance of terror, they have provided the West some forty years of freedom from world war. Industrial spies prevent the ravages of monopoly by transferring technology, increasing choice, and speeding world growth. Nations and city states historically protected their technological advantage by imposing death penalties on workers who would emigrate and take their secrets with them. Despite these precautions, other nations and city states have "acquired" the secrets of glass blowing, silkweaving, porcelain-firing, steelmaking . . . and silicon chips.

DEREGULATION

About halfway through any economic revolution, it is recognized that the system is the problem, that the thicket of regulation designed to restrain industry (or commerce or craft) has been all too successful, and that stagnation has become the result. A process of deregulation is proposed and accepted, whereby the whole regulatory mechanism is dismembered piecemeal. Sickly industries are urged to fight their way back to health or disappear, while new businesses are allowed and even encouraged to compete against traditional industries.

British liberalism, which grew out of her Industrial Revolution, was in fact the massive deregulation of the outdated mercantile system. The regulations surrounding the craft guilds were thrown off in stages, some during the Commercial Revolution, much of the rest in the wake of the Industrial Revolution. Although apprentices were still bound over for seven year terms in Dickens' day, this practice did not survive the second round of Industrial Revolutions leading up to the first World War.

BYPASS

"Bypass" has a very precise technical meaning in the 1980s: It refers to competition in the telecommunications industry, where unregulated carriers "bypass" the regulated service with cut-rate alternatives. Such short-cutting is encouraged by some authorities, who are thus able to force the sheltered phone companies to cut expenses and rates. Since communications represents a growing component of the cost of doing business, bypass helps national firms become more competitive in global markets.

In a broader sense, bypass refers to any technological advantage that permits frustrated users to escape from a monopoly, regulated service, or government-controlled institution. The classic example is the bypass of the protected and inefficient textile guild monopolies by the merchants of the Commercial Revolution when they introduced the putting-out system of cottage industry.

Videocassettes of movies bypass government-controlled broadcasting (which is usually mired in uplift and national propaganda) as well as high-priced movie theaters with inflexible schedules. Censorship of the erotic or political content of films can also be bypassed by the new technology. Personal computing and software allow young people to learn at their own pace at home according to their own interests rather than those imposed by an educational authority, however enlightened. Soon, medical diagnosis and advice will be available in the form of smart programs, so the patient may at the very least have the benefit of a top quality second opinion, and at best avoid the costs of second-rate medical advice. Similar bypass of the legal and judicial systems can be expected.

Bypass of the telephone system began as an underground activity. "Blue boxes" were electronic tone-generators that allowed amateur electronic experimenters, or "hackers," to fool the switching and billing mechanisms of the world's largest computer, the telephone system. In the early seventies, these devices opened the question of long-distance charges that were maintained at an artificially high level by regulators in order to cross-subsidize local telephone service. As increasingly efficient satellites all but eliminated the costs associated with long-distance, however, the justification for distance-sensitive tolls disappeared. Thus bypass, with its roots in the technically efficient underground, is another beneficial form of slither.

ANARCHY, REBELLION, OR SOUND ECONOMICS?

Americans regard with some resentment the economic development of Asian countries, since so much of it came through piracy, espionage, counterfeit, smuggling and stolen jobs. They have forgotten the role these practices played in its own economic development. They think of the transfer of jobs to the Third World as a defeat, whereas it is in fact a great victory. America could not maintain its growth while everyone else stagnated. And in fact, there are more jobs in America, more cars, more fine clothes in the closet, more television sets, more VCRs, more cultural variety than ever before. And now there are many parts of the world which live as well as America used to live. Because of this, America remains the inventive and spiritual center of a prosperous and rapidly growing free world. As long as developing countries want to steal North

American techniques, designs, and technology, America and the West will prosper and grow. It is when they stop borrowing—and stop growing—that leadership is lost, recession threatens, and real trouble begins.

SEARCH

Of all the institutions peculiar to economic revolutions, none is more heartrending than the search for values. If the old values are honored only in the breach, if hypocrisy, cynicism, despair, and anarchy lose their power to fascinate, if intellectualism fails and systems are corrupt, then the mind turns for truth to the past, to feelings, or to the senses. Five institutions prevail at this time: historicism, romanticism, eroticism, mysticism, and the escape to the commune.

Historicism is a natural expression of the feeling that we have been here before. At the height of the British Industrial Revolution, in 1775, the year Adam Smith was putting the finishing touches to *The Wealth of Nations,* while James Watt was perfecting the governor and condenser of his steam engine, and while the American Colonies were locked in a struggle for secession, Edward Gibbon's *The Decline and Fall of the Roman Empire* appeared and became an immediate best-seller. From the counting houses to the government benches, from the salon to the boudoir, Britain lifted the curtain on the end of empire and pondered her fate. Would Britain in fact survive the surrounding chaos? Karl Polanyi observes:

> In actual fact prosperity was just around the corner, a prosperity of gigantic proportions which was destined to become a new form of life not for one nation alone but for the whole of mankind. But neither statesmen nor economists had the slightest intimation of its coming.

Shakespeare's Histories were among his most popular plays during the Commercial Revolution in England, and they were rich in lessons, inspiration, and warnings, just as Barbara Tuchman, America's favorite historian today, uses the cataclysms of the past to illuminate the present. Her most important work, *A Distant Mirror,* draws a warning picture of the decline of the French in the years leading up to the Commercial Revolution; the late Fernand Braudel's monumental study of Europe's Commercial Age is rich in lessons as we move into the Information Revolution. Renaissance Italians were obsessed with Imperial Rome, whose achievements they carefully studied in order to surpass them. Machiavelli's *History of Florence* and Vasari's *Lives of the Artists* came out at the start of that city-state's economic decline. Hardly a sentient being today in the West has failed to draw the parallels of today's cataclysms and the Industrial Revolution; it is the very stuff of luncheon addresses, more common than chicken and peas.

The main thrust of historicism is the romantic return to the past. Britons of the Industrial Revolution reading Walter Scott's tales of knighthood, Americans of the Information Revolution eating up westerns or burying themselves in Tolkien's medieval recreations in *The Lord of the Rings* are no different than Elizabethan playgoers hurrying to *Macbeth* or *Julius Caesar.*

A skillful artist uses this interest in history to make a case for the present. Michelangelo's Sistine Chapel ceiling revisits the past to strengthen the faith of his age. Judy Chicago's traveling exhibition of ceramics and needlework, *The Dinner Party,* which identifies and celebrates 999 of the greatest women in history, makes a comparably powerful statement about women's place in contemporary society.

ROMANTICISM

Romanticism is feeling unleashed—self-sacrifice to something eternal, something bigger than oneself. When intellect fails, when growth ceases, when progress ends, when values fail, when cynicism tires, romanticism soars. We become, as Mumford tells us, obsessed with nationalism, nature, the primitive, the isolated individual, and the revival of old theologies and supernaturalisms.

Tiring of the Greco-Roman heritage of rationalism as the British Industrial Revolution broke out around them, Europeans turned to their pagan origins. In the words of cultural historian Sir Kenneth

Clark, "Romanticism was a northern movement, a rediscovery of those natural forces, mists, mountains, dark rivers, impenetrable forests that are part of the European imagination but which have lain dormant during two centuries of Mediterranean authority."

First, the British and French writers foresaw in the surrounding skepticism and cynicism a need for feeling and belief. The most successful novel of Britian's enlightenment was *Pamela* by Samuel Richardson, which set the pattern for sentiment. About the same time, France's de Marivaux raised delicate feelings to a delicious art form in a highly successful series of novels and plays. In 1775, *The Sorrows of Young Werther* gave the young Goethe an instant reputation throughout Europe. Werther, the anti-hero, was a helpless victim of his own tumultuous feelings. His extravagant clothing was widely imitated, his uncontrollable feelings became fashionable, his meaningless suicide swept Europe like a disease. Similarly, Jean-Jacques Rousseau's noble savage made us nostalgic for some supposedly lost natural simplicity, which our children might regain through education. Walter Scott reminded us of the nobility of feudal knighthood, the dearest vision of all.

Oh, Arthur, oh, Lancelot, oh, great hearts of yore, where are you now that we need you? The sweet anguish of chivalry, of passion in search of the pure, of a life of noble service, of an all-encompassing love, recognized and eulogized by a great poet— what solace in these miserable, petty times! When the spirit of Obi-Wan Kenobe sends Luke Starwalker off to fight the Empire with his "May the Force be with you," whose heart can resist?

As the sixties drew to a close, American romanticism found its voice in Yale law professor Charles A. Reich, whose *Greening of America* proclaimed Consciousness III:

> This is the revolution of the new generation. Their protest and rebellion, their culture, clothes, music, drugs, way of thought, and liberated life-style are not a passing fad or form of dissent and refusal, nor are they in any sense irrational. The whole emerging pattern, from ideals to campus demonstrations to beads and bell bottoms to the Woodstock Festival, makes sense and is part of a consistent philosophy. It is both necessary and inevitable, and in time it will include not only youth, but all people in America.

"Here are the eyes that see the world" writes romantic Theodore Roszak in 1969, in *The Making of a Counterculture*, "not as commonplace sight or scientific scrutiny sees it, but see it transformed, made lustrous beyond measure, and seeing the world so, see it as it really is." Enthusiasm becomes the supreme value. Unfortunately for its promoters, it is a faculty which easily tires.

Another popular form of romanticism during an economic revolution is nostalgia for the future. Be it Jules Verne as Europe struggled through its Industrial Revolution, or Ray Bradbury and George Lucas, Robert Heinlein and Arthur Clarke in our own, cultural historian Arnold Hauser has a word for them all:

> The escape to the past is only one form of romantic unreality and illusionism—there is also an escape into the future, into Utopia. What the romantic clings to is, in the final analysis, of no consequence, the essential thing is his fear of the present and the end of the world.

EROTICISM

If the Information Revolution began with the uptight fifties, with prudish and ill-informed marriage manuals mailed to the inexperienced in plain brown wrappers, the sixties brought a complete reversal. Bookshelves sagged under the weight of erotic novels, manuals on spouse-swapping, and erotic masterpieces of other cultures and other economic revolutions. The learned tome by Masters and Johnson on the nature of the orgasm became a global best-seller. The magazine of the revolution was *Playboy*, which made a clean breast of female anatomy and promoted the philosophy of the singles' bar and the etiquette of the one-night stand. Fashion hurried to the spotlight from one erogenous (or erroneous) zone to the next. Industrialization of the sexual act appeared in the form of the vibrator. Pleasure was heightened and inhibitions lowered in an ubiquitous cloud of pot. If you weren't getting yours, you weren't really trying.

Perhaps the most extravagant symbol of the erotic age was Betty Dodson's New York Academy of Liberating Masturbation. Here middle-class matrons met to learn about labial anatomy, clitoral stimulation, appropriate vibrators, orgasm, and other things their mothers never told them because they didn't know.

The heightened atmosphere of eroticism requires ever stronger stuff to squeeze hormones from overworked glands. The erotic titillation of the cinema, the novel, and the girlie magazine moved on to harsher stimulation, provoking the liberated woman, who had only just burned her bra, to put on the bluestocking of censorship.

"The whole age lived in a state of constant erotic tension," wrote Jan Huizinga in his classic study, *The Waning of the Middle Ages,* or in our terms, the closing years of the Small-Business Age. Their tournaments, like our hockey games, became ritual acts of conquest and rape. The lance, like the hockey stick, was the rampant phallic symbol aimed at penetration. Like the swinging Club Med vacations of the sixties, "Pilgrimages are the occasions of all kinds of debauchery; procuresses are always found there, people come for amorous purposes." The most popular book of the day was not the Bible but *Roman de la Rose,* "a veritable treasure-house of amorous doctrine, systematic and complete."

WITCHCRAFT, MAGIC, AND CULTS

If the liberation of women from economic purdah, always an issue at times of economic transformation, often took erotic form, there was a harsher, more perverse side. Their treatment as witches, a recurring feature of economic revolutions, inevitably resulted in continued subjugation. Even in our enlightened times, the cult of witchcraft has had a broad appeal for the young alienated from a vacuous industrial culture, and it returned in the 1960s, carried in on a breath of smoke.

Barbara Tuchman, in *The Distant Mirror,* writes:

Times of anxiety nourish belief in conspiracies of evil, which in the 14th century were seen as the work of persons or groups with access to diabolical aid. Hence the rising specter of the witch. By the 1390s witchcraft had been officially recognized by the Inquisition as equivalent to heresy. The Church was on the defensive, torn apart by the schism, challenged in authority and doctrine by aggressive movements of dissent, beset by cries for reform. Like the ordinary man, it felt surrounded by malevolent forces, of which sorcerers and witches were seen as the agents carrying out the will of the Evil One.

In the irrational sixties, flirting with witchcraft had little to do with pacts with the devil. American novelist Erica Jong studied the craze in her 1981 picture book, *Witches:* "The attraction of neo-paganism, witchcraft, the occult, as well as to Eastern religions is an indication that our established Western religions . . . have become too worldly, too concerned with the preservation of their own hierarchies; they have come to mirror the worldly powers they were designed to balance. They are no longer truly spiritual entities."

Ms. Jong would have us see witchcraft not as a fight against the Church, but a search for our own ancestral roots:

> The revival of interest in witchcraft is part of the whole neo-pagan movement. Often people are attracted to witch-craft for the wrong reasons—the desire to hex their enemies, to attend orgies, to shock their parents. But there are poignant and quite reasonable bases for the attraction to witchcraft: the desire to return to a religion that honors nature; the desire to acknowledge the potent force of sexuality in our lives; the desire to question the failings of organized religions; the desire to learn ancient techniques of meditation and healing.

Magical powers are honored in hundreds of films, including the most successful; in hundreds of plays, including those of Shakes-peare most particularly; and in thousands of books, including the world's first best-seller from the new printing presses, *Malleus Maleficarum (The Hammer of Witches,* 1484), "the most impor-tant and most sinister work on demonology ever written." It spread the hysteria of witchcraft throughout Europe. Ritual mur-ders of women attributed to the Christian persecutors of this pagan cult are widely believed to have reached nine million: more than the death camps of the Nazis, more than all the wars up to and including World War I.

COMMUNES

With the collapse of the old system, and often before the appearance of the new, there arises a desperate desire to escape from
"civilization" and to live a meaningful life. The breakdown of the
feudal system during the Small Business Revolution led to the
reform and resurgence of the monasteries. The vow of poverty was
a relative thing; civil life was brutish and uncomfortable even for
the nobility, and monks often had servants (or lay brethren) to do
the actual work. Until corruption returned with the dying age, the
reformed monasteries, and the Cistercians in particular, provided
challenge, purpose, and accomplishment to their brethren, and
technology, growth, and instruction to the surrounding community.
    The basic monastic formula, one third reflection, one-third study,
one third work, had been devised in the sixth century by Benedict
or Nursia, and over the centuries it had proved attractive, cohe-
sive, productive, and satisfying. Such a life compares favorably to
most alternatives during times of economic collapse.
    Even royalty can tire of its excesses as an economic era nears its
end. It is well known that Marie Antoinette and her friends played
at shepherd and shepherdess in carefully countrified costumes as
the Commercial Era collapsed. It is less well known that Isabeau,
queen of France at the close of the Small Business Age, indulged
in exactly the same regressions and excesses as her world crumbled around her, according to her biographer, that specialist in
pre-revolutionary decadence, the Marquis de Sade.
    Communes during the American Industrial Revolution (1870–1920)
were watched with great interest around the world: Those of the
Oneida Community were particularly well known, probably because of their open attitudes toward sexual freedom. They in turn
were influenced by the idealistic factory-communities started by
the pioneering British industrialist, Robert Owen. Similar interest
was shown in the various hippie communes as the Industrial Age
ground to a halt. Spirituality is always a factor in organizing a
commune, and ashrams of various religions are a growing feature of
rural America. Some have moved offshore for a maximum freedom, like the Jonesville religious community in Guyana, which
concluded its search for values in collective suicide.
    It is reported by NASA space consultant Gerard O'Neill that the
Soviets are raising children in monastic communes as preparation
for life in space colonies and for long-distance travel to the further

reaches of our solar system and beyond. The virtues of religious conviction and life under strictly reduced conditions would qualify colonists of the high frontier just as they did the pilgrim colonizers of the New World sometime earlier.

Chapter 5

REACTION

Once it gains a foothold, the new economic system begins to spread. But while economic innovators may be successful in establishing themselves in thirteenth century Venice or Florence, in sixteenth century Amsterdam or London or nineteenth century New York, they meet determined and sometimes overwhelming resistance from a threatened establishment as they expand across the West. Once established, the forces of reaction may persist for centuries, stifling change and growth.

As the Small-Business Revolution introduced a secular spirit into society, and as burghers and independent farmers gained power and independence, the Church and the nobility reacted with a bold and compelling strategy for the reestablishment of faith: the Crusades. Belief was strengthened and treasuries enriched as Christians were urged to pillage, plunder and destroy a more evolved civilization.

While the northern Italian city-states introduced reason and experiment to society with the Commercial Revolution, a generally corrupt church responded to the creation of spiritually more virile sects by attacking them as heresy and imposing the Inquisition, a system so vile it makes Naziism pale by comparison, for they succeeded in imposing "the final solution" on the Cathars of southern France. Otto Friedrich describes these reactionary forces in *The End of the World*:

> The Inquisition was uncontrollable. The inquisitors themselves were appointed for life, and anyone who interfered with them, or criticised them, or even questioned them, was subject to arrest, incarceration or torture. There were powerful economic reasons for the continuing pursuit of heresy, since the Inquisition by now claimed a large share, usually one third, of all the property

of anyone condemned as a heretic. . . . And since the inquisitors' first demand of their victims was their confession, and since the sincerity of the tortured defendant's confession could be proved only by his denunciation of his friends, neighbors, and accomplices, the inquisitors' search proved unending, their field of battle unlimited.

As the Industrial Revolution spread across America in the decades before the first World War, and tiny regional factories began to federate into national corporations, the muckraking press and the politicians joined forces to limit the power of the industrialists. Antitrust became such a powerful reactionary force that it gave shape to American industry for generations, and prevented it from reaching its natural global size.

Thus each revolution provokes the reaction that brings it to its end. Nothing could be more normal or less surprising. Gradually the reactionary forces are converted, ignored and mocked, or die. The radical ideas of the revolution are refined, and become the wisdom that guides the age. If reactionaries are too powerful, however, there is a danger that they will prevail, that they will silence, convert or destroy the creative elements of the economy. Innovation becomes disrespect, the search for growth, vulgarity, the desire for wealth, common venality. This is the English disease. It is as old as growth itself. It infects peaceful duchies and great republics. Much of Europe suffers from it today. It infects the Third World, like a sleeping sickness.

In 1981, American historian Martin Wiener published *English Culture and the Decline of the Industrial Spirit, 1850–1980,* a careful and brilliant analysis of the forces that ended the Industrial Revolution in Britain. Wiener's book, which is rapidly becoming a bible for the current British renewal, suggests the aristocratic drive to turn the industrial wealth-makers into gentlemen was so powerful that a century later it still prevents innovation and growth.

The gentrification of the materialistic, mechanistic inventors and entrepreneurs took but one generation, a mere nothing to the feudal aristocracy. The school system and the universities swallowed their children and graduated them as idealistic public servants well suited to run India and the empire, but ignorant of science and industry and unfit for venture and risk. Once the schools and colleges had turned them into gentlemen, they were above vulgar ambition and useful pursuit. They, too, looked on businessmen as "objects of scorn and moral reproval, and industry was noted chiefly as a despoiler of country beauty."

"If Oxbridge [that is, Cambridge and Oxford] insulated the sons of older elites against contact with industry," Wiener argues,"it also gradually drew sons of industrial and commercial families away from the occupation of their fathers, contributing to a 'hemmorhage' of business talent. The educated young men who did go into business took their antibusiness values with them. As businessmen sought to act like educated gentlemen, and as educated gentlemen . . . entered business, economic behavior altered. The dedication to work, the drive for profit, and the readiness to strike out on new paths in its pursuit waned."

As for the founders of industrial enterprise, they were invited to join the landed gentry by taking their money out of their business and putting it into land. "As capitalists became landed gentlemen, Justices of the Peace and men of breeding, the radical idea of active capital was submerged in the conservative ideal of passive property, and the urge to enterprise faded beneath the preference for stability."

As the turmoil of the Industrial Revolution was gradually smothered under the "village values" of the English gentry, the problems of England were laid on the doorstep not of a self-gelded establishment, but of the entrepreneurs of the Industrial Revolution. Then, as America took over the vigor and vulgarity of economic growth, civilized disdain was transferred from the English Midlands to the work-and-money-mad New World. Finally, as the Industrial Revolution receded in time, it was as though it had never happened: The clear line of chivalric value from Arthur on down was restored to virginity.

The triumph of chivalry over the entrepreneurial spirit, the failure of the nation to nurture the authors of its wealth and greatness, the massive rejection of all they stand for—this is the English disease. These attitudes are to be found everywhere in the world where there is inherited wealth. The quest for stability is a natural expression of a people caught in the throes of untrammeled growth, and it provides a fitting balance to the relentless pursuit of efficiency. When, however, it invades a people to its core, when it lasts not for a generation but a century, when it stands united against the creation of wealth and the entrepreneurial venture, it ceases to be a counterbalance and becomes a disease.

This disease is part of the British legacy to her one-time colonies, those parts of the map still shown in red. Canada's founding as a nation in 1867 dates from the height of British anti-industrialism, and its national goals of "peace, order, and good government" are the purest expression of the disease. It acquired all the right attitudes of a civil service and an educational system designed to rule an empire, but without any empire to rule; and to contain the excesses of industry, but without any industry to contain. As in the mother country, entrepreneurialism was treated as impertinence, risk thought of as impudence, and business failure considered shameful. As a consequence, with the Empire's collapse Canada quickly became an economic colony of the United States, a "moonlight culture" reflecting rather than generating light, in Spengler's famous phrase.

Yet even the long feudal night was disturbed by the dawn of change, and there are signs the disease is losing its grip on the British soul. As the world shifts from industrial to information values, from material technologies of steel and chemicals to the ethereal world of bits and bytes, quirks and quarks, photons and genes, the British might once again let their creative cat out of the bag for a generation or two and dazzle the world anew.

PART TWO

REVOLUTIONS
PAST

WESTERN ECONOMIC REVOLUTIONS

Feudalism is a stable economic state that can last for centuries. In Japan it lasted right down to the Meiji Restoration in 1868. The anonymous risk-takers who awakened the West from its feudal snooze in the tenth and eleventh centuries with their towns, small businesses, guilds, and private farms were interrupting an economic movement that was just getting under way. A marriage of faith and order, feudalism could still inspire William and his Norman troops to conquer both Moslem Sicily and the kingdom of Britain, and impose this powerful system on the unenlightened inhabitants.

All the more marvelous, then, was the courage of the authors of the Western economic awakening to bypass secular authority and install their new institutions in the interstices of feudal Europe. They were not revolting against Church or Faith, they were taking it in their own hands, secularizing it. This, too, was a risk which threatened ecclesiastical authority and inspired the Inquisition.

In the preceding section we looked at economic revolutions in the abstract and noted a number of recurring patterns demonstrating the economic order behind the random events of political and social history. It is time to apply them to specific revolutions.

The first pattern is the two-phase, fifty-year cycle that launches each new economic age. As we work our way through our historic revolutions we will notice that with each repetition the pattern becomes more clearly defined and more closely followed. This may be because the forces underlying economic growth are themselves more developed and powerful, or alternately, our records are more detailed and precise.

The second pattern is the regular appearance of a new functional class (administration, small business, finance, industry, etc.,) complete with its own hierarchy of risk-takers, staff, and workers, and its striking and irreverent new mode of thought. The accumulation of layers of economic classes makes each successive age richer (in all dimensions) than the last.

The third pattern is the speedy takeover of the new approach by the older economic classes, and the thoroughness with which they integrate it into their affairs. Thus, it is not so much the economic intitiatives of the new class, but the integration of the new economics throughout the system which creates the new wealth.

If these patterns stand up to historic inspection, they will prove useful in helping us predict the future of the present revolution, and future revolutions, and in helping less developed nations awaken their own economic growth.

Chapter 6
THE FEUDAL ECONOMY

800 A.D. ONWARD

The feudal economy was a sophisticated and complete work of relationships between the nobility and their vassals (lesser nobles) and serfs (laborers). They were tied together not by monetary arrangements with limited responsibilities, but by an unequal system of duties and privileges from which there was no escape.

The system was by no means unique: It was actually the final, rigid stage of the agricultural economy, typical of many civilizations past and present. Only a small number of civilizations have managed to pass beyond it into the small-business or craft economy, and fewer still (such as the ancient Egyptian, Greek, Roman, Moslem, and Chinese, as well as our own) succeeded in evolving into a commercial economy.

The feudal or manorial economy was strictly hierarchical. Land was the sole basis of wealth, and it belonged in turn to emperor, king, baron, and knight, and also pope, bishop or abbot, and priest. The nobles held their land in exchange for service, and they were provided with sufficient vassals and serfs to assure their station in life, keep them in armor and horses, and free them for extended military service on demand.

Between battles, nobles were expected to sharpen their skills with hunting (which also provided them with meat) and to joust in tournaments. They were also expected to administer their fiefs with all the severity required to maintain order and respect. They were thus the ancestors of today's government.

Many of the characteristics of today's bureaucracy trace their origin to the feudal system. The hierarchy, with its carefully graded privileges and responsibilities, is essentially feudal, as is the sense of "noblesse oblige," where one's sense of duty and honor rises with one's position in the hierarchy. The senior executive in government today, like the military commander, is working for far more than his emolument. Many contemporary political systems have a completely feudal and entirely honorific monarch as head of state, and most which don't have some ceremonial substitute, such as a nonexecutive president.

The line of evolution of the feudal lords is clear and direct. As the economy evolved beyond the feudal stage, many became part of the king's court or parliament, trading in offices, collecting taxes and fees, making and executing laws. Using skills developed in administering their estates, some nobles would eventually become merchant bankers. The large Florentine family banking houses that launched the Commercial Revolution grew out of the landed magnates who had successfully turned their feudal estates into diversified, revenue-producing holdings.

It would, however, be romantic to assign to the feudal nobility the trappings and graces of later ages. Most warlords lived uncomfortably in timbered blockhouses (the great stone castles came after the Crusades) with cold walls and straw covered floors. The serf was a despised and degraded creature who lived in a mud hovel with an earthen floor and a smoke hole in the thatched roof. Feudal life was mainly a subsistence system, with limited diet and no prospects for improvement.

The only part of the economy that was monetized and showed any growth was the information sector—that is, the Church. Priests traded salvation and other ethereal products for a goodly share of all their flock produced. Though the priesthood included men of great spiritual and intellectual achievements, this period of Church history was, more often than not, characterized by corruption and depravity.

Priests were the militant side of the Church, in daily contact with the world. More highly regarded on the spiritual plane were the monks, whose waking hours were divided equally among spiritual, physical, and intellectual exercises remote from the follies and vanities of the world. Monks also had control over the mystery of writing, a sacred act performed on meticulously prepared sheets of sheepskin (parchment) or calfskin (vellum). As an instrument of power, it was kept from the profane.

Monasteries were the inns of their day. They welcomed travelers—and pumped them for news, which was processed into intelligence and passed up the hierarchy of the Church. Their libraries contained manuscripts both sacred and profane. Their scholarship was shared throughout the religious community. They provided what teaching there was for the children of the nobility. They kept the arts and crafts alive. They, more than any since, appreciated the value and uses of information as the very basis of the religious economy.

Given the brutishness of feudal life, accepting the asceticism of the monastery was hardly a sacrifice. There were lay brothers to act as servants and laborers. Advancement came quickly to the monk or nun with ability, connections, and strength of character. He or she would establish a branch plant in the wilderness and become its abbot or abbess for life.

Corruption of monastic life in the closing years of the feudal regime was a matter of distress to the truly religious, an embarrassment to the Church, and the butt of humor to the laity. It would be the subject of constant reform during the coming Small-Business Revolution.

During the Feudal Era, there was a minuscule business community providing crafts and trade in the occasional town surviving from Roman days, but for the most part it was a premonetary economy, organized into self-sufficient entities. Taxes and tithes were more often paid in kind than coin.

Throughout the dark centuries, the Church grew by religious conversion and expanded across Europe. When conversion slowed as the millennium closed, the system stagnated. Internal wars became a welcome diversion and chance for plunder, and the Church oscillated erratically between the vilest corruption and zealous devotion and reform. The ground was prepared for change.

The arts of the Feudal Era were almost exclusively confined to the monasteries. "Medieval art," says Arnold Hauser in his four-volume *Social History of Art,* "was a vehicle for ecclesiastical propaganda." Its task, he says was "to put the masses of the people into a solemn but on the whole a somewhat vague and indefinite religious frame of mind."

Monasteries since Benedict's day had devoted some part of their efforts to copying and illustrating manuscripts, which grew exceedingly ornate and demanded the work of many specialists. There were *miniatores* (painters), *antiquarii* (calligraphers), *rubricatores* (who painted the elaborate initial letters), and *scriptores* (assistants). Throughout this period the making of books was of far greater consequence than writing them, and few from this time are still read.

"Apart from book-illustration," says Hauser, "monks also engaged in architecture, sculpture and painting, were active as goldsmiths and enamel workers, practised silk- and carpet-weaving, started bell foundries and book-binding workshops, glass factories and ceramic workshops.'' They also trained artists for the richer courts and parishes of that not yet wealthy time.

Secular arts were largely confined to poetry. The writing and reciting of heroic lays was an essential component of the feudal war machine, and important military fiefs often maintained a full-time minstrel who knew by heart the history of great battles dating back to Charlemagne and who passed them onto the next generation. Thus the minstrel was the last professional artist.

Chapter 7

THE SMALL-BUSINESS REVOLUTION

TENTH TO TWELFTH CENTURIES

PHASE ONE: ESCAPE TO FREEDOM

Incorporation is the great institution of the Small-Business Revolution. Through accepting the rules of a simple charter, independent towns, independent smiths and millers, and independent shopkeepers are absolved from service to the noble and are free to exist and do business with each other and with manors, churches, and monasteries. Workers are free to sell their labor, farmers their produce, farmwives their lace and homespun. Land, home, mill, smith, and business now become private property and can be bought and sold, pledged and lost.

With the town comes the market by which it is supplied, where the farmer, smith, and miller buy and sell their wares. With trade comes the merchant, and with the merchant comes specialized production and the fair, where goods from afar may be traded or sold.

The familiy farm dates from this time. Prior to the Small-Business Revolution, serfs worked the land for the warlord or his vassal and were little more than human cattle. As productivity grew with the new technology, opportunities opened to leave the manor, clear or drain a new piece of land, and start a farm of one's own, selling the surplus to the towns.

Much of Europe was colonized in the process, often in large scale developments. The solid band of green forest running across England and northern Europe as far as Russia was everywhere breached by the broadax, and great portions of Holland owe their origins to the enthusiasm which ex-serfs brought to drainage projects in their quest for their own piece of land.

Although outraged at first by the disappearance of their serfs and vassals, some noble families were quick to join the monetary economy. By taking rents instead of service from their underlings, they made money on a scale that allowed them to buy their own freedom from service in the king's wars and enjoy the produce of the new craftsmen, saddlers, armorers, tailors, glazers, cutlers, and others whose specialties were becoming institutionalized as family names.

To colonize seashores, control floodplains, drain marshes, fell forests, and turn them into farms demanded organization and entrepreneurial skill. Corporations were established and contracts let to develop uninhabited regions.

To establish towns, to trade, run a craftshop or a mill, also demanded corporate organization and an entrepreneurial bent. The charter of incorporation was the kiss that awakened the economy from its long sleep.

To run a big fair, such as those of Champagne to the southeast of Paris, demanded extensive organization. Each of these fairs lasted for several months and had a well developed code of rules and court of justice, housing for foreign contingents, exemptions and laissez-passers for traveling merchants, and a system for reconciling payments as the fair drew to a close, all of which laid the basis for future trade.

To move from preeconomic manor to country estate demanded corporate organization on the part of the nobles as well. The economic awakening of the West meant learning to incorporate, contract with others, and run a business. The first Western economy was a Small-Business Age.

The Small-Business Revolution started in Northern Italy and in Flanders in the tenth century, giving these widely separated regions a head start on the rest of Europe that would last for centuries. Like a tidal wave in slow motion, it gradually spread across western Europe and reached a backward England in the twelfth century. In its wake were thousands of independent towns bursting their walls, hundreds of soaring cathederals, scores of lively universities, tens of thousands of technologically sophisticated mills and monasteries, and hundreds of thousands, and soon millions, of thriving private farms.

The reformed monasteries of the eleventh and twelfth centuries, with their renewed dedication to poverty, were the carriers of the wealth-making know-how. St. Bernard's Cistercian abbeys, the most austere (and fastest growing) of the new orders, were models of agricultural, industrial, and commerical organization. Established in the wilderness, they encouraged regional growth.

They conducted research into agricultural and mechanical technologies, such as wind and water mills, which they were quick to adopt and share with their sister institutions throughout the West. They ran schools and model farms, passing on their knowledge of breeding, crop rotation, water power, and metallurgy to their surrounding communities. They exchanged market information, traded throughout their continent-wide network, and founded industries (the British wool industry was established by the Cistercians). At the height of the Small-Business Era, there were some forty thousand monasteries throughout Europe. Without them, there might never have been a Small-Business Revolution, and Western civilization would have been very different—had it survived at all.

Parallel with the growth in agriculture was the spread of the town. Northern Italy led the way, partly because it was the least devastated by the fall of the Roman Empire; in part, thanks to its ties to the all-powerful Chruch; but mainly because of its close contact with the highly civilized Arabs, from whose learning and science, crafts and commerce they had much to gain. Historian Lauro Martines describes the economic explosion in his study of the Italian city-states, *Power and Imagination*:

> Rude little settlements like Prato and Macerata burst into thriving towns; and ancient cities like Milan, Pavia, Cremona and Mantua were borne up once again in a rising flood of people, property, transactions, commerce and feverish activity in the building trades. The river towns and obscure ports—Florence, Pisa, Genoa—exhibited spectacular dynamism; and the tiny cities of the northern plain, Piacenza, Verona, Crema, Padua—eagerly received foreign merchants or as eagerly dispatched their own.

"Europe was suddenly covered with towns," writes Fernand Braudel, "more than 3000 in Germany alone. Some of them, it is true, were little more than villages, despite their city walls, harbouring a mere two or three hundred souls. But many of them grew to become towns of a new and unprecedented kind. . . . It was the medieval city which, like the yeast in some mighty dough, brought about the rise of Europe."

PHASE TWO
ELEVENTH CENTURY

With the towns came the great incorporated institutions, the guilds, cathedrals, and universities. The principal industry of the Small-Business Age was textiles, and the principal textile was wool. This industry was dominated by the Flemish, who in the eleventh century were making and shipping thousands of bolts of cloth to the fairs of Flanders and Champagne, and through them to Italy and elsewhere in Europe. Productivity was maintained by technological innovation, mainly in the development of vertical looms and factory production.

Flanders soon had more looms than wool. A lively import trade was developed by the Cistercians, who taught the British sheep-breeding and husbandry and used their wide network on the continent to market their produce. Britain's damp climate favored fat sheep with long-staple fleece, which made the best cloth, and exports soon reached thirty to fifty thousand sacks per year.

A sack of wool could be produced for four to six pounds sterling, and sold for twelve to fifteen pounds in the Low Countries, of which the king of England took five or six pounds in taxes to help pay for his wars. Such high export taxes encouraged the development of an indigenous cloth industry in England, and English wool merchants began to be seen in the trading centers of Europe.

The guilds, which today are little more than unions of artists or professionals, were, at their origins in the West in the twelfth century, a syndicate of the town's business owners incorporated to defend their privileges, maintain prices, and keep out competition. The richest and most powerful guilds were the merchants, who traded abroad on behalf of the town and brought back wholesale goods. Later, craft guilds appeared, and they divided and subdivided into specialties as the town's economy grew.

The guilds were the center of manufacturing in the early town. A "master" owned a shop, in which he and his journeymen and apprentices lived, where they crafted their products, and where these were offered for sale. The richest, freest, and most powerful of the crafts guilds were the masons. They built the town's houses, walls, and bridges and roamed Europe creating its cathedrals, the dramatic expression of the new prosperity.

Though the age was directed to creating wealth, the size of a master's fortune was limited by guild ordinance and religious principle to one suitable to his station and no more. There was a just price and a just profit for every transaction. No businessman (read, gentleman) was to corner a market, buy up all the supplies, create a large backlog, lower his prices, or otherwise compete with his colleagues on any basis other than quality. (These constraints survive in the doctors' and other professional guilds today.) Merchants' profits were limited by what they could carry with them on caravan or in the hold of a ship. They were small businessmen in thought and deed and were forced by circumstance and the spirit of the time to remain that way.

This small-business culture of the guilds found its expression in drinking and benevolent societies, which looked after guildsmen and their families in all the vicissitudes and pleasures of life. The performing arts, confined to the Church in feudal times, were taken over by the guildsmen and secularized. Feast days were occasions of the most elaborate processions of floats, each a rolling stage sponsored by a different guild; they moved from square to square, stopped, performed there its appropriate Bible stories, then moved on to the next. The artistry, playfulness, and mechanical genius behind these elaborately profane passion plays was basic to the staging of a contemporary musical comedy or Christmas pantomime. No money was charged or collected: This was the guilds' contribution to the community for all they had received from it, and they competed with great energy and fervor.

Secularization could well be said to be the spirit of the time. Through incorporation into guilds, scholars and professors found at least partial freedom from Church control. First, scholars incorporated themselves into universities and hired professors to teach them. Their pay was tied to performance, and they were fired if they failed to meet expectations. Later it was the professors who incorporated themselves into universities, setting the rules and charging students appropriately. Both models flourished, and the spread of universities created a host of lawyers, doctors, theologians, and educators—a professional class still organized in guilds after eight prosperous centuries.

While the merchants and craftsmen were bound by guild rules to restrain their quest for wealth to modest proportions appropriate to their middle rank, no such scruples applied to the nobles, who, if they had the wit or the proper advice, could acquire great wealth through the appropriate exploitation of their estates. Thus three distinct cultures coexisted: the small-business culture of the new middle class; the churchmen, anxious to appropriate the new wealth to God's purposes; and the noblemen, eager to profit from and control the new economy.

No longer brutish warlords, nobles sought to institutionalize their new status through refinement and chivalry. The chatelaine was transformed into a great lady, to whom selfless love and devotion were due. Courts of love were formed where high-born troubadours sang of forlorn but ravaging passion, and the new emotion was debated, distinguished, and codified. Tournaments demonstrated that the new knights maintained staunch hearts and fearful skills inside their mannered exteriors.

Neither the Italian city-states nor the Flemish cities of the north were by any means the most civilized of the developing regions. That distinction belonged to Languedoc (now known as the French Midi), which was centered in Toulouse. "Its merchants shipped cloth and leather to the trade fairs outside Paris, and the wines of the Bordeaux region to England," writes chronicler Otto Friedrich in *The End of the World, a History*. "The sea-captains of Genoa and Pisa appeared, bringing the silks and spices of the Levant in exchange for Toulouse's oil and wax, rope, lumber and fish."

Along with its commercial success, Friedrich tells us, "under the twelfth century sun of Languedoc, there occurred one of those almost miraculous flowerings of cultural life," including Romanesque architecture, infinitely sophisticated sculpture, and the poetry of the troubadours. The Provencal poets "not only created great art, but provoked the creation of great art in Italy and Spain and even Germany."

One of the great creations of Languedoc was a sect of Christianity noted for its purity and great beauty, the Cathars, whose virtues shone all the more brightly compared to the "violence, sottishness, lust and stupidity" of the regular clergy (to quote the Archbishop of Rouen), who were "zealous in avarice, lovers of gifts, seekers of rewards. They justify the evil-doer for bribes and deny justice to the righteous" (to quote Pope Innocent III). "Hence the insolence of the heretics, the scorn of rulers and people for God and the Church."

It is said that France was at its greatest and most influential in the twelfth and thirteenth centuries, and that Languedoc, its southwest quarter, was truly paradise. Mankind, historians say, may not have known a happier time. This, not Arthur's mythic castle, was Western civilization's Camelot.

REACTION

At each economic revolution, some one class finds its interests or status threatened by the advance of the new class and the new economic spirit transforming the economy, and it seeks by whatever means necessary to suppress change and return to past values and privileges. Fearing that secularizing of culture and the monetizing of the economy would lead to loss of control, it was the reactionary religious forces of the Church, very much in disarray and suffering from widespread incompetence and corruption, which sought to arrest or deflect the forces of the Small-Business Revolution.

Disturbed by the adulation of the chatelaine, the spread of romantic love, and the rise in the status of women, the Church instituted the cult of the Virgin. Once tolerant and adaptive to the old religions, it institutionalized witchcraft and heresy by creating another religious institution, the Inquisition, which promoted conformity through terrorism, torture, and murder.

The abundant surplus of the awakened economy was channeled into those two unique but typical institutions, the cathedral and the Crusades. Though at first they appear to be supreme expressions of faith and of the great power of the Church, they were in fact, like the Inquisition and the schism to follow, signs that the Church had passed its great period of growth, that it was losing its grip on the economy and the heart and needed some bold action to restore faith and control.

Much of the wealth which went into building the cathedrals came from the Crusades. And the compliment was returned: "In the conflict between East and West, between Christianity and Islam" wrote Von Reinhard Bentmann and Heinrich Lickes in *Churches of the Middle Ages*, "these buildings became huge monuments to victory, symbols of an awakening consciousness."

It was the pugnacious and piratical Pisans who set the economic precedent the Crusades would follow. In 1062, they mounted a combined religious and plundering expedition on the Moslem stronghold of Palermo in Sicily. Those who think of Sicily today as an arid desert strewn with sun-baked rocks would not recognize the Islamic paradise of the eleventh century. Palermo the Golden was studded with "delicately structured Chateaux de Plaisance with artistically laid out streams and gardens, and shady courts under whose arcades Arab love-poets recited their latest works to an appreciative audience and learned scribes copied the manuscripts of classical authors.''

The Pisans easily defeated the Arabs, who were otherwise occupied fighting the Normans. According to Bentmann and Lickes, ''the ships of the Pisan fleet were hardly able to carry the vast load of treasures—gold, jewels, carpets, precious furnishings, spices, works of art, architectural ornaments, thoroughbred hunting animals, ivory chests. . . . The monument that grew out of this great victory and the immeasurable plunder it afforded was to be the cathedral complex erected outside the city of Pisa, one of the most unforgettable groups of buildings in all European architecture.''

With this successful model to guide him, and faced with cynicism, schism, political disunity, and the economic decline of the Church, the reform pope Urban II solved all his problems with one bold idea: a great Crusade to "rescue" the Holy Land from the Turks. It was a gesture so successful that it would be repeated eight times by opportunistic popes over the next two hundred years.

The Crusades were enormously profitable to the Italian cities, charged with outfitting the venture with its maritime requirements. Vast plunder was returned from the more successful of these expeditions, and much of this found expression in a spate of soaring gothic cathedrals. Among the first to profit were those at Chartres, Amiens, and Rheims.

Both the Crusades and the cathedrals had their desired effect of rebuilding the faith of the West. To quote Bentmann and Lickes again, enthusiasm for these projects was immense:

> Rich and poor, men of distinction as well as peasants and labourers, joined in to pull the carts bringing sustenance to the builders and stone for the masons to the building site, all the while singing pious songs in ecstasies of delight, confessing their sins aloud and imploring God to heal the sick as they followed behind vessels containing relics. Building the cathedral was an enormous, protracted act of expiation *ad maiorem dei gloriam,* to the greater glory of God.

By promoting the Crusade, the Church institutionalized religious war against fellow Christians such as the Cathars of Languedoc, whose genocide and the destruction of that happy region's economy and culture marks the sad beginning of the Church's darkest days. Fearful of the new secularization and monetization of the economy, it institutionalized simony (the selling of offices) and otherwise monetized sin, sacraments, virtues, repentence. Every one of its sacred rituals and offices had its price. Soon there were two, and at one point three, popes squabbling for control and dividing its revenues.

AFTERMATH

This happiest of times, the golden twelfth and thirteenth centuries, when dreams of freedom, prosperity, and meaningful lives were first realized, was based on the growth of towns, which in turn was based on the reclamation and colonization of unexploited land. Once the useful land was filled, the towns stopped expanding. Ghent, in Flanders, was typical: enlarging its walls four times during the golden years, each time expanding further and more boldly than before. Its fifth expansion, the most ambitious, took place as the Small-Business Revolution ended, and it remained embarrassingly unfinished until this century.

When there were no more lands for colonization, every vassal or serf's dream of a farm of his own was blighted. Once growth slowed, every journeyman's dream of a shop of his own was scotched. Henceforward, only those who could pay could have land; only the master's son could hope to acquire a shop.

As the age passed its prime, rules became stricter and lawyers multiplied. The guilds, once instruments of freedom and promise, became prisons, fettering innovation. The nobility, having bought their freedom from military service to their liege, lost their main justification for the privileges they enjoyed, and softened by silken dalliance at the courts of love, no longer commanded respect. God's carefully ordained social system was coming apart.

Chapter 8
COMMERCIAL REVOLUTIONS

The Commercial Revolutions carried the economic advances made in the Small-Business Revolution to a higher level of activity. A self-sustaining commercial economy is essentially a system in which five components are balanced:

1. *A long-distance trading network, with a diversified group of products and services.* The Small-Business Age merchant travelling with his goods is little more than a glorified peddler, unable to attend to other business and out of touch with world events and opportunities while en route. One major loss can bring ruin. By remaining at home rather than accompanying his goods by ship or caravan, the sedentary merchant is able to amplify his operation far beyond that of a single venture and to increase the magnitude of his profit while reducing the impact of failure of individual ventures.

2. *A banking operation, carried out in connection with the above.* The merchant-banking firm maintains a network of factors (agents) throughout its trading area, with whom it is in constant contact, sending instructions and receiving reports of transactions, opportunities, and other market intelligence. The bank provides the merchant with capital and clients, information, and the opportunity for leverage, favor, or monopoly.

3. *A system of production.* The trading cycle is primed with world class product(s) manufactured at home and shipped far and wide in exchange for exotic goods.

4. *A distribution network*, whereby the products of long distance trade are brought to market: either to other merchants or directly to customers. This network requires warehousing and wholesale operations (developed by the Dutch).

5. *Collaboration of state and Church.* Building a long-distance trading network requires the power of the state; maintaining it,

the power of empire. The state also sets the terms of trade. In the commercial system, the instruments of wealth are the trading network, the profits on the transfer of funds, and the interest on large-scale, long-term loans. Since usury was prohibited by the Church and profits were coveted by the state, ingenuity was required to disguise the making of money (which complicates the task of the economic historian).

The Commercial Revolution came relatively easily to the Italian city-states. The Venetian model was based on empire and monopoly access to the East. The Florentine model was based on production, banking, and distribution. Both models lasted for half a millennium. The nations of Europe found the Venetian and Florentine formulas difficult to master and harder still to combine into a balanced system. Much of the anguished history and distinguished achievement of Europe is contained in the attempt.

THE COMMERCIAL REVOLUTION IN VENICE

At the time of the Crusades, at the height of the Small-Business Revolution, Venice was an outpost of the East, a trading outlet on the continent for the products of Constantinople, Syria, and Alexandria. Spread over some sixty islands, the city had to trade to survive, importing even its food and water. As a consequence, it had no great landed families; its ruling class was mercantile, exclusively concerned with trade. From 1100, the principal activity of the state was the building of ships and galleys at the Arsenal, and these it leased to the merchants of Venice, sold to the Crusaders, and exported to the East.

The origins of the Commercial Revolution in the West can be traced to this Venice at the end of the twelfth century, when a novel method of financing ships and expeditions appeared. Merchants divided the cost of vessel and expedition into twenty-four carets (or shares), taking some themselves and selling the rest to other merchants and to small businessmen eager and ready to make a play. This shared the risk, brought new capital into the game, increased the level of collaboration throughout the economic community, and greatly speeded the pace of trade and shipbuilding. It was a momentous innovation for the West.

This new system of financing had been in place about a generation, when at the beginning of the thirteenth century, the French organized the fourth Crusade, focused on Egypt and Alexandria. Venice was chosen as its staging ground, and twenty thousand Crusaders assembled there in 1203.

Enrico Dandolo, the doge (or duke) of Venice, had contracted to build a transport fleet to take them to Egypt, for the then huge sum of eighty thousand francs. Money ran out before the ships were completed, and the wily doge agreed to finish construction of the fleet only if the Crusaders would attend to some of Venice's business en route to Egypt: a disciplinary visit across the Adriatic to Zara, a coastal port that had rebelled against Venetian control.

The Crusade never reached Alexandria. Dandolo, blind and aged, took personal charge of the attack on Zara and, when that caper was successfully completed, skillfully persuaded the adventurers to lay siege to Constantinople, Venice's erstwhile master now at odds with Rome. The entire fleet arrived in the Byzantine capital in 1205, sacked the city, and carried off its wealth, giving Venice control of the eastern Mediterranean shipping lanes, and of a series of outposts that stretched from Constantinople home. By subverting the Crusade from its religious purpose, the doge brought Venice a monopoly of trade with the East and, with it, economic leadership of the West.

While the primary purpose of the network of outposts was to protect trade routes, these colonies, which included the fertile island of Crete, became consumers of Venetian products and providers of wines, grains, and materials. The West had its first taste of empire, and the economic fruits were sweet.

The Venetian state was in total charge of the economy from the start of the revolution, and it laid out strict rules for trade development. It owned the ships, which it chartered to local merchants. It concentrated on the import of Eastern products by sea, forcing the merchants of Europe to come to Venice to trade. Foreign merchants, and in particular the Germans, were made to live in ghettoes and obliged to accept Venetian goods in exchange for those they brought from the north.

These rules also prevented the merchants of Venice from becoming too powerful; cartels of any sort were swiftly put down, and so the republic's enormous wealth was widely distributed. The share system offered opportunities to even the most modest capitalist. As long as Europe needed spices, drugs, silks, and cottons from the East, and Venice held the monopoly, everyone prospered.

For a hundred years, Venice had it all its own way. Toward the end of the thirteenth century, however, its traditional rival, Genoa, was moving in on the European market, sailing her fleet out the straits of Gibraltar and trading into the European markets from the north. Genoese fleets were also attacking Venetian galleys right up the Adriatic to her very front door. It was a new game.

Challenged by its rival, Venice was soon running scheduled annual sailings of its own to England and Flanders. They carried damask from Damascus, calico from Calicut on India's southwest coast, cottons and silks, paper and glass, alum and dyes, spices, wine, and fine foods; they returned with Flemish cloths and Arras hangings, tin and iron, lead and pewter, brass and cutlery, leather and hides.

No longer were the merchants of Europe compelled to come to Venice to trade: Competition was forcing the empire to fight for its markets with everyone else. Venice was getting lazy. Its merchants bought estates on the mainland or went into manufacturing. The doors were closed to new wealth and power by the aristocrats in power. It had not allowed large firms to emerge or banking to become international. Yet because of its continuing monopoly of eastern Mediterranean trade, assured by its outposts and colonies, it remained a world power right down to the eighteenth century. This monopoly model of trade and empire was followed by the Atlantic nations over the centuries.

COMMERCIAL REVOLUTION IN FLORENCE

A somewhat different approach to the Commercial Revolution took place in Florence toward the end of the thirteenth century. Democratic government was being established in the Italian city-states. In 1250, Florentine merchants managed to wrest control from the aristocrats and created a government run by the "popola," or businessmen. About 1275, a number of highly successful patrician merchant families, among them the Bardi, Peruzzi, and

Frescobaldi, expanded into banking, establishing networks of agents, or factors, in the Italian city-states and throughout the East and Europe. Instead of traveling with their goods, which limited them to one project at a time, these new merchant bankers stayed home and ran a number of concurrent business ventures by letter. They contracted with ship captains to share in the profit of expeditions. They established a courier service to speed instructions to their factors and business associates and to keep themselves informed of developments affecting their interests. Through the city, they launched the golden Florin, Europe's first universal coin and one of the first of many financial institutions of the Commercial Revolution.

In the Small-Business Age, partnerships were the only form of joint business venture, with each partner responsible for any losses incurred. This limited the size of ventures to those which could be personally financed and handled. The universities, however, were studying Roman law, looking for commercial precedents and modifying them to Western conditions. By following Roman example, limited (-risk) companies were allowed for business ventures, raising incorporation to a higher economic level. Once risk was limited to the size of one's investment, merchants could spread their capital over a score of ventures, some goods-producing, some trading, some moneylending, some estate-holding. And they accepted money from smaller investors and shared the profit with them. They also took day-to-day deposits from other businessmen, offering security in exchange for the use of the money. In this way their operating capital was greatly expanded. Thus was capitalism born (a word not used until the nineteenth century).

These merchant bankers soon managed enormous sums of money, which they loaned to princes in exchange for monopolies on trade. The Bardi managed to secure a monopoly on wool exports from England in exchange for loans to King Edward II. The Naples dairy market was acquired the same way. The Florentine merchant bankers were also in a position to offer rulers and popes the use of their courier service, and to transfer payments for them throughout Europe. Big was Beautiful, and they grew bigger still.

In the first phase of the revolution the Florentine merchants brought Mediterranean goods to the fairs of Champagne and traded them for untreated wool cloth from Flanders, which they brought back to Florence to finish (full, shear, and dye) in their workshops. This finishing process tripled the value of the cloth, which was widely sought after by princes of Church and state. Yet when the Bardi obtained exclusive raw wool export privileges duty-free from the king of England in exchange for loans, the shift began from merely finishing cloth to the whole manufacturing process from bag to bolt, with quality rising and profits expanding accordingly. The revolution was entering its second phase.

No longer had these great merchant bankers anything in common with the guilds. In fact, with their monopolies, strict regulations, and small-business mentality, the guilds were becoming an embarrassment. Nonetheless they controlled production through their monopolies. So another structural change was needed: a way of producing goods which was more efficient and less limited than that of the guilds. This was found in the "putting-out" system of cottage industry. In the nearby countryside, as well as in the city, the merchants established a network of cottagers who were provided with tools and materials, usually looms and wool, and produced the finished product. In this way, the merchants slithered around the monopolies of the cloth-making guilds.

By 1317 the transformation of the Florentine wool-manufacturing process was complete. The revolution was over, and the Bardi had become the wealthiest family in Florence. Yet in order to keep the raw wool coming, they had to continue making loans to the British kings. The foppish Edward II, who had seriously weakened the English state, was deposed and replaced by the Boy King, Edward III, who in turn was soon at war with France, for which he needed yet more funds. He called on his faithful Lombards. In 1337, the Peruzzi, the Frescobaldi, the Acciauoli, and the Bardi were in over their heads, and clamoring for collateral. In 1340, involved in a war that was obviously not going to end quickly, Edward renounced his debts. First the House of Peruzzi tumbled, then the Acciauoli and Frescobaldi, and in January 1346, the mighty Bardi succumbed.

In that same 1346, the plague, which had killed thirteen million in China, left countless dead in India, and devastated Persia, arrived in the Crimea, where the Turks were laying siege to the Genoans, behind the walls of Kaffa. The plague hit the Turks, leaving blackened and bloated corpses, which survivors catapulted over the walls and into the Genoan camp. The Genoese, infected and dying, escaped in their galleys and sailed for home, collapsing at Messina in the summer of 1347. The plague had arrived in Europe. By January of 1348 it had reached Genoa. In Florence it came with the rains of spring.

"Death on such a scale made all the traditional forms of life meaningless," writes chronicler Otto Friedrich in *The End of the World, a History*. Where once there were two human beings, now there was one. Horror and terror were the universal emotions. but when it was done, one thing was clear: Those who survived were twice as well off as before. Among the survivors of the plague and the financial and political chaos of the mid-fourteenth century were the Albertis, rather slow in their methods, but living proof that to survive was to thrive.

THE ALBERTI BROTHERS

(case history)

In 1302, the Alberti brothers of Florence invested their inheritances in a merchant-banking partnership dealing in gray (untreated) woolens purchased from the Flemish at the Champagne fairs near Paris. They brought the bolts of cloth home to Florence, finished them in the Florentine manner and then sold them through their agents abroad.

In addition to their capital, they employed moneys borrowed from other Florentines at fixed interest (disguised as a bonus, since the Church forbade borrowing money at fixed interest as usury). They sent a factor (a paid agent) to the Champagane fairs to select and buy unfinished cloth on their account and to sell bolts of finished fabric. The accounts were settled at the end of the fair, paid in florins or in bills of exchange. The agent then returned to Florence with his unfinished woolens.

In Florence, the brothers maintained a plant where the famous Florentine finish was applied to the rough Flemish cloth. Since finishing usually tripled the value of cloth, this was the basis of their operation: the same as had been established in the previous centuries; the same as it was carried on by the pioneer merchant bankers, the Peruzzi, Bardi, and Frescobaldi; the same as would be done by the Medicis in the fifteenth and sixteenth centuries. Textiles were *the* basic industry until the nineteenth century, and since rank was established by what one wore, the manufacture of luxury fabrics was *the* business for centuries.

Running this kind of business had its particular problems: If the merchant hired the wrong kind of agent, he might abscond with the cashbox. If he wasn't furnished with frequent instructions, the agent might act on his own, or fail to act, and business would suffer. Since the clients were wealthy nobles and prelates, the problem of aging and bad debts was constant and demanded the strictest attention. The

Alberti had a special problem: One of the brothers, Neri, had borrowed heavily from the firm. When the business cycle turned sharply downward and Neri could not repay, the brothers dipped deep into their personal coffers to keep up interest payments to their lenders, who might otherwise withdraw their capital and put the firm under. Much of the Alberti family fortune disappeared this way during the tough decade 1310–20.

Success of the new multiagent, long-distance trading and banking business depended on the adoption of the new accounting systems. By changing over from the old paragraph style of entry of the Small-Business Age to the Arab's more sophisticated double-entry system, merchants were able to keep an accurate picture of their various dealings, keep track of a score of agents, and use their capital to best advantage. It took the Alberti nearly a generation to get on top of the new system, but once it was mastered, it made sure every florin was working for the firm.

Just as the Alberti family firm was getting a grip on the textile-finishing business, the market began a major restructuring. The Champagne fairs were being bypassed by the big firms, the Bardi, Peruzzi, and Frescobaldi, who had established agents in the big cities and were doing business directly, using bills of exchange to settle their accounts. Because they were bigger and had close dealings with princes of state and Church, they were forewarned of problems, wars, changing fortunes, and opportunities.

The larger, older firms were buying their wool directly from Britain and processing, spinning, weaving, and finishing it in Florence themselves, rather than buying it half-finished from Flanders, as the Alberti were doing. This put the Alberti at a competitive disadvantage when it came to selling their product.

But it wasn't easy to get an export license from the British. The big Florentine banking firms had acquired theirs in exchange for extensive loans to the British kings. For some undisclosed reason (prudence, fear, or lack of capital), the Alberti stayed out of this side of the banking business. When Edward defaulted in the 1340s, bankrupting the older firms, the Alberti suddenly found themselves the biggest bankers in the West.

Now the rewards came their way. The Papal Curia sought them out to collect taxes, make loans and transfer funds from the further corners of Europe, and the firm prospered. Having survived adversity, however, the Albertis were finally defeated by success. The firm split into several branches, and what was worse, it became involved in local politics, resulting at one point in banishment from Florence. Their place at the head of European banking passed into the hands of the Medici.

During the turbulent years following the crash of the banking titans, Florence matured from a landlocked medieval frontier town into the capital of a stable city-state with its own seaport and merchant fleets, its own domestic industries and international network of banking and trade. Where a small handful of merchant bankers had taken on entire countries, (and were brought down by them), the new houses which emerged from the chaos of the plague years maintained a low profile. They were more diversified in their activities, more sophisticated in their business technology (bookkeeping, insurance, instruments of credit), and more careful in the structuring of their holding companies and working units so that the fall of one would not endanger the whole.

As the Bardi, Peruzzi, and Frescobaldi had realized much earlier, the secret of the luxury textile trade is to improve quality and variety constantly. By now the Italians had diversified into silks, first using imported raw silk and then, as their freshly planted mulberry trees matured, breeding their own silkworms.

"Weaving of silk was much more demanding than weaving of wool," writes social historian Richard Goldthwaite in *The Building of Renaissance Florence*. "Looms were more elaborate, and the highest skills were required to weave the patterns for the damask, brocades and figured satins the industry was noted for." The industry needed wide support from artists and craftsmen, including "goldbeaters, who made the gold and silver threads for the most luxurious figured cloths, tailors, embroiderers and related craftsmen, who made the cloth into clothes, belts, hats, purses, liturgical vestments, altar hangings, and all those other luxury items of 'high fashion' for which Florence is famous; and designers, who planned patterns for figured cloths and styled the finished pieces."

Gold poured into the republic faster than it could be spent, and goldsmiths flourished. Their jewelry plate and ornaments found an expanding market in a world whose growing wealth was concentrated in the hands of plague survivors, who, with this dreadful memory always in mind, were not inclined to save.

Another characteristic of Florence's economic growth was the decision of the banking houses to invest their wealth in the city and to continue in business—and not to invest it, as merchant families were inclined to do, in country estates. As a class, the Florentine merchant-bankers sought status through great works, great palaces, great learning, great art. With the world's luxury and financial markets so closely intertwined, with a population incredibly rich in highly skilled craftsmen and artists and cultivated merchants, magnificence was simply good business. There was a self-sustaining symbiosis of taste, quality, creativity, and commerce, much imitated by the monarchs of Europe but never surpassed.

THE MEDICI

(case history)

After the Alberti came the Medici. They were one of seventy-two merchant banking firms in Florence when Baldassarre Cossa, rather a rascal, was elected pope. Baldassarre was a friend of Giovanni de' Medici, who had loaned him the money to buy his cardinal's hat. "After Cardinal Cossa's election as Pope the Medici had begun to enjoy an exceptionally profitable relationship with the Papal Chamber, by which the Curia's revenues were collected and disbursed," writes Christopher Hibbert in *The Rise and Fall of the House of Medici.* "Within a few years, the Medici bank became not only the most successful commercial enterprise in Italy, but the most profitable family business in the whole of Europe."

"The structure of the Medici bank closely resembled that of a holding company," writes their economic biographer, Raymond de Roover, "with this fundamental difference: it was a combination of partnerships rather than of corporations or joint stock companies. At the peak of its prosperity, the Medici bank had five branches in Italy (Milan, Naples, Pisa, Rome and Venice) and four beyond the Alps (Avignon, Bruges, Geneva and London). Besides the bank, the Medici controlled three manufacturing establishments in Florence itself: two woolen 'shops' and one silk 'shop.' Each of the branches and the 'shops' was an autonomous partnership, or separate entity, which had its own capital, its own partners, its own books. However, the Medici had a controlling interest—at least 50 percent in all of them."

To this severe picture, biographer Christopher Hibbert adds some softening touches. "As well as undertaking all the customary services of a bank, the Medici houses undertook all manner of commissions for their customers, supplying tapestries, sacred relics, horses and slaves, painted panels from the fairs of Antwerp, choirboys from Douai and Cambrai for the choir of St. John the Lateran, and even on one occasion, a giraffe. They were importers and exporters of all manner of spices, of silk and wool and cloth. They dealt in pepper and sugar, olive oil, citrus fruits, almonds, furs, brocades, dyes, jewelry, and above all, alum, a transparent mineral salt essential to the manufacture of fast, vivid dyes, and widely used in glassmaking and tanning.''

The achievements of the Renaissance were legion and extended deeply into philosophy. They provided an alternate value system to Christianity by replacing a morality based on sin with one founded on the dignity of man. The Medici paid scholars to translate Plato, and the classics became widely available as a guide to thought and action. For after all, classical Rome and Greece were full-blown commercial empires, and the West was still on the doorstep.

The Medici differed from the average successful banker or businessman in the depth of their culture, and in the imagination by which they made it manifest in institutions. Their great library, the finest in Italy, soon became the model for that of the Vatican. Their respect for the arts helped raise the status of the artist from an anonymous craftsman to that of prince of creativity; and Michelangelo, the prince among artists, was adopted, raised, and sponsored by the Medici family. To confirm the importance of artists, the Medici founded the Accademia del Disegno, the first of the academies of art, which, by giving the artist a new way to learn his trade and achieve mastery, freed him forever from the guild apprentice system. Soon all Europe would have its academies.

In the fifteenth century, the Medicis were chosen by the people to become hereditary leaders of the now-stabilizing Florentine state. As businessmen, they were learning the importance of state involvement in ongoing prosperity. Goldthwaite reports on the "reign" of the Medicis:

> Beyond encouraging the planting of mulberry trees and boosting the port of Livorno, it investigated the possibilities of direct trade with India; it reclaimed large tracts of land for agricultural purposes in the lower Arno valley; it set up a monopoly for the marketing of iron from the island of Elba and undertook searches for other metals on the mainland; it opened new quarries at Carrara. . . ; it experimented with the manufacturing of porcelain; it spied on the Venetians to learn how to set up commercial glass works; it promoted the entire range of luxury crafts at court by gathering jewelers, wood carvers, goldsmiths, miniaturists, distillers, clockmakers, ceramicists, cosmographers, and a host of others working together at the Uffizi.

Here was a model to guide the kings of France, in many ways much more appealing than the monopolistic model of the Venetians.

REACTION

By 1320, the Commercial Revolution was established in northern Italy. The great structural changes had occurred and the new institutions were in place. If there was anything lacking, it was nationhood. Northern Italy was a hodgepodge of independent city-states. While a shakeout was going on, while the largest and most successful of cities were consolidating their hold on their surrounding countryside, while Venice, Genoa, Florence, and Milan were becoming capitals of small countries, each was jealous of the other. Factious wars were endemic. This was their tragic flaw.

Stuck within the narrow mind-set of the Small-Business Age, the rest of Europe was not ready for the Commercial Revolution. The Church continued to insist with fervor that it was unchristian to seek a large profit, and usury to lend money at interest, to profit from another's needs. North of the Alps, Europeans were having trouble enough keeping the small-business system operating now that growth had stopped, especially when for three years in a row the climate had ruined the crops and farmers were forced to eat their seed corn to survive. Marginal farms were abandoned. People starved. Even before the plague arrived, the economy had failed.

For the next two centuries, while Italian commerce prospered, the rest of Europe stumbled through the no-man's-land between the corporate and commercial economies, suffering the worst stream of miseries since the seven plagues of Egypt. In 1336 the Hundred Years' War between France and England began its dreary course. In 1348, the Black Death arrived. In 1378, the Church found itself with two popes, one in Avignon, one in Rome, each complete with court, college of cardinals, and pack of tax collectors. Brigands roamed the forests and highways.

"It was a time of default," writes Barbara Tuchman, the age's most eloquent critic, in *The Distant Mirror*. "Rules crumbled, institutions failed in their functions. Knighthood did not protect; the Church, more worldly than spiritual, did not guide the way to God; the towns, once agents of progress and the commonweal, were absorbed in mutual hostilities and divided by class war; the population, depleted by the Black Death, did not recover. The war of England and France and the brigandage it spawned revealed the emptiness of chivalry's military pretensions and the falsity of its moral ones. The schism shook the foundations of the central institution, spreading a deep and pervasive uneasiness."

In the fifteenth century despair took the form of a cult of death:

"Artists dwelt on physical rot in ghoulish detail: worms wriggled through every corpse, bloated toads sat on dead eyeballs. A mocking, beckoning, gleeful Death led the Danse Macabre around innumerable frescoed walls." Lovers picnicked in graveyards, where merchants hawked their wares.

Sexual license exploded into orgiastic bacchanales. The most read book of the day was Jean de Meung's *Roman de la Rose,* a bible of eroticism where the holy grail is the rose—that is, the petaled genitals of his lady love. The Church provided example and not restraint. Ruling dynasties, such as the Visconti of Milan and the Borgias, vied for immortality through debauchery and vice.

Denied all leadership, the religious masses turned to cults and mysticism. Wave after wave of flagellants toured Europe, scourging themselves and inviting others to join in this sure road to God's forgiveness. Flagellant parades often led to attacks on the Jewish quarter. Witchcraft and devil worship exploded and were viciously repressed. Mystical sects, such as the Beghards, were enormously popular, in part because they encouraged free love, communal sex, and nudity, but also because, like today's communes, they provided both refuge and meaning to the unemployed and the dispossessed.

The business of the Church was irreparably damaged by the papal schism, with its double call on the community's resources. "To keep each papacy from bankruptcy," Tuchman writes,"simony redoubled, benefices and promotions were sold under pressure, charges for spiritual dispensations of all kinds were increased, as were chancery taxes on every document required from the Curia. Sale of indulgences, seed of the Reformation, became financially important. Instead of reform, abuses multiplied."

PORTUGUESE COMMERCIAL REVOLUTION

EARLY FIFTEENTH CENTURY

There were a number of reasons why Portugal should be the next to undergo a Commercial Revolution. She was a seagoing nation, hardly more than a narrow strip of Atlantic coast. The halfway station on the sea route from Venice and Genoa to Flanders and England, she acquired a cosmopolitan flavor, with Christians, Muslims, and Jews, Genoans, Britons, and Dutch all crossing paths and trading news, ideas, and tales.

In 1385, according to Fernand Braudel, Portugal cleaned house with a "bourgeois" revolution. She had driven out the Moors who had occupied the southern end of the country, the Algarve, and forced them back to the north shore of the African continent, something Spain would need another century to accomplish. She had also begun to diversify her agriculture, with cork and olives and grapes.

Portugal had been treated lightly by the plague and had managed to avoid the century of war preoccupying the French and English in their quest for nationhood. King John I, who had liberated Portugal from Castile and married Philippa of England, spawned six sons to assure his succession, including the man who would set Europe's course of growth and expansion and assure Portugal's wealth for centuries to come.

INFANTE DOM HENRIQUE

(case history)

Prince Henry was the third of six children, far enough down the succession never to be chosen king, but close enough to his father to be an instrument of state. The three brothers, close to the same age, shared the old ideas of conquest and glory that characterized the nobility during the Small-Business Age. Chivalry demanded a test of manhood, winning one's spurs in some glorious exploit. A magnificent tournament was planned where all Europe would note the arrival at maturity of the royal princes.

Prince Henry persuaded his brothers and father that, instead of a tournament, the money would be better spent on a mini-Crusade against Ceuta, the Moorish trading center at the gates of the Mediterranean, across the Gibraltar straits. This would be a true test of valor, as well as a blow for Christ, and would also advance the commercial interests of Portugal.

The expedition was a success, pillaged treasure amply repaying its costs. Ceuta became a Portuguese possession, although it required the return presence of Prince Henry to assure its new loyalties. During these months he learned about the commerce of Africa and the rich Muslim trade routes centering on Timbuktu, where gold and ivory and spices moved by caravan back to Islam; he learned the Muslim secrets of commerce and long-distance trade. But Prince Henry also learned that commerce was not something one captured. Once he had won Ceuta, the trade patterns shifted, the merchants slipped away, and he was the master of nothing but fortifications, wharves, and a handful of empty shops. Thus he passed from a small-business outlook to a commercial one. He was a new man.

Back in Portugal, as governor of the Algarve, Prince Henry determined to acquire the commerce of Africa, not by overland conquest but by opening trading routes down the coast. To do this required a great deal more knowledge of navigation than the Portuguese possessed, and a new kind of ship that could sail against the prevailing winds blowing down the African coast. So he brought scholars and cartographers, mathematicians and instrument-makers, shipwrights and navigators, to his headquarters in Sagres, put them on his payroll, and encouraged them to develop the charts, instruments, and ships needed to reach the heart of Africa by the sea.

If you study a map of the Horn of Africa, you can hardly see Cape Bojador, but to Portuguese explorers, in their single-masted square riggers, it was the end of the world, a long narrow point jutting miles into the sea, surrounded by reefs and forming a barrier perhaps more psychological than real. Henry had sent out a number of expeditions to round the cape, and each time they returned to say it was impossible. Finally, at Henry's urging and with his trusted friend at the helm, the cape was rounded, and like the sound barrier six centuries later, it turned out to be little more than wind and noise.

At last the think tank at Sagres came up with a new design for a ship. Using the round, clinker bottom style of the northern hull with its center rudder post, which slipped so well through the water, two masts of square-rigged sail, and a third mast aft with a triangular lateen-rigged sail borrowed from the Muslims, Henry's team came up with a ship that could sail much closer to the wind, making the return trip against the prevailing northerlies much shorter, and maneuvering that much easier. This was the caravel, the ship that Columbus would use fifty years later to find his way to the New World. And back.

Expedition followed expedition, plumbing the depths of Henry's purse. Surprises came as islands were discovered: Madeira, the Azores and Canaries. Following the Venetian model, Henry determined to settle the islands. At first the settlers made mistakes. They took rabbits as well as plants to a colony, the rabbits ate the plants as fast as they could be grown. Try another island. Soon there were crops growing on plantations: grapes (source of the famous Madeira wine) and wheat.

Each year, the expeditions pushed further down the African coast, eventually finding the fabled ivory, spices, and gold dust, and bringing it home. By the late 1440s, after twenty years of costly exploration, the returns started coming in: a thousand ounces of gold dust every month, a thousand slaves per year, ivory and spices. When Henry died in 1460, Portugal had profitable colonies on the islands, a monopoly on the African trade, and a mission to continue down the African coast, up the further side, across to India and the East Indies, and to bring home cottons, spices, and treasures that would take the rest of the century to unfold.

But more important, he had shown that exploration, not conquest, was the route to national wealth.

Two mistakes prevented Portugal from becoming the Venice of the Atlantic. It had turned down Columbus's offer to sail West on its behalf, and it never caught up with the riches pouring in from the New World. Nor had it developed markets for its products in the north, and it was forced to depend on the wholesalers of Antwerp for its sales. Nevertheless, prosperity rewarded the Portuguese for centuries, supported by gold finds in Brazil.

Although both France and England benefited from the general growth arising from Portugal's African and Indian ventures and Spain's success in the New World, they bungled their Commercial Revolutions through a preoccupation with greatness and statehood. France's aristocracy and court bled her resources; Britain's glorious Elizabethan Age was built more on the sands of piracy than on a bedrock of commerce.

Nevertheless, the English did manage to open the first stage of a Commercial Revolution in the century following Henry VIII's break with the Catholic Church in 1534. Merchants were active, and Henry supported them with a navy. Moneys and lands confiscated from the monasteries, however, flowed to the landed, not the merchant class. Elizabeth, with the help of her economist, Gresham, was more successful in her commercial policies, establishing a stock exchange, and monopoly companies to exploit the Muscovy trail and the East Indies trade. It was during her reign that the putting-out system began to be employed, the Newfoundland fisheries began providing low-cost fish, and the first magnificent returns arrived from pirate expeditions to the Spanish Main.

Lacking an economic priority, the arbitrariness of Elizabeth's decisions was like a dress rehearsal for the dreaded English disease of the nineteenth and twentieth centuries. Policies were on-again, off-again. Colonies would be started and abandoned. The interests of the landowners always superceded those of the merchants. Policy was aimed at full employment rather than trade, and found expression in a series of economically devastating laws designed to keep wages low and manpower available. Technological developments, especially those promising productivity gains, such as William Lee's knitting frame, were banned.

When James took the throne at Elizabeth's death, the situation deteriorated, for the Scottish king looked down his nose at tradesmen. The single greatest economic feature of the hundredth anniversary of Henry's revolution against the Roman Catholic church was the tidal flood of emigration to the new world.

DUTCH COMMERCIAL REVOLUTION

1580–1620

While the secret of sustainable growth eluded the French and the British, the Dutch put the winning combination together in the generations before and after 1600, leading to centuries of prosperity continuing through to the present day. They managed to combine the best features of the Venetian and the Florentine models into an ideal Commercial Revolution and economy. As the West's first truly successful and complete economic revolution, it stands comparison with the American and Japanese Information Revolutions and deserves attention as a model for future generations.

The Netherlands managed to escape from the double restraints of an aristocracy and the Catholic church. It had next to no government and no expensive pretensions to greatness that might interfere with its single-minded pursuit of economic growth.

It had developed a profitable and efficient three-way trade between Amsterdam and the Baltic and the Iberian peninsula. It knew its markets and its sources, and had even developed a system of newspapers to keep its merchants informed of developments in commerce from all over the world.

It had the world's most developed and efficient agricultural system. Its canal-based transportation network, interlacing the country and the city, extended deep into Europe and had open access to the sea. Its ceramics industry was able to take over the porcelain trade when Chinese originals were no longer available. Its textile manufacturing facilities were the state of the art, with frequent technological improvements. Its shipyards were superefficient, with wind-driven sawmills, mast-stepping hoists, a standard design of ship that was much cheaper to operate than any competitor's, and a system of mass production based on standardized parts and precut timbers stockpiled in advance. Its trading fleet was bigger than the rest of Europe's combined. Its ships sold profitably to any who came, and a flourishing secondhand market developed.

It had perfected the warehouse system and its accompanying financial instruments, so that ships from all over could unload and trade their cargoes for goods needed at home. In its heyday, Amsterdam's harbor was a forest of masts, and its canals were bustling with lighters laden with goods from all over the world.

Amsterdam had a stock-exchange and a banking system both borrowed from Italy, as well as a central bank. There were joint-stock companies, willing investors, and expeditions mounted to the farthest corners of the world. The Dutch East India Company, set up in 1602, two years after the British, was much better financed and much more successful than its British counterpart, paying original investors 20 to 40 percent per annum for over a century.

Hollanders practiced free trade. Perhaps that is merely the prerogative of the world leader, but while her competitors assembled complex barriers and restrictions to protect hothouse industries at home, the Dutch let the market decide what would flourish or die. When her clients bought Dutch goods and services, there were no taxes or subsidies padded into the bill.

When the Londoner looked to the Thames, he counted two Dutch masts for every British spar. The French, though they copied

the institutions of the Dutch, always put greatness before commerce, and inevitably failed to find the sustained growth they so
desperately needed to fund their royal extravagances.

BRITISH COMMERCIAL REVOLUTION

CLOSING PHASE 1680-1720

Quite suddenly, there was a breakthrough in Britain. The Dutch
Commercial Revolution had lasted fifty years, from 1570 to 1620,
before the instruments of sustained growth were in place. Around
1680, the British began two generations of surging economic
growth and reform that greatly stimulated their economy and set
the stage for the Industrial Revolution of 1770.

The turmoil surrounding the Stuart kings, with several beheadings,
revolutions, and restorations, had established that Parliament and
not the king was making decisions and setting priorities. The
Glorious Revolution of 1688, which ended the fuss, put Dutchman
William of Orange, with his British wife, Anne, on the throne. If
ever there was a king who understood commerce, he was now
wearing a British crown.

One of the greatest successes of British economics was the
funding of the national debt, taking it from the shoulders of the
king and making Parliament responsible on behalf of the people.
Though it scandalized many sober Englishmen, such was the
quality of British paper that even the Dutch, seeing a good investment, hurried to buy their share of Britain's national debt. This is
the origin of the Treasury Bill system that the United States and
other nations find so attractive today.

In 1694, Parliament authorized the creation of the Bank of
England. This was a private company, but it held a monopoly on
issuing banknotes, controlled the money supply, and set the discount rate. It managed its affairs so scrupulously, it soon became a
national institution and was much imitated abroad.

In 1688, a group of maritime insurers meeting at Edward Lloyd's
coffeehouse formed their famous consortium. By the nineties, as

press censorship ended, Lloyds of London was issuing a thrice-weekly news sheet of world commerce. By 1702, there was a daily newspaper in London serving a population that had reached 550,000 the largest in Europe. By decade's end, there were eighteen dailies. Britain was learning to read—and to make use of what it learned.

The revolution was fueled by an explosion of joint-stock companies: 150 founded between 1692 and 1695. Parliament acted speedily to support the restructuring. In 1697, ground rules were laid to order the trade in stocks and assure the soundness of the brokers, and in 1698, the first modern stock exchange was founded in London. Over the next twenty years, the total value of issued shares quintupled. Parliament ended the monopolies of the old Levant and Muscovy trading companies and allowed new ventures in old waters. The era of "aggressive capitalism" had begun.

In an excess of religious zeal, the French had massacred and expelled its Protestant minority. Many of these highly talented Huguenot craftsmen found their way to England, setting up industries that stoked the revolution.

The British colonies, particularly those banded together in the New England Confederation, prospered and multiplied. There were now over a quarter of a million colonists. Because of the prevailing mercantilist theory, the colonies had one-sided rules applied to their trade by the mother country which were detrimental, stultifying, short-sighted, and unnecessary. The colonies brought much wealth to England, and though the rules would lead to the American Revolution, the freedom won by the thirteen colonies only increased their English trade.

Economic revolution was by no means the only route to commercial development. Even a failed revolution, such as Elizabeth's or Louis XIV's, can be a time of enormous creativity and institution building, as well as much economic growth. Nor are they, as has been suggested, necessarily periods of cultural greatness, although this often follows as an expression of surplus wealth. What is most characteristic is a single minded pursuit of wealth, with all rules bent in that direction, venal and unromantic as this may seem.

It was suggested by the German sociologist Max Weber and the British socialist R. H. Tawney that Protestantism or Calvinism is the key to growth. While these theories may appeal to the prejudices of protestants, they no longer stand up to economic history. Venice and Florence and Portugal managed to cut a path for

Western growth at a time of oppressive Catholic power, and the Crusades may be seen as the economic ventures that first amassed the capital which triggered the West's Commercial Revolution.

On the other hand, a tolerant cosmopolitanism, rather than nationalism, is an identifiable characteristic of centers on the verge of economic revolution about to take off. Perhaps this is because such a revolution implies the abandoning of deeply held values and rules, and this is eased by the presence of others who function effectively by systems other than the ones locked so deeply into our hearts. The success of California in general, and the San Francisco/Silicon Valley area in particular, is related to the high level of tolerance there, just as New York's "melting pot" approach of the late nineteenth century layed the groundwork for America's Industrial Revolution.

Chapter 9
INDUSTRIAL REVOLUTIONS

Unlike previous revolutions, which had occurred many times before in classical civilizations, the Industrial Revolution was unprecedented in World History. No previous civilization had made the vital leap into powered machinery and factory production. Craftsmen of the Small-Business Age had developed some interesting wind- and water-powered machinery and factory production techniques (printing) but were impeded in their growth by lack of commercial financing, distribution, and sense of scale, and these technologies remained largely unimproved throughout the Commercial Age.

The Industrial Revolution in Britain (1780–1830) followed closely on the heels of the closing phase of her Commercial Revolution (1680–1720), which had installed a distribution infrastructure and financing mechanism, but which still depended on the putting-out system of cottage industry for production.

The great achievements of the brief Commercial Age (1720–1780) in Britain were the development of transportation (highway and canal systems), the use of steam power to drain the new deep mines, the improvement of iron-making, and the explosion of publishing and literacy. Scientific thought achieved a great boost from Royal Society meetings and publications (from 1660) and the monumental work of Isaac Newton on universal mechanics (*Principia*, 1687) and calculus. Laws protecting intellectual property (patents and copyrights) encouraged and rewarded invention and thought.

The Industrial Revolution was carried by a wave of mechanical invention that enormously increased textile production and transportation speed. An overlooked contribution, however, was the idea that common people should have access to paying jobs and cheap products and transportation, an idea that greatly expanded the economy.

Britain's wealthy received their income from rents from common people and were distressed at the idea of extending them privileges previously reserved for themselves. They regarded the economic revolution as subversive, since it raised the expectations of the poor. They considered the new technology as an assault on the establishment. They treated industrialists as venal, vulgar and dangerous. Rather than joining the revolution, they succeeded in ending it: The pace of British inventions sharply declined after 1830.

The twin achievements of the Industrial Revolutions were the expansion of the economy through mechanized production and the introduction of systems thought. Its twin weaknesses were an overemphasis on inflexible systems and on material things.

THE STATUS QUO ANTE

The first (or "Venetian") phase of the Commercial Revolution in England lasted from Henry VIII's disestablishment of the Catholic church in 1534 to the death of Elizabeth in 1603, in which colonies, long-distance trade and some industry had been installed in the economy. The second (or "Florentine") phase extended from 1680 through 1720, endowing the country with the instruments of commerce: banks and trading houses, with their innumerable instruments of credit, trade, insurance, and exchange, warehouses, stock exchanges, bank clearinghouses, new forms of companies, and in particular, great government companies trading with the Indians of North America (Hudson's Bay Company), the West Indies, or the Far East.

By 1780 "England was the minimal state: no such ever has existed before or since," claims British historian (and editor of the New Statesman) Paul Johnson in *A History of the English People*. "There was no professional police force, and only a tiny army subject to annual parliamentary vote. The country was governed by unpaid country gentlemen meeting as magistrates four times a year. The civil service, even including the highly efficient postal, customs and excise system, was minute."

The eighteenth century was a time of great invention and innovation and of widespread self-confidence throughout the Western world, but most particularly in Britain. Scientific innovation, sparked by the foundation in 1660 of the Royal Society of London for Improving Natural Knowledge, blazed up with the theories of Isaac Newton, lighting the eighteenth century mind with ambitious dreams. Publication exploded, from scientific papers to newspapers, dictionaries, encyclopedias, and histories, culminating in 1775 with Adam Smith's brilliant speculation, *The Wealth of Nations*.

In the 1750s roads improved. In the sixties, attention turned to canals, which made transport so cheap they halved the price of coal. New iron-making techniques, combined with skill in machining, provided inventors with new materials. New machines poured forth to mechanize the making of textiles. If few people realized an Industrial Revolution was in the making, there were still those with money to invest in long-term ventures, especially as interest rates dipped to 3 percent.

Agricultural productivity was growing even faster than the population, and Britain was exporting grain. Most farmers had a loom in the cottage, and some, in the Midlands and West Country, were so busy spinning yarn and weaving cloth that farming had become a sideline. Regional networks of clothiers, merchants, agents, and subcontracters arranged the putting-out of wool and yarn, and mechanized finishing shops, where the cloth was fulled, dyed, fluffed, and sheared for market, sprouted overnight in the favorable climate.

The farmer himself worked the loom. Wife and children sorted, carded, and spun, trying to keep the shuttle loaded with yarn. Nottingham and Lancashire cotton spinners could use Jim Hargreaves' jenny, which spun a half-dozen threads at a time good enough for the weft, though the warp still had to be spun by hand. Arkwright's water frame made thread strong enough for the warp, but it was too big for the cottage and needed the power of a mill. Crompton's spinning "mule" made thread so fine and strong a weaver could make muslins. Home and export markets were taking off. So many people were making so much money the country ran short of coin to pay them all.

BRITISH INDUSTRIAL REVOLUTION
PHASE ONE: 1780–1805

Whether we describe the Industrial Revolution as the beginning of factory production or as the application of power and machinery to mass production, the 1780s is what Walt Rostow would later call the "take-off" period. Steam power had been around since the turn of the century, but it was terribly inefficient, and it was oscillating, not rotary, so the only way it could be used to power a factory was in pumping water up to a millpond to drive a waterwheel.

James Watt was an instrument maker at Glasgow University, where he learned about steam engines, heat, and energy. Newcomen's engine wasted its energy by cooling the cylinder after each stroke to condense the steam and pull the piston back. In the mid-sixties, Watt added a separate cool condenser, which left the cylinder hot and achieved a fourfold gain in efficiency. But it took him twenty years to perfect the double-acting rotary engine with governor that was to make his fortune, that of his partner, Matthew Boulton, and of the five hundred or so customers who installed his machine in their mills before his patent ran out in 1800.

By the time it was fully evolved, Watt's engine was a self-regulating system complete with feedback. The same phrase could be used to describe a factory, the other major component of the Industrial Revolution. According to Andrew Ure, the industry's first consultant and spokesman, in his enormously influential *The Philosophy of Manufactures*: "The term *factory*, in technology, designates the combined operation of many orders of work-people, adult and young, in tending with assiduous skill a system of productive machines continuously impelled by a central power.

"This title," continued our verbaceous consultant, "involves the idea of a vast automaton, composed of various mechanical and intellectual organs, acting in uninterrupted concert for the production of a common object, all of them being subordinated to a self-regulated moving force."

This concept grew from the foresight, boldness, and inventive genius of Richard Arkwright, Ure told his clients, and his main achievement was "the distribution of the different members of the apparatus into one co-operative body, in impelling each organ with its appropriate delicacy and speed, and above all in training human beings to renounce their desultory habits of work, and to identify themselves with the unvarying regularity of the complex automaton. To devise and administer a successful code of factory discipline, suited to the necessities of factory diligence, was the Herculean enterprise, the noble achievement of Arkwright.''

To Arkwright and his followers, our consultant and historian attributes the following statistics:

	1770	1834
Annual consumption of cotton in British manufactures in millions of pounds	4	270
World consumption in millions of pounds	10	480

"This prodigious increase (almost two orders of magnitude) is, without doubt, almost entirely due to the factory system founded and upreared by [Arkwright] the intrepid native of Preston.''

Founding and uprearing a factory was no easy matter: There was little precedent. The machinery was new and unproven. Sometimes the workers rebelled and smashed the machines. There was a lot of republican talk inspired by the French Revolution. And inflation was pushing interest rates to perilous heights. Investors, however, were interested in factories and machines, and the market was there, and the excitement of being part of the future.

THE REVOLUTIONARY MILL

(case history)

The industry was given a great boost in 1785 by the invention of a weaving machine by the Rev. Dr. Edmund Cartwright, who saw the problem as an exercise in logic. Since weaving involved the repetition of only three movements, "there would be little difficulty in producing and repeating them,'' wrote the minister, in complete ignorance of the problems involved. "Full of these ideas, I immediately employed a carpenter and smith to carry them into effect. As soon as the machine was finished, I got a weaver to put in the warp, which was of such materials as sail cloth is usually made of. To my great delight, a piece of cloth, such as it was, was the produce.''

"As I had never before turned my thoughts to anything mechanical, either in theory or practice, nor had ever seen a loom at work, or knew anything of its construction, you will readily suppose that my first loom must have been a most rude piece of machinery,'' he wrote. Indeed, it took two more years of work to perfect his power loom. On August 1, 1787, the patent was issued, and the machine was installed in a factory that Edmund Cartwright had constructed, using a Newcomen steam engine to raise water to a millpond, which drove the water wheel powering the mill.

Edmund had three famous brothers, George, an explorer; Charles, a naval commander; and John, a political figure of radical tendencies (the abolition of slavery and the vote by secret ballot were causes he espoused). Intrigued by Edmund's success, John decided to mount a factory to spin and weave wool in Retford, and to use steam power as well as his brother's inventions. This was the ill-starred Revolutionary Mill, named for the Glorious Revolution of 1688.

In the mid-1780s it was relatively easy to raise money for mechanical endeavors. A partnership was established of twenty shareholders, and the mill was constructed in the summer of 1788, a four-story building 30 by 123 feet. A long correspondence with Messrs. Boulton and Watt of Birmingham followed, in an attempt to acquire a steam engine, which had recently been improved to provide rotary power. Since the first of these machines had been installed only two years before, there was little experience upon which to make decisions. After much vacillation on Cartwright's part and much patience on that of Matthew Boulton and James Watt, a large thirty-two horsepower machine was installed, which meant that John could include Edmund's latest invention (almost as famous as his power loom), a wool-combing machine.

For a number of years the mill flourished, employing upwards of six hundred hands. John Cartwright treated his employees well, providing medical care and good food for the orphans and pauper apprentices from the workhouses. He was well regarded in the community and asked to stand as their representative to Pitt's reform government. Whether his benevolent attitude toward his employees was responsible for a series of disastrous losses is not clear, but in the late 1790s the mill was losing more money than the partners could afford, and attempts were made to sell it. In 1806 it was finally broken up and sold in parcels.

Edmund, too, failed as an industrialist. His mill closed, and he lost money on his weaving and wool-combing inventions. But these devices had so changed the face of British industry, Parliament voted him an appreciative grant of £10,000 in 1809.

The rush to mechanize the wool-spinning and -weaving process in the nineties was only one of a series of enthusiasms that gripped industry during the first phase of the Industrial Revolution. Before it, there was the race to industralize cotton spinning and weaving; after it, linen and then silk production were mechanized. There was the race to put in canals, to build bridges and macadamize the roads, to light the factories with illuminating gas, allowing longer hours of work in the winter, as well as work in shifts.

PHASE TWO: 1805–1830

The patent held by Watt & Boulton expired in 1800, and Watt could no longer hold back the flood of invention. That year Richard Trevithick patented a high-pressure steam engine so much more powerful than its predecessor that it could be mounted in a boat or a carriage and used as motive power.

Canals crisscrossed the nation by the 1790s and could absorb no more investment. Profits were pouring in, and when the war with France ended at Waterloo, capital started to build up like a dam ready to burst.

By 1829 there was a railroad running from Manchester to Liverpool, designed to carry freight but surprisingly successful with passenger traffic. In the thirties the dam burst.

There were two decades of unprecedented growth. A quarter of a billion pounds sterling was invested in the iron roads, while construction employment peaked in the 1840s at 300,000 men. The demand for iron rails, engines and carriages, and the coal to run them created further employment. A further spurt to trade from faster transportation spread the boom throughout the economy.

Each new wave of invention pushed its predecessors another step ahead by lowering costs, increasing efficiency, raising quality, and extending markets. When the first World Exposition of industry opened at the Crystal Palace in 1851, there was hardly a corner of life that had not been deeply touched by industrialism.

REACTION

That first world's fair in 1851 marked the zenith of Britain's soaring flight. Thenceforward, the pace of innovation would slow, never again to speed up. Britain would coast through the next century with no significant innovations, no synergistic rush of creativity, just as Italy coasted for centuries on the creative surge of the Commercial Revolution. What went wrong?

The more money the industrialists made for themselves, their employees and investors, the fewer friends they had. Locked away in the north behind clouds of smoke and heaps of slag, they failed to defend themselves when attacked by opposition politicians looking for an issue to embarrass the government, journalists eager to exploit the feelings of their new readers and sell newspapers and magazines, and above all, the landed gentry, who saw the new entrepreneurial class as a threat to their status and values.

"English snobbery played a devastating and destructive role. The machine men were not welcome in society," writes Paul Johnson. "England became an industrial country against the current of social approval."

The instruments used by the landed gentry against the vulgar and venal entrepreneurs, as previously described in the chapter "Reaction," included the "public" schools, universities, the press, parliament, and the honors list. They deprecated, ostracized, investigated, educated, and above all assimilated the entrepreneurs, whose wealth-creating initiatives were brought to an end. As a result, an angry and sorry Paul Johnson tells us, "The modern history of the English is a tragic record of missed opportunities, of chances recklessly squandered or thrown to the winds, of great men dying in despair, of genius and energy poured into the sands of thoughtless indifference, of advancing reason slowed to the pace of a glacier, and of the slow, confident retrenchment of privilege, injustice and obscurantism."

In this climate of disrespect and envy, politicians and journalists jumped on the wealth-makers for grinding the faces of the poor and exploiting and corrupting children in their "dark satanic mills." There are a whole series of myths created by the "Whig historians" of the nineteenth century and by the socialist historians of the twentieth which dominate our thinking about capitalists and industrialists, and which contemporary historians and economists are endeavoring to undo.

"There is, however, one supreme myth which more than any

other has served to discredit the economic system to which we owe our present-day civilization," writes economic historian Friedrich Hayek in *Capitalism and the Historians*. "It is the legend of the deterioration of the position of the working classes in consequence of the rise of 'capitalism' (or of 'manufacturing' or the 'industrial system'). Who has not heard of 'the horrors of early capitalism' and gained the impression that the advent of this system brought untold new suffering to large classes who before were tolerably content and comfortable? . . . The widespread aversion to 'capitalism' is closely connected with this belief that the undeniable growth of wealth which the competitive order has produced was purchased at the price of depressing the standard of life of the weakest elements of society.

"That this was the case," Dr. Hayak continues, "was at one time indeed widely taught by economic historians. A more careful examination of the facts has, however, led to a thorough refutation of this belief."

The myth stems in part from the widespread romantic notion of the eighteenth and nineteenth centuries that praised the noble savage and eulogized the peasant close to his land and in harmony with nature. His supposedly Eden-like state was lost when the farmer was uprooted and forced to work in noisy and filthy factories.

That is not, however, how the noble savage sees it, as C. P. Snow reminds us in *The Two Cultures*: "With singular unanimity, in any country where they have had the chance, the poor have walked off the land into the factories as fast as the factories could take them."

Evidence for the monster myth of child oppression in the factories comes from the now-discredited report of the parliamentary investigations of the Sadler committee of 1832, which subsequent critics have accepted at face value. "Its report was emphatically partisan, composed by strong enemies of the factory system for party ends. . . . Sadler permitted himself to be betrayed by his noble enthusiasm into the most distorted and erroneous statements." That criticism comes from no less an authority than Friedrich Engels, Karl Marx's chief collaborator, who had written extensively and sympathetically on the subject in *The Conditions of the Working Class in England* in 1844.

All of Sadler's criticisms of the manufacturers were refuted. Still, they were "on the record," and they have been cited time and again to prove the deliberate cruelties of the industrialists toward the children in their employ.

There are a number of reasons children were among those employed in factories. The apprentice system, still legally in force, limited employment to those who had been formally trained in residence while young. The state was particularly concerned that orphans and workhouse children were apprenticed and learned a trade. In addition, there was a carry-over from the putting-out system when families worked together spinning and weaving cloth. Factory employers tried to provide work for whole families.

Whatever the reasons, country children were worked much harder on the farm and in the cottage than in the factory, and there was a steady improvement in standard of living and conditions of work in the factories from the beginning. While the cost of living rose 11 percent from 1790 to 1831, the year of the Sadler committee, urban wages improved by 43 percent, according to T. S. Ashton, one of the leaders of the postwar movement to demolish the monster myth. The real misery was suffered by those cottage-industry workers who tried to compete with the tumbling price of manufactured cloth by working their families ever-longer hours for ever-falling rates.

Perhaps the last word on the English Industrial Revolution can be given to Engels, the middle-class revolutionary and textile manufacturer whose writings did so much to foment revolution:

> Sixty, eighty years ago, England was a country like every other, with small towns, few and simple industries, and a thin but proportionately large agricultural population. Today it is a country like no other, with a capital of two and a half million inhabitants; with vast manufacturing cities; with an industry that supplies the world, and produces almost everything by means of the most complex machinery; with an industrious, intelligent, dense population, of which two-thirds are employed in trade and commerce, and composed of classes wholly different; forming, in fact, with other customs and needs, a different nation from the England of those days. The industrial revolution is of the same importance for England as the political revolution for France, and the philosophical revolution for Germany; and the difference between England in 1760 and in 1844 is at least as great as that between France under the ancient régime and during the revolution of July. But the mightiest result of this industrial transformation [Engels concludes ominiously] is the English proletariat.''

Prince Albert, who was responsible for the tremendously influential World Exposition of 1851, with its Crystal Palace and industrial displays, died in 1860, around the same time as the last of the engineer celebrities, George Stephenson and Louis Brunel. Britain had already lost her competitive advantage in cotton; America had ten times the trackage in railroads; Germany would soon surpass her in steel production. British investors looked abroad for opportunity.

As the challenge of running the empire and spreading civilization was taken up by the young, talent which should have gone into business and industry went into the civil service. Thus the crippling English disease (the triumph of gentlemanly values over economic growth) was exported around the globe. British industry had gradually lost its reputation, which soon was confined to matters of taste and sensibility, men's fashion, literary and dramatic culture, and international finance.

AMERICAN INDUSTRIAL REVOLUTION

PHASE ONE: 1870–1895

The Civil War began April 12, 1861, when eleven agrarian Southern states, determined to keep their states' rights (and their slaves), seceded from the Union and attacked Union forces at Fort Sumpter near Charleston. It lasted four years, until April 9, 1865. The Thirteenth Amendment to the Constitution passed by Congress that autumn prohibited slavery as an unconstitutional denial of liberty without due process of law.

It was a war between a commercial economy and an industrial one. At the outset, Southern families were issued looms and asked to weave fabric for uniforms—the old putting-out system of production dating from the Commercial Revolution in Italy. Northern factories spun cotton (smuggled in from the South) and manufactured munitions and matériel with the latest industrial technology.

"Because of the new weaponry that was developed—" writes Thomas Kiernan in *The Road to Colossus,* "—the ironclad, the submarine, sea and land mines, the breech-loading rifle, the Gatling gun (forerunner of the machine gun), the swivel cannon, the mortar—the Civil War was the first large-scale 'modern' war in history. It was not just the radically new weapons that gave war production its distinctly modern cast, however; it was also the new systems of manufacturing that were developed in response to the need for greater productivity.''

The Civil War taught the government, commerce, small business, and industry to collaborate in the pursuit of progress. Secretary of War Edwin Stanton summed up America's new understanding ''that its public political interests are identical with its private economical dealings. Let Providence deem that henceforth the government shall go forth with industry arm in arm, for if we are to suppose ourselves a nation blessed and guided by Providence, so it must be.''

''The American economy grew at unusually rapid rates following the Civil War—'' writes econometrician Jeffrey Williamson, ''—rates which had never before been achieved for so long a period. Indeed these four decades (1870 to 1910) were critical ones during which the United States passed from a phase of primary product export and experimentation with early industrialization to a position of unsurpassed modern industrial power.''

Ralph Waldo Emerson spoke for the nation when he wrote, in *Works and Days,* ''Such is the mechanical determination of our age, and so recent are our best contrivances, that use has not dulled our joy and pride in them; and we pity our fathers for dying before steam and galvanism, ether and ocean telegraphs, photograph and spectroscope arrived, as cheated out of half their human estate. These arts open great gates of a future, promising to make the world plastic and to lift human life out its beggary to a godlike ease and power.''

Out of the ashes of the war arose ''corporate America''—not a nation of corporations, but one in which all components were working together for progress, like today's ''Japan Inc.'' The engine of growth was steam, puffing across America in a race from east to west. The two coasts were joined by the Union Pacific in 1869, which suddenly reduced the time to get from New York to San Francisco from three months to eight days.

Almost from the beginning, American railroad building surpassed that of Britain in terms of total miles of track: twice as much in 1840, three times as much in 1860, ten times as much in 1890. By the turn of the century, a third of a million miles of track crisscrossed the nation in an interconnected system.

The impact of this frenzy of construction was enormous. In addition to the railroads' direct expenditures on and employment in construction, they made huge demands on other industries, increasing employment and production in iron and steel, coal and coke, locomotive works and suppliers, coach and wagon works, and station builders and suppliers. By speeding up the inland movement of goods, they forced development of steamship lines and construction. Like yesterday's automobile makers, railroads were driving the economy.

The financial sector was the first to benefit from the railroad boom. The railroads were both the instruments of capital formation and the focus of investment. The capital markets of America became centralized in New York. Investment banking firms sprang up to handle railroad securities as well as the large capital flow from European investors eager to participate in the growth of American railroads.

In *The Visible Hand*, Harvard economic historian Alfred Chandler credits the railroads with creating "all the present day instruments of finance . . . and nearly all the techniques of modern securities marketing and speculation. Bonds became the primary instrument of railroad construction." Mortgage bonds were followed by income and debenture bonds, convertible bonds and preferred stocks. "Traders sold 'long' and 'short' for future delivery. The use of puts and calls was perfected. Trading came to be done on margin." By 1860, he concludes, "the New York financial district, by responding to the needs of railroad financing, had become one of the largest and most sophisticated capital markets in the world."

Once the railroad arrived, freight handling exploded. A rail car could make four trips between cities while a canal barge made one, and the railroad carried fifty times the freight of a comparable canal. Because of the greater speed of delivery the manufacturer was able to reduce the amount of his product tied up in transit by one or two orders of magnitude, releasing capital for investment.

The railroad transformed business management in America, creating problems we are only now beginning to resolve. A hierarchical structure was developed to cope with the problems of managing a decentralized operation dependent on precision scheduling. Middle management was introduced to look after specialized departments: finance, traffic, machinery, construction, and repairs. By 1870, there were seven levels of management in a well-organized railroad.

In addition to structural changes in railroad management, Chandler points out that accounting underwent its first major overhaul since the Commercial Revolution of the fourteenth century. "A constant flow of information was essential to the efficient operation of these new large business domains. For the middle and top managers, control through statistics quickly became both a science and an art. . . . During the 1850s and 1860s [they] invented nearly all of the basic techniques of modern accounting. By 1860 the railroads probably employed more accountants and auditors than the federal or any state government."

More than anything previously, the railroad embodied the idea of system, a dynamic assembly of components, a whole bigger than its parts. Newton had determined the universe to be an interactive system. In the 1850s the laws of thermodynamics were in place, explaining the universe's energy system. By putting a governor on the steam engine, Watt invented the feedback system, almost two centuries before the computer arrived.

Systems. The industrial age was a time of systems, and the events which are the mileposts of the Industrial Revolutions can be measured in terms of system development. From this perspective the revolution itself is a system of temporary institutions and transformations whose function it is to advance the great social system of civilization to the next stage in its development.

As railroad investment peaked, new outlets for capital were required. There was capital for Bell and the telephone system; for Edison and the electrical system; for the great theatrical touring systems. Cities raised money for the water and sewage system. States funded the education system. Then there was the health system, the insurance system. With the German development of the internal combustion engine came the great systems of the second phase of the revolution: automobile and highway transportation, and aviation. And the system of systems that was to make the future happen: the assembly line of Ransom Olds and Henry Ford.

During the first phase of the American Industrial Revolution, the medical profession underwent a profound change, as did the whole health system. At the beginning of the period, the doctor was a badly trained, wretchedly equipped, and poorly paid professional. The hospital was an almshouse dispensing charity to the poor and homeless. Any wise, respectable person would be treated at home.

In this technology-obsessed era, there was a great emphasis on equipment. From stethoscopes to X rays, from anesthesia to antiseptics, a series of technological innovations gave the doctor the opportunity to see what was going on and the means to intervene safely to change it. Medical education turned from a joke to a science. Nursing became a profession. Knowledge multiplied. Most important, the idea of surgeon as master mechanic so permeated society that operations became fashionable.

As for the hospital, writes sociologist Paul Starr in his Pulitzer prize-winning study, *The Social Transformation of American Medicine,* "From refuges mainly for the homeless poor and the insane, they evolved into doctors' workshops for all types and classes of patients. From charities, dependent on voluntary gifts, they developed into market institutions, financed increasingly out of payments from patients. . . . The sick began to enter hospitals, not for the entire siege of an illness, but only during its acute phase to have some work performed on them. The hospital took on a more activist posture; it was no longer a well of sorrow and charity, but a workplace for the production of health."

Beginning with Morse's telegraph, which slowly moved into the market in the forties and fifties, and the transatlantic cable, which caused a sensation when it connected the continents in the summer of 1866, many of the myriad inventions and systems pouring out of the inventors' studios would now be called office automation. Telephone, teletype, tickertape, and wireless were the communications side of the industry, while the typewriter, the cash register, comptometer, fountain pen, addressograph and Hollerith card punch belonged to the business-machine side of the industry. There were fortunes to be made. Edison, who had started one of the original research laboratories, where he had perfected the tickertape and the electric light system, was determined to continue to mine this vein. He invented the dictaphone—or so he thought. It turned out to be something else.

THE PHONOGRAPH

(case history)

There were always a number of things going on at any one time in the Edison lab in New Jersey. One of these was a telegraph reader-player in which the dots and dashes of Morse code were embossed in a moving paper tape. Another was a telephone improvement, designed by Bell, in which the diaphragm was outfitted with a needle point to communicate with the deaf. Edison noted that the former made an almost talking sound when the embossed tape whirred by the reader, and that the latter pricked his finger when he was shouting into it. Edison put two and two together, shouted "halloo" at the telegraph reader, which embossed the sounds in the paper tape, and discovered they could be faintly heard on playback. At last the great inventor had an original idea.

By the fall of 1877, he had glued tinfoil to a cylinder attached to a crank and equipped with recording and playback heads. He then made the world's first record, the famous "Mary had a little lamb" recitation. This device was patented in the winter of 1878 and was the subject of much press attention. That spring, a company was formed to exploit the device as a curiosity. As no practical use turned up, the ten-day wonder was soon forgotten. Edison had turned his attention to the invention of an incandescent light bulb and the development of the public electricity system.

Ten years later, in 1888, borrowing developments from the rival invention laboratory of Alexander Graham Bell, Edison returned to the phonograph. The combination of a wax cylinder and electric motor provided two minutes of sound at a constant speed. A shaving device permitted the cylinder to be reused. In partnership with millionaire businessman Jesse Lippincott, Edison launched his invention through the North American Phonograph Company as a dictating machine.

Lippincott decided to rent the machines through subsidiary companies organized on the states'-rights basis developed by the telephone interests. The Delaware company made money in 1889, because it had a contract to provide dictating machines to government offices in Washington. But secretaries, mostly male, preferred real dictation to this mechanical substitute, and in 1891 the company faltered and fell back into Edison's hands.

Edison firmly believed in the business application of his device and thought Lippincott's mistake was renting the machines; so Edison arranged that they be sold. There was considerable interest in placing the device in public places, like a jukebox, with entertainment cylinders and a slot for the public's nickels, but Edison was opposed. "He could not or would not countenance the potentialities of the phonograph as a medium of entertainment," writes industry historian Roland Gelat in *The Fabulous Phonograph*. "He insisted that it was not a toy. He resented its use for amusement. And for years he deliberately discouraged the development of the phonograph as a musical instrument."

The subsidiaries, however, could sell the machines any way they wanted, and the demand for entertainment was insatiable. "The nickel-

in-the-slot phonograph met it with immediate success. The strains of
Sousa marches and Stephen Foster melodies quickened the tempo of
phonograph business from Massachusetts to California.'' Thus the
phonograph industry was launched over its inventor's indignant protests.

PHASE TWO: 1895–1917

European inventors had long tried to industrialize entertainment. Printing, of course, had industrialized printed entertainment
in the fifteenth century. Music boxes and player pianos of increasingly elaborate design brought increasingly complex music at the
turn of a handle, the push of a pedal, or the throw of a switch. But
the phonograph was a new class of instrument, with a far greater
range of expression than any previous entertainment machine. The
moving picture projector soon followed it out of Edison's studio,
and together they opened up a market for industrialized entertainment that would reach 3 percent of the gross national product in
Western nations and become a force for the globalization of culture
and the informationization of the economy.

Another industry taking shape in the second phase of the revolution was retail distribution. Mail-order catalogues and chain and
department stores owed their origin to the first phase of the
revolution, but they acquired their characteristic style and explosive growth in the nineties and after. Advertising, also a product of
phase one, took on its dominant characteristics and impressive
growth in the years leading up to the First World War. Automatic
vending machines were another product of this era. Marketing
became a standard subject at American universities in the prewar
years. Installment buying and its accompanying discipline, credit
checking, reached their maturity between the turn of the century
and the outbreak of the war.

Behind the restructuring of American industry in the revolution's second phase was the enormous success of the railroads,
which had turned disconnected regions into a nation. The need for
national companies created the federations and amalgamations
within each industry that led to the infamous trusts.

"The Gunpowder Trade Association had been formed in 1872
when overproduction resulting from increased output and a surplus
of Civil War powder threatened to collapse prices," writes Ameri-

ca's corporate historian, Alfred Chandler in *Strategy and Structure*. This was three years after the completion of the Union Pacific, at the beginning of phase one. Henry du Pont had managed to buy a controlling interest in his larger rivals during the 1870s depression. He controlled the association.

The structure of the gunpowder industry remained unrationalized, unconsolidated, until a family crisis in 1902 (early in phase two) forced a restructuring. "The administrative end would have to be reorganized, numerous selling organizations or administrative organizations done away with, and we would have to establish a system of costs in order that an economical manufacture could be established throughout the business," wrote Pierre du Pont. The various companies were bought out for cash or shares in the new E. I. du Pont de Nemours Powder Co.—a classic trust which made it possible (here Chandler quotes Pierre du Pont again) "to operate the properties in one name, through one set of selling agents, and under one management, or operation."

This pattern of phase-one federation/phase-two consolidation runs right through the development of modern American industry. And the pattern of holding company or trust, which characterized the first phase, was developed just seven years after the du Ponts created the gunpowder association, and ten years after the railroad crossed the country. It is described by Stewart Holbrook in *The Age of the Moguls*:

> The beginnings of the Standard Oil trust were to be seen in 1879, when stockholders of Standard and all affiliated companies turned their stocks over to three employees of Standard. These three men then legally owned the various companies. This legal fiction was the work of Samuel C. T. Dodd, John Rockefeller's attorney. Through the fiction, John Rockefeller and his associates could swear all sorts of things in court and not commit perjury.

The problem was, no company could hold stock in another company, unless specifically permitted by charter and approved by state legislation, and most states were inalterably opposed. In 1889, New Jersey amended its legislation to permit the formation of holding companies, and with Standard Oil as a model, the rush to form trusts was on. Soon Standard Oil was selling details of its magic formula to other would-be trusts.

The instrument of trust was the giant holding company. "Chartered under the friendly statutes of a few states—New Jersey, Delaware, Maine and West Virginia—holding companies exercised control by trading their own stock for the stock of companies that joined the new combinations," reports Alex Groner in *The American Heritage History of Business and Industry in America*, adding that "the organizers or promoters often retained a controlling interest in the holding company itself."

Either through voting trusts or holding companies, the result was monopoly. Sugar refining was at one point 95 percent controlled by a single company; Pullman Cars owned 85 percent of their market; tobacco production was 80 percent owned by J. B. Duke; Standard Oil and Bell Telephone were famous examples, as were General Electric and International Harvester.

The press kept the public angry about these constraints to competition, while Congress worked out new legislation (the Sherman Antitrust Act dates from 1890) and the Supreme Court interpreted it. The structuring of American industry was carried out in a politicized climate of antagonism and attack.

In phase two of the restructuring, from the mid-1890s onward, Chandler tells us, "Administrative innovations were much more important to the development of American business than legal ones:

> The transformation of a loose alliance of manufacturing or marketing firms into a single consolidated organization with a central headquarters made possible economies of scale through standardization of processes and standardization in the procurement of materials. . . . Consolidation permitted a concentration of production in a few large favorably located factories. By handling a high volume of output, consolidated factories reduced the cost of making each individual unit. They could specialize further and subdivide the process of manufacturing and also were often able to develop and apply new technological improvements more easily than could smaller units. [During this restructuring,] the factories or sales offices, formerly managed by heads of member firms, became operated by salaried plant managers or sales representatives.

Thus in the second phase of the American Industrial Revolution, the trusts had moved from legal fictions to get around the law into operating companies with their own logic, run by salaried execu-

tives with layers of middle management, and exploring and de-
lighting in economies of scale. If the first phase of the revolution
had made the Robber Barons of distribution famous (Rockefeller
with his oil well and pipeline shenanigans; Vanderbilt and his
underhanded tricks to build a railroad trust), in the second phase, it
was the experts of production and finance who would grab the
headlines and the public imagination. Andrew Carnegie, John
Pierpont Morgan, Meyer Guggenheim, Henry Ford, and Pierre du
Pont were tycoons whose reputations still smoke, while Rockefeller became another word for wealth.

With economies of scale established by the operating trusts, the
next important development of the revolution's second phase was
the assembly line and mass production, which is generally attributed to Henry Ford and his Highland Park Model-T assembly plant
in 1914. Not true, says Alex Groner:

> The "Father of Automotive Mass Production" was Ran-
> som E. Olds, who had started his business on a shoe-
> string in 1899 on East Jefferson Avenue in Detroit. Olds
> built an 'assembled' car. Engines came from the Dodge
> Brothers' machine shop. The Lelands, father and son, made
> his transmissions. The "Merry Oldsmobile" looked like
> a buggy steered by a tiller—crude and spidery compared
> with the massively built, elegant French cars; but its
> cost was less than four hundred dollars against five to ten
> thousand for the imported models. . . . In 1901 Olds
> turned out four hundred and twenty-five cars; and the
> following year he turned out twenty-five hundred. He
> was the first to preach and practice the idea of a cheap
> car for the masses.

There is no doubt that Ford's work on the assembly line made a
success of the industry. Coupled with his brilliant marketing schemes
and his enlightened labor policy, it not only put America on
wheels, it changed the way Americans worked. The impact of his
methods is equivalent to the changes in production being introduced by the Japanese in the current revolution.

In many ways, the successful development of the Ford Motor
Company was an anomaly. In 1904, automobile supersalesman
William C. Durant took over the failing Buick Motor Company,
and in four years built it into the leading automobile company in
America, selling a third more cars than Henry Ford, who was then
just introducing the Model T.

Noting the success of J. P. Morgan, who had put together the mammoth $1.4 billion United States Steel trust, Durant decided that the motor industry was ripe for plucking. Chandler picks up the story:

> On September 8, 1908, Durant formed the General Motors Company, a holding company, which by the end of the year owned stock in Buick, Olds, and the W. F. Stewart Company, bodymakers in Flint. Within the next eighteen months, largely through exchanging General Motors stock for the stock of purchased companies, Durant came also to control all or sizeable blocks of stock of Cadillac, Oakland, six other automobile companies, three truck firms, and ten parts and accessory companies.

If the pattern of American industry had been set before the outbreak of World War I so had the antitrust mood, in part by muckraking journalists of the yellow press, in part by politicians who discovered that attacking the trusts was good for votes. On the other hand, they did not want to disturb the wealth-making machine. This conflict was exemplified by President Teddy Roosevelt, who pretended to go after the villains and built a reputation as a trustbuster without really doing anything except making government bigger. His successor, William Howard Taft, was slightly more successful with some spectacular trials, including General Electric, U. S. Steel, International Harvester, and Standard Oil but it's not certain that even this was effective. As a rule, government antitrust actions succeed only when the trust itself had been rendered obsolete by the marketplace.

As a result of the press's attacks, the tycoons sought to improve their reputations by putting conscience money into foundations and institutions dedicated to ends that the government would later assume when taxes outgrew needs. The most famous of the philanthropists was Andrew Carnegie, who built thousands of public libraries and installed thousands of organs in churches.

As at the conclusion of previous revolutions, the pattern of innovation shifted from technologic and economic to social. While the number of major ideas developed by the business community slowed, the social innovations of the New Deal and the expansion of regulation and government departments were dominant characteristics of the between-the-wars Industrial Age.

JAPANESE INDUSTRIAL REVOLUTION

1868–1918

In the middle of the nineteenth century the Japanese were humiliated by American, French, and British traders determined to open the Japanese market to their products. Confronted by a modern industrial and military power they did not understand, the Japanese were forced to concede humiliating trading rights to "barbarians."

Japan was a feudal state, run by a regent, or shogun, in the name of a token emperor. There were nearly three hundred regions, or clans, each run by a warlord and paying tribute to the shogun in Tokyo (then known as Edo). Actual administration was carried out by the samurai, who were trained in both the martial arts and administration and who carried swords and were licensed to kill.

Below the samurai in descending social order were the peasants, who created the wealth but lived at subsistence level; artisans (or guildsmen), who made the few products the people enjoyed, and the lowliest of all, the merchants, who created nothing and who lived for nothing but money. Since foreign trade was prohibited, there had been no Commercial Revolution. Japan in midcentury was five hundred years behind Europe in economic growth.

The samurai, educated and aristocratic, foresaw the worsening humiliation of their country by the West. Rebelling against the shogun, they restored the emperor to power and installed a military national government, modeled on Western lines, whose purpose was to make Japan as strong as the West in both miliary and economic might. Their success is one of the great stories of economic growth, perhaps the greatest in history, although, as we shall see, it was fatally flawed.

PHASE ONE: 1868–1895

In the words of the leading Japanese economic historian, Kamekichi Takahashi, "The key that unlocks the mystery behind Japan's 'miraculous' modern economy is in the understanding of that first stage.'' The new national government in Tokyo was composed largely of the samurai from the Western clans who had put down the shogun and restored the emperor. They were determined on two complementary courses: to abolish all traces of the shameful feudal regime; and to build a powerful Western economy safe from the humiliations imposed by the West on China, Saigon, Cambodia, Burma, and India. England, the first industrial nation, was to be their model and tutor, but they would take what they could from the French, the Germans, and the Americans, who were rejoicing in the first stages of their own Industrial Revolutions.

In the view of the young samurai, the situation was desperate, their need for strength urgent, their nationalism paramount. To accomplish the impossible, their energy had to be boundless, their integrity unassailable, and their policies fair. What followed was a military operation, a fifty-year war in which the samurai accomplished all of their objectives. By the end of World War I, Japan was a world power, an economic force, a great trading and manufacturing nation with a thirst for further conquests both military and economic.

To end the rice-based feudal economy, the samurai government replaced the tribute payments made by the peasants to the warlords and samurai with monetary pensions. To pay the pensions, they taxed the peasants, who had been given title to their land and the right to sell their rice or land as they pleased. The almost three hundred territories of the warlords were abolished and replaced with a prefectural system of regional government, as in France. The warlords were given titles, as in Britain. A parliamentary system was established on the British model, with an elected government headed by a prime minister.

Unlike a revolution, the restoration was almost bloodless; the various classes were compensated and found new roles to play in the samurai-run economy. As historian William Lockwood put it, in *The Economic Development of Japan*, ''the Meiji Restoration was not the story of a rising business class, which burst the bonds of feudalism to establish its supremacy in a mercantile state. Still less was it a democratic revolt transferring political power to representatives of the mass of peasants and workers.'' It was more like a right-wing military coup, with the military dressed in Western business clothes and determined to install a Western economic democracy; they were equally determined to avoid even the slightest taint of the corruption which, they observed, had contaminated all previous attempts at national economic development in the world. For the samurai, honor and nation is all.

Economic reforms were the other order of business. To the samurai governors, the merchants were narrow and venal and could not be expected to seek the larger economic interest of the state. The artisans were too small in their thinking to create a modern industry. The samurai would be the government, the financiers, the industrialists, and would bring to each a spirit of service to the state. They would develop a unified world-wide industrial intelligence operation in the military style. They would establish a world-class strategic industrial system and service it with a world-class infrastructure of communications, railroads, shipping, highways, banking, and insurance.

They believed that the private sector was essential to accomplish these activities, and were diametrically opposed to socialism. Where necessary, however, they were prepared to start an industry in government and transfer it to the private sector at giveaway prices as soon as circumstances warranted. Thus it was that the government found itself at the root of all progress, that government spending soon rose to the highest per-capita level in the world, and that despite a number of errors, it was also the most effective the world had then seen, or has seen since.

One characteristic element of the first Japanese miracle was the establishment of a coordinated intelligence operation superior to any known before. Students were sent abroad and sent back reports. When they returned, they were given key posts to put their knowledge to use. Foreign experts were brought in, often at salaries ten times higher than their employers, to teach the needed skills. Delegations to the West were numerous, and debriefings intense. Translations of Western publications were commissioned or subsidized. Diplomats had the most onerous intelligence chores. And as soon as trading agents were established abroad, they were expected to provide intelligence reports on the minutia of the Western economy. As this information was brought home, it was coordinated and analyzed and used both strategically and tactically throughout the whole samurai community, as in a war.

Another samurai reform was the introduction of the new corporate structure, just finding its role in the United States. The joint-stock company was a product of the Commercial Revolution in Italy and Britain, but it was undergoing a restructuring in America under the influence of the continental railroads. The samurai found this multilevel hierarchical approach much to their military taste and were quick to adopt it. It also helped solve one of their most important problems, finding and utilizing capital where none existed. The banks were joint-stock companies, and they trapped the payments made to the warlords and put them to work. Thus the joint-stock company had a higher purpose beyond the making of money, and this suited the samurai ideal of patriotic industrialism.

By these various means, in the first quarter-century of the restoration "the foundations were laid for the building of the defense industries and for the steady expansion of the civilian economy." Yet, as Lockwood also tells us, it would have taken a wise observer to see it, for there were few indications in the standard of living or life-style of the people, the size and number of factories, the miles of railroad, or the use of steam power. Inland transport was still largely by handcart and packhorse, and exports were still as they had been: agricultural products and handicrafts. As Dr. Takahashi says, in *The Rise and Development of Japan's Modern Economy*:

> The main reason why the samurai-class pioneers made great headway in the economic world, was because they accepted the idea that apart from the assimilative development of the modern economy, there was no other route to the guarantee and growth of Japanese independence, no other route to a prosperous and strong nation.

PHASE TWO: 1895–1918

The first phase produced the inflation and other forms of slither typical of an economic revolution, and the government responded in the 1880s with a program of stabilization and restraint that was severe enough to refund the national debt. The road to prosperity reopened in the late eighties. Capital formation accelerated. Industrialization became intense. The railroads boomed. Japanese trading companies (the sogoshosha) began to take over from the foreigners. Trade moved to Japanese freighters. At last, their ships were coming home.

Now the time had come for the samurai to show their might. By provoking a war with the Chinese (1894–95), they greatly advanced their economic goals. As it proved victorious, the reparation payments helped end Japanese dependence on foreigners and put them on the gold standard. It also made Japan a colonial power. William Lockwood adds to the list of benefits gained:

> Politically, the war reinforced the power and prestige of the oligarchy for another generation, winning unified support for Japan's aggressive entry into the arena of Far East imperialism. Economically, it exerted a stimulus no less immediate and far-reaching in consequences. Arms expenditures accelerated the upswing in prices already under way. New banks and small industrial and trading concerns mushroomed under the recently promulgated Commercial and Banking Acts of 1890 and 1893. Military requirements doubled the merchant marine in 2 years. A boom developed in a number of industries producing war supplies.

It is hard to avoid the conclusion that war had become the samurai's principal instrument of development. From then onward, they tried to have a war every ten years. "Obtaining these strategic advantages [from China]," writes Lockwood, "and redoubling her armament program, Japan now prepared in turn for the challenge to Russia in 1904. . . . Again a conflict of limited duration, fought on foreign soil, hastened the development of financial institutions, marine transport, and industrial technology, without itself imposing an insupportable drain on Japan's still meager reserves."

Ten years later, it was World War I, from which Japan again emerged as an economic winner (as did the United States). Enormous profits came from the sale of armaments and supplies at inflated prices. Imports of strategic materials declined, forcing their development at home. Merchant shipping revenue soared, and as Takahashi states with unconcealed pride, among the "wartime blessings" brought by "the golden chance of World War One" were "the large profits earned in international trade transactions during the war years":

> Japanese specialists in international trade had already developed quite far by the end of the Meiji era, but during the war as the power of European trading houses declined, the Japanese became even more active. They even advanced into trade between third countries (e.g., trade not directly involving Japanese imports or exports) and, as a result, they made huge profits, establishing themselves as powerful international traders.

PART THREE

THE INFORMATION REVOLUTION

AN INFORMATION
REVOLUTION?

It is widely believed that we are currently undergoing an economic revolution comparable in depth and scope to the Industrial Revolution, and that the sudden, explosive growth of the information, service, and high-tech sectors is symptomatic of this fundamental economic shift.

Deep changes in the basic structure of the economy abound. Management and labor relate in new ways, as jobs move offshore, and unions struggle to find their new role. Centuries-old traditions of women's place are being suddenly altered. Work returns to the home, where it was before the Industrial Revolution. The structure of the corporation is flattening from the thousand-year-old hierarchy. These and other structural changes strengthen the revolutionary hypothesis. Dramatic advances in the standards of living of Europeans, Americans, and in several Westernized Asian countries since World War II also suggest a revolutionary change in economic activity.

What happens if we apply our two-stage, two-generation model of economic revolution to the present period of structural change? As with past revolutions, a new post-industrial and non-mechanical technology emerges to form the basis of the new economy. Automation, television, computers, reactors, lasers, jets, rockets, and satellites become important industries.

Every past economic age has ended in a thicket of regulation, special privilege, social rigidity, and hyper-taxation and the last generation of the Industrial Age is no exception. By the 1960s much Western industry was careless of quality and ethics, out of touch with its clients,

no longer innovative, heavily taxed and increasingly regulated, enormously large and profitable, and increasingly
under attack.

Past revolutions have been marked by economic slither,
institutional collapse, social alienation, and the romantic
search for new values. During the sixties and seventies,
all these forces can be clearly identified. By themselves
they are insufficient signs of economic revolution: They
all can be found in the thirties as well. Yet when combined with changes in business and technology, the case
becomes very strong.

The pain of birth is endurable because it promises new
life. Looking back through Western economic history, the
periods leading into economic revolutions have often been
turbulent and disturbing, leaving a trail of the dispossessed. Yet the emergence of a new economy has inevitably been a time of great technical and cultural creativity
and astonishing economic growth.

Chapter 10
INFORMATION REVOLUTION

PHASE ONE: 1950–1975

The United States came out of World War II the unquestioned industrial leader. As economist Michael Hudson reports in *Global Fracture*, it "stood at the pinnacle of its power and appeared invincible in the military, political and economic sphere." American industry, enormously built-up during the war and undiminished by bombing or sabotage, was favored with the world's largest homogeneous domestic market and a government geared to production. America guided the design of world economic institutions and the terms of world trade. As symbol of its power, it owned almost three-quarters of the world's gold.

World War II fathered a brood of Faustian technologies: atomic energy, jet aircraft and rocketry, computers and solid state electronics—the triggering technologies of the revolution soon to get underway. It brought a new world view to isolationist America, and a new respect for scientific research and education, which returning veterans were encouraged to explore.

Perhaps the most compelling new technology was television, our electronic window on the world. TV was destined to do for the Information Revolution what printing had done for the Commercial Revolution: spread the new awareness. Soon there were stations, networks, and sales and repair outlets in even the poorest countries, and highly polished and popular American programming began reducing national characteristics to a common global denominator.

Business was another culture that was leveling national borders. In 1950 the Diners Club credit card appeared. In 1956 the first trans-Atlantic telephone cable, TAT-1, was put into service. And in 1957 Boeing's 707 and Lockheed's DC-8 reduced the Atlantic to a six-hour flight. Second-generation computers crunched the most varied operations into a single bottom line. These four innovations shrank the business globe to executive size. The era of multinational enterprise was inaugurated, along with the celebrity jet-set.

As leader of the postwar West, America drew new energy from confrontation with the Communist world. Rapidly increasing state funding earmarked for "defense" poured through the economy. A test war against communism was pursued in Korea. Purges of "commies and pinkos" preoccupied the nation as it rearmed and rebuilt the West. By the mid-fifties, Italy, Germany, and Japan were pronounced rehabilitated and were relaunched as economic partners. The 1957 Treaty of Rome set Europe on the road to unification.

America was the hothouse producing new technology. Some came from government labs and think tanks. Much came from the universities, with the highly specialized Massachusetts Institute of Technology setting the pace. Private R and D centers, like MIT's neighbor, the Arthur D. Little Company, were very productive, as were some private foundations, particularly in medicine. Experiments with venture capital in Boston encouraged spin-offs and start-ups along peripheral Highway 128. All profited from government funding, largely in the form of contracts, most of which were for defense.

Perhaps the most fertile sources of new technology were the laboratories of large corporations, many of which dated back to the American Industrial Revolution at the turn of the century. The largest of these was Bell Labs in northern New Jersey, dedicated to keeping the giant AT&T telephone system on top of the burgeoning demand for communications. Their most important creation was the transistor, designed as a permanent replacement for the millions of unreliable radio tubes in telephone-line amplifiers. The tiny transistor, and its even tinier descendant, the microprocessors, would sweep the world, changing everything in their way.

Espionage spread the new technology to Communist countries. Licensing arrangements brought it to U.S. allies. Piracy, fakes, knockoffs, and counterfeits brought it to the Third World. Nothing could contain it, as the story of Masaru Ibuka and Akio Morita illustrates.

THE SONY CORPORATION

(case history)

During the war, Masaru Ibuka worked on heat-sensing bombs for the Japanese navy. After the defeat, he and his young engineering assistant, Akio Morita, started an electronics business under General MacArthur's strict occupation rules, with $500 capital borrowed from Morita's rich father, a distinguished sake brewer. They made ricecookers (a disaster), voltmeters (a modest success), and shortwave converters for civilian radios, which had customers lining up in the streets.

A more ambitious plan to build tape-recorders nearly proved fatal, until Morita demonstrated his ingenious skill in marketing products for which there was as yet no demand. Soon their recorders were used in courtrooms, schools, police stations, broadcasting networks, and even private homes. Morita contracted with the musical-instrument maker Yamaha to distribute the tape recorders. Sales were disappointing. Morita then made a crucial decision: He would build his own sales organization.

Meanwhile in America, Western Electric, the owner of the patents on the transistor, was pushed by the Justice Department to share its important secret. Licenses were offered for the new technology for $25,000. Ibuka, who dreamed of making a transistor radio, tried to persuade MITI, the Japanese government's international financial watchdog, to let the young firm buy a license. The government said no, the company is too small, the technology too ambitious. Then, after a year of arguments from Ibuka, MITI agreed in the spring of 1954.

Western Electric warned Ibuka that although the transistors worked well at audio frequencies (they were used for hearing aids), they would not work at higher radio frequencies. Ibuka was sure he could improve them. Then in the summer of 1954 came the shocking announcement: Texas Instruments, Inc. had succeeded in making radio-frequency transistors, and its subsidiary, Regency, was marketing a transistor radio. Thanks to MITI's delay, the prize was lost.

Both encouraged and disappointed by the American success, Ibuka's team succeeded in improving the transistor in the following months, and in mid-1955 the young company was on the road to fame with its own transistor radio. From then on, they would stun the world with their technical leadership (Ibuka) and marketing acumen (Morita).

In 1958 the firm changed its name to Sony, and introduced a shirt-pocket sized transistor radio that would circle the world. "This was a breakthrough for Japanese industry," says Sony admirer George Gilder in *The Spirit of Enterprise*. "Instead of just copying American products and improving them, Sony led the way—leaving other electronics companies—American as well as Japanese—to follow."

Shortly after, Ibuka had so improved his transistor that it would work at the higher FM and television frequencies. The Sony line continued to expand with solid-state electronics and laid a trail of innovations into the eighties.

When Japanese firms wanted to expand internationally, they made deals with foreign distributors through giant trading companies known as sogoshosha. Morita, however, was opposed to traditional Japanese ways. He set up a Canadian and then an American distribution system and soon had branches in 147 countries, and the Sony pocket transistor was spreading popular music, Western culture, and the Sony name to the corners of the world.

Sony was not the first company of the Japanese invasion. Japanese cameras had paved the way. Nevertheless, Ibuka's insistence on quality and innovation, and Morita's on popular products and global marketing put Sony and Japanese electronics on the path of world leadership. Those who credit government intervention and the large financial cartels for Japan's success in world markets would do well to study the case of Sony, perhaps the world's most innovative company since Edison hung up his smock.

Soon the Japanese miracle would be repeated around the Pacific rim. European industry, thanks to Marshall Plan aid, was finding its footing. Growth in population and wealth was unprecedented. Between 1948 and 1973, the world's total industrial expansion increased 350 percent, from $2 trillion to $7 trillion; the population went from 2.5 to nearly 4 billion; per-capita income almost doubled, jumping from less than $1,000 to nearly $2,000. While much of this growth was in the developed West, many Third World countries began the climb from poverty.

Other material accomplishments of the opening phase of the Information Revolution (as noted by the perennially optimistic Hudson Institute) included a raising of life expectancy in the less developed world from forty-two to fifty-three years, and from sixty-five to seventy-one years in the developed countries. Agricultural land increased worldwide by 16 percent, and despite tremendous urbanization, it has even increased in the United States, largely through irrigation and swamp drainage. Widespread fears to the contrary notwithstanding, known mineral reserves increased

4,000 percent and world per-capita grain and food production soared.

While growth rates were high for the United States, they were even higher for other developed countries, with the result that despite the boom, America's share of world production fell. In 1950 Americans produced 39 percent of the world's industrial output. By 1970 this had fallen to 30 percent. In 1950 America produced 46 percent of the world's steel and 76 percent of its cars. By 1970 America steel had fallen to 20 percent and cars to 31 percent of world production.

STRUCTURAL CHANGES

1950–1975

With their materialistic outlook, economists and policymakers of the time focused on industrial production, which was shrinking; they ignored services, which were growing rapidly, and information activities, growing most rapidly of all. At the beginning of the period, about four out of every ten in the work force were industrial workers, two were service workers, one was a farmer, and three were information workers. At the end of the period, nearly half were information workers, a quarter each were in services and industry, and the farm worker was one out of forty. Within the pace of a generation, the work force was transformed.

During this time frame, the nature of the work place also changed. In 1950 multinational enterprises (MNEs) were responsible for 17 percent of American manufactures; by 1974 this had risen to 62 percent, or about a third of the non-communist world's Gross National Products. The average growth rate of leading MNEs was two to three times that of most countries, including the United States. Comparison of annual sales to GNPs indicates that by the end of the period, the biggest of the MNEs were larger than many Western countries: General Motors was bigger than Switzerland and all but 22 nations; Royal Dutch Shell was bigger than Iran, Goodyear than Saudi Arabia.

Consumers all over the world were growing familiar with names like Olivetti and Volkswagen, Michelin and Nikon, Volvo and Philips, Sony and Fiat, and were getting used to eating in foreign restaurants, drinking imported wines, or just ordering up a pizza, hamburger, or egg foo yung. World products and services were taking over the marketplace, and a Western culture—still largely American—was taking hold of the "boomies," that explosive postwar generation crowding the urban West.

Corporate growth in America was constrained by powerful national taboos on collaborative behavior. Mergers were government inspected to prevent even the possibility of lessening competition. This was supposed to help the domestic consumer, but in reality it placed American firms at a global disadvantage. To grow, they were forced to diversify—that is, acquire companies in areas in which they had no experience or natural interest. This resulted in huge "conglomerates" with no recognizable character or purpose, executives who could take no pride other than "the bottom line", and products whose quality was secondary to more urgent corporate goals.

Despite the momentous changes in the world marketplace, the major leaps made by other countries, and structural changes in the work force and the economy, America remained a confrontational society, with labor, corporation, and government locked in antagonistic relationships, and with lawmaking, law courts, lawyers, and lawsuits the biggest growth industry of all.

THE ASSAULT ON INDUSTRY

1961–1973

"Camelot" was ushered in in January 1961, when John Kennedy took office. In his farewell address, outgoing president Dwight Eisenhower warned of the grave implications of the "conjunction

of an immense military establishment and a large arms industry,''
because of "the potential for the disastrous rise of misplaced
power." In addition to the dangers of "the military-industrial
complex," he warned of "the prospect of domination of the
nation's scholars by federal employment," and "the equal and
opposite danger that public policy could itself become the captive
of a scientific-technological elite." It was well he was leaving;
events and forces were getting out of hand.

In February 1961, immediately following President Kennedy's
inauguration, twenty-nine major manufacturing firms and forty-
four of their officials were convicted of rigging bids and fixing
prices in the sale of electrical equipment from 1955 to 1959. Judge
Cullin Ganey noted the involvement of "virtually every large
manufacturer of electrical equipment in the industry, . . . a shocking indictment of a vast segment of the economy," as he sen-
tenced seven of the executives to thirty-day jail terms and fined the
major offender, the General Electric Company, a total of $437,000.
Press and public expressed disappointment, shock, and betrayal.
Attorney General Robert Kennedy thought the sentences were light
in the circumstances. President John Kennedy told Congress that
"morality in private business has not been sufficiently spurred."

On the morning of April 12, 1961, Flight Major Yuri Alekseyevich
Gagarin took off from the Baykonur space station in a 2.4-ton,
8.5-foot Vostok space capsule for a 108-minute round-the-world
trip, at speeds exceeding 17,500 miles per hour. This act of daring
(two dogs from a previous flight had died on reentry) earned
him a place in history. That morning, around four AM Washington time, a journalist phoned NASA publicity head Shorty Powers
for comment on the news and was told, "We're all asleep down
here." In the words of space historian David Baker, "To the press
that Thursday morning it seemed an apt quote for why America
had, once again, and almost exactly three and a half years after
Sputnik I, been beaten in the space race."

Nineteen sixty-one was a transition year for American television as
it moved from black and white to color and from the golden era of
live studio productions from New York to a second golden age of
videotaped drama series from Hollywood about institutional America: Ben Casey, Dr. Kildare, The Defenders. Bonanza's Ben
Cartwright and his sons were in the third of fourteen seasons of
weekly morality plays that would be seen by four hundred million
people in ninety countries by the end of the decade.

It was a surprise to many when in the spring of 1961, President
Kennedy's new appointment to head the FCC, Newton Minow,

called television programming "a vast wasteland" that was "squandering the public's airwaves" with mindless and often violent entertainment. "It is not enough to cater to a nation's whims—you must also serve the nation's needs," Minow told the nation's broadcasters at their Washington convention. Minow's "vast wasteland" phrase became the rallying cry of those impatient for television to become more than entertainment, and who failed to appreciate its great strengths. It led to the founding of the Public Broadcasting System in 1967.

The cause of a mysterious four-year outbreak of genetic birth defects in Europe was discovered by Dr. Widekund Lenz of Hamburg in late 1961. Expectant mothers who took the German sedative Contergan between the thirty-eighth and forty-first days of their pregnancy could give birth to babies with defective arms; and from the forty-first to forty-fourth days, with defective legs. Chemie Grunenthal, GmbH, of Stolberg, West Germany, the drug's developer and manufacturer, denied any connection between the birth defects and the product the world would come to know as thalidomide.

During the outbreak, some 10,000 West German babies were born with genetically damaged limbs, of which only 5,000 would survive. In England, 805 were born with genetic defects, of whom 652 were still alive. Forty "phocomelia" cases were reported in Ottawa before Dr. Lenz's theories were reported in the February 23, 1962, issue of *Time* magazine. In the United States there were only 10. It seems Dr. Frances Kelsey, of the Food and Drug Administration, had resisted the "very rigorous" demands of the William S. Merrell Company of Cincinnati that their version of thalidomide (Kevadan) be approved for American sale.

The American reaction was swift. President Kennedy called for stronger drug legislation. To strengthen the call, he awarded Dr. Kelsey the gold medal for distinguished federal civilian service. Legislation passed the Senate on October 3, and the House on October 4, 1962. The pharmaceutical industry was henceforth subject to the most rigorous control. Never again, it was hoped, would the industry "get away" with another thalidomide.

The mood of distrust of the chemical industry was reinforced by the appearance in September of Rachel Carson's *Silent Spring*, which depicted in graphic terms the physical destruction of animals and plants by the unrestrained use of pesticides. To a reviewer from the *Chemical and Engineering News*, this was an irresponsible, uninformed, and unbalanced attack on a great industry, but in the rising antibusiness climate of the period, many were inclined to agree with the distinguished naturalist Loren Eisley, writing in the *Saturday Review*: "It is a devastating, heavily documented, relentless attack upon human carelessness, greed and irresponsibility."

The 1960s in America were growing into a full-scale replay of the 1830s in Britain, where government, the literary community, the educational and institutional establishment were attacking and rejecting the industrial sector as venal, ruthless, and unprincipled. Industry was totally unprepared for the assault.

When Ralph Nader attacked the auto industry, General Motors, and the Corvair in *Unsafe at Any Speed, The Designed-in Dangers of the American Automobile*, stunned chief officers of the corporation struck back at him in the one area where he was invulnerable: his monklike private life. When a congressional committee revealed that the corporation had commissioned private investigators to dig up dirt on this pure-hearted ascetic, the damage to corporate America was multiplied. Beside this, GM's $475,000 fine was minor.

For all his faults, Nader was indeed a monk, a reincarnation of Savonarola, who, at the height of the Commercial Era in Florence, attacked the venality and materialistic corruption of his society with such eloquence that the great painter Botticelli was inspired to burn his own paintings. Perhaps Nader's attack on our leading wealthmaker became the focus for our collective guilt over our incredible economic growth. Or, perhaps unconsciously, we were ready to kiss the tired old Industrial Age good-bye and get on with the future.

By middecade, the Vietnam War pitted America's technological might against a tiny, long-oppressed Third-World colony in search of liberation. Defoliation, napalm, and body counts became the vivid symbols of mindless productivity on color television. President Eisenhower's warnings about the evils of the military-industrial complex seemed to be coming true. Young people from the largest generation in history were forced to take sides. Eighty percent chose country and establishment. But a remarkable twenty percent grabbed the headlines with a barrage of activities and a courageous stream of protest for which to some there seemed no reply but violence; it culminated in the death of four student demonstrators at Kent State University at the hands of the National Guard. It was to end the war.

At the heart of the protest was a sense that business and government had grown beyond human scale, and that Western values had been lost in a vast bureaucracy. Megadeaths, megalopolises, megaversities, and multinational corporations larger than most countries were equally disdained. Pushed by the escalating war in Vietnam and a growing desire to control civil unrest and corporate irresponsibility through regulation, government grew and grew.

Regulatory programs proliferated. So many government departments were created that new systems of management were brought in from industry to keep track of them. If morality could not be legislated, perhaps opportunity could. The meaning of democracy was explored through forced integration and bussing; economic values were enlarged as ecologists demanded clean air and water irrespective of cost; social benefits were extended regardless of the contribution of recipients; and an army of inspectors and social workers was mustered and released on the land to enforce the new morality.

In fact, what was happening was a massive shift in employment from industry to government. Prosperity and inflation were pushing us all into higher tax brackets, and while industry automated and flourished, government grew fat on taxes, and padded the payroll with specialists, clerks, and special assistants, plus new buildings to house their new multitudes, and computers to keep track of them all. Back in 1955, the year Parkinson issued his first report on public-service proliferation, information workers became the most numerous group in the economy, larger than the industrial work force, which had peaked in 1953 and was starting its downward slide.

By the late sixties, the forces of slither were buffeting the Western economies. Inflation, which had started in Britain in the summer of 1954 and spread to the rest of the West the following summer, continued to mount. Unemployment was rising. The industrial community was no longer growing, no longer creating jobs. Hijacking had broken out, hobbling airline travel with the expense and inconvenience of security. Terrorism was rapidly becoming institutionalized. Youth was everywhere restless.

The rejection of industrial values during the sixties was turned into a romantic movement by these revolutionary forces. The introduction of the birth-control pill (a great technological accomplishment) created the basis for the sexual revolution and the women's movement. Freedom included not only protest against industry, government and oversized institutions, but sexual liberation. Bra-burning, mate-swapping and pot-smoking were not only signs of protest but acts of personal liberation.

"There is a revolution coming," wrote Charles Reich in *The Greening of America,* at the end of the decade.

It will not be like revolutions in the past. It will originate with the individual and with culture, and it will change the political structure only as its final act. It will not require violence to succeed, and it cannot be successfully resisted with violence. It is now spreading with amazing rapidity, and already our laws, institutions and social structure are changing in consequence. It promises a higher reason, a more humane community, and a new and liberated individual. Its ultimate creation will be a new and endearing wholeness and beauty—a renewed relationship of man to himself, to other men, to society, to nature and to the land.

The search for new values was underway. Phase one of the revolution was coming to a close.

1975–TRANSITION YEAR

On Wednesday morning, October 1, 1975, a planeload of celebrities, led by Norman Mailer and Warren Beatty, arrived at Philippine Coliseum in Manila to watch the world heavyweight championship bout between Muhammad Ali and Joe Frazier. At 9:45 P.M. on Tuesday, September 30 at the Montreal Forum, at 2:45 A.M. Wednesday at Wembley Stadium in London, and at corresponding times in a hundred other cities all over the world, sports fans gathered to watch the global event on closed-circuit TV.

In the Fort Pierce–Vero Beach area of Florida, guests gathered in the six thousand homes which that evening would receive the fight via satellite and pay-TV. Home Box Office had chosen the "Thrilla in Manila" to highlight the inauguration of its Pay-TV network, a major gamble by its parent company, Time, Inc.

The fight was carried east from Manila by Lani Bird, hovering some twenty thousand miles above Hawaii, then across America to Vero Beach by Westar, the first of America's domestic satellites. Before the fight, the cable-TV industry had been so depressed that one regional convention earlier in the year was canceled for lack of delegates. Now suddenly everyone wanted to be on the cable and subscribe to HBO. The tide had turned. A new industry was born into a new age.

Some years, such as 1066 and 1492, are remembered for single events. Some, such as 1984 and 2000, take on mythic proportions long before they arrive. Nineteen seventy-five is one of those special years that went unrecognized at the time. A dismal period for the Dow Jones, for those who had lost their jobs or their businesses, for those lining up on alternate days to buy gasoline for their cars and trucks, 1975 was nevertheless a watershed. It marked the end of the dominance of smokestack America and signaled the birth of a new global economy. As the Information Age continues to spread its wings, 1975 will come to be recognized as the year the world changed course.

Some weeks after the fight in Manila, the *Wall Street Journal* began transmitting facsimile pages to its regional printing plant in Orlando, Florida, offering a daily edition throughout the Southeast. Once the *Journal* had been set in type at the Massachusetts printing plant, page proofs were converted into digital signals by a scanner, then beamed up to Westar I and down to a page-sized camera via the Orlando dish, one page every three and a half minutes. Here was another use for the satellite, one that other publishers would use in creating national and international editions.

The financial community regularly used international satellites to whisk money around the world, working the Asian markets while Wall Street slept, keeping the multinational branches greased with the same modest reserves. Now domestic satellites were drastically cutting the cost of telecommunications. Less than twenty years after Sputnik, that chirping basketball, took to the skies, three-thousand-pound satellites were erasing national borders and hurrying us into a global economy.

Arthur C. Clarke, the futurist who had published a plan for a geostationary communications satellite in 1945, issued his famous edict: "Don't commute, communicate." Urged on by the quadrupled price of oil, people were beginning to do just that. Fiber optics, hair-thin optical wave-guides, began replacing copper wires in telephone systems, and large corporations, led by Corning Glass in the United States and Northern Telecom in Canada, were positioning themselves for a multibillion-dollar market. The Information Revolution was beginning to find its economic base.

Northern Telecom was also pioneering the private exchange, an electronic switchboard that allowed corporations to make drastic cuts in the cost of doing business. The company was helped along by a 1975 U.S. ruling permitting non–telephone-company equipment to be attached directly to the AT&T system. The integrity of the world's largest monopoly was breached, and an interconnect industry was born. For those who didn't happen to own a corporation, the new law brought the answering machine.

Nineteen seventy-five was the also the year of the pocket calculator, which was rushing toward a $2.5-billion year. Pioneered in 1969 by Commodore International, the calculator business attracted an aggressive group of competitors from all over the world. In five years prices had fallen from hundreds of dollars per unit to thirty. Along the way, various firms were crushed in the avalanche.

The adding machine was once a very expensive and cumbersome mechanical device full of motors, levers, gears, and cams—a symbol of the industrial age now made obsolete by the new technology. The evolution of the pocket calculator also symbolized another striking change. Before 1975 it took years to gear up for mass production of machinery-based products. In 1975 the rules changed. Now products could be upgraded and down-priced simply by changing the software or improving the design of the silicon chip. One of the victims of the new technology was Bowmar Instruments, which was unable to maintain the breathless price-cutting pace. Teetering on the edge of bankruptcy, the one-time market leader struggled for four months to meet the thirty-dollar price. Bowmar salesmen were setting up a booth at the Consumer Electronics Show in Chicago in June 1975, when they saw to their horror that five of their competitors, including Commodore, were about to offer a ten-dollar calculator. On the night before the show, the Bowmar team abandoned their half-finished booth, packed their bags, and went home.

Bowmar was a victim of the learning curve, a relentless Information Age law that describes the rapid fall in prices as production and design experience is acquired. Bowmar's new $7-million plant in Chandler, Arizona, was picked up by General Instruments at forty-five cents on the dollar.

The microchip fueled the revolution. Though the silicon chip was the basis of the explosive growth of new industry, Silicon Valley chipmakers were undergoing the worst time in their twenty-year history. Consumption of chips continued to rise throughout the recession, but wild marketing swings, rumors of shortages, and double orders "just to make sure" had prompted the chipmakers to overexpand. Now they were caught in a glut of their own making.

In the past, silicon chips had either been special-purpose devices for electronic calculators and watches, or else building blocks for the computer industry. But in 1970 Ted Hoff of Intel Corporation created the computer-on-a-chip, and the general-purpose microprocessor was born, computing's second wave. By 1975 Hoff's microprocessor had gone through two generations, and competitors were racing Intel down the learning curve.

Another law of the information industry is that no manufacturer will buy a new component, however powerful and miraculous, from any single supplier, no matter how stable, until a second source is available to guarantee its supply. In 1975 many second sources emerged for the one-chip computer. Manufacturers from every industry rushed to improve traditional mechanical products by making them "smart." The Singer Corporation brought out a smart sewing machine, with a quarter-inch chip replacing the gears and cams previously needed for fancy stitching. Smart gasoline pumps that electronically metered the flow of gas could be read from the booth; they made self-service stations possible and kept records as well. Letter scales calculated postage when the zip-code was keyed in. Meat and grocery scales calculated price. Cash registers dropped their mechanical keys and wheels to become point-of-sale terminals, keeping an electronic record and updating inventories at the same time. Intelligent microwave ovens offered touch-set controls. Taximeters stopped ticking in 1975. Automakers developed computerized ignitions that were capable of saving 20 percent on gas but which—because automakers weren't yet concerned about the learning curve in their industry—wouldn't be phased in for several years. Secure in their domestic markets, the automobile manufacturers believed they had the luxury of time.

If the microprocessor transformed traditional products, it also started a new group of information industries. The most important of these was the microcomputer—or home computer, as it was beginning to be called. In January 1975, using one of Ted Hoff's chips, a small Albuquerque electronics firm called Micro Instrumentation Telemetry Systems (MITS) brought out the Altair 8800, the first microcomputer, and managed to sell several thousand of them that year.

Hobby clubs sprang up across California—notably, the Home Brew Computer Club in Palo Alto, home of Stanford University and heart (perhaps "brains" would be a better term) of Silicon Valley. Attracting a brilliant mixture of free-wheeling engineers and Berkeley radicals, the club advocated "computer power to the people." A critical mass of activity soon exploded. Soon there would be the PET from Commodore, the TRS-80 from Radio

Shack, and most famous of all, the Apple. Within five years home computers would become a billion-dollar industry.

What were home computers good for? Magazines cropped up and suggested possible uses: Control the energy in your home. Do your taxes. Keep a phone list. Play games. Games? Serious computer people were scornful. This was surely another California craze.

The videogame industry, which had started back in 1972, took off in 1975. Every game on the shelves was sold long before Christmas. Leading the field was Nolan Bushnell's "Pong," already popular in bars and waiting rooms. Bushnell's firm, Atari, which pioneered the industry, was turning out three thousand games a day. Such was the success of home videogames that TV watching in 1975 took its first dive: a small, unexpected drop in network viewing that experts of the time attributed to a statistical error. Pay-TV, videogames, and home computers were beginning to compete with broadcast TV for use of the home screen.

The videocassette recorder (VCR) industry was also born in 1975. Sony introduced its new product in time for Christmas. For $2,295 a consumer could buy a nineteen-inch Trinitron receiver and a Sony Betamax packaged in a single piece of furniture: "A Xerox for TV," said Sony marketers. Since RCA and Philips were about to launch their $400 videodisc systems, some analysts believed Sony had made a mistake. But Betamax, already tested in Japan, could record programs off the air. A videodisc machine could not. RCA, as it turned out, didn't launch its videodisc players until 1981, by which time VCRs were outselling Japanese automobiles in dollar volume in some countries and had become Japan's leading export.

In the office of 1975 the new technology was starting to emerge. Montreal entrepreneur Steve Dorsey went beyond the "power typewriters" of Xerox and IBM, adding a video screen and the new floppy-disc memory to create the word processor. Dorsey founded the number-one firm, AES, Ltd., lost it, and went on to found the number-two firm, MICOM, now wholly owned by Philips.

In the mid-seventies the newspaper industry, staggering under escalating costs and increasing competition, began to install video-display terminals (VDTs) and computer photocomposers to set "cold type," replacing the Linotype machines with their pots of molten lead. Hard-bitten columnists and reporters happily surrendered their typewriters for terminals; editors called up stories on their screens and processed them electronically. Wire stories could be fed directly into the computer, where editors could choose and cut without having to keyboard them again. The productivity gains were dramatic. More important for society, the press was learning firsthand what the revolution was all about.

In 1975 the digital watch took off, forsaking jewelry stores for drugstore counters. Within two years, Seiko, the industry leader, along with two other Japanese, three American, two Swiss, and one Soviet firm, were producing two-thirds of the watches sold. The Swiss industry was devastated. Ironically, the quartz watch had been invented by a Swiss and rejected by his employers as a novelty. In 1970 the first electronic watches appeared at two thousand dollars. By 1975 they had dropped to thirty dollars, following the same learning curve as the calculators. Eight hundred Swiss companies closed; forty thousand Swiss jobs were lost. Eventually the Swiss industry restructured and found niches in the market it once owned. Today, as before, successful Japanese wear top-of-the-line Swiss watches, while Japanese electronic time-pieces more accurate than the finest mechanical watch are built into two-dollar pens.

By 1975 information technology had begun to provide an alternative to many old industrial ways. Noisy, dirty mechanical methods could now be bypassed by clean, efficient, inexpensive, smart technology. Now that the information alternatives were in place, the learning curve could tell us when each institution, each machine, each industry would be transformed or bypassed.

Consumers, tiring of their seventy-year love affair with the automobile, began flirting with consumer electronics. Each year the old technology was costing more and was worth less; the new calculators, watches, games, recorders, computers, and word processors were costing less and were worth more. By 1975 the revolution had found its technological foothold. It was only a matter of time until institutions, governments, and thinkers would take note.

The first to feel the brunt of the change were the old-line industries, such as steel and autos, and they soon made their fears clear to governments. If entire national industries could be destroyed (such as Swiss watchmaking), the industrialists argued, then governments should rethink their role. Industrial Age governments sought to restrain manufacturers in their relentless pursuit of profits. Each year new regulations were added to the old, creating an increasingly dense thicket.

Americans as politically opposed as Gerald Ford and Ralph Nader felt the same way about the burden of regulations. Regulation was inflating consumer costs, encouraging inefficiency in protected key sectors, stifling innovation, and dulling competitive forces.

In early 1975 President Ford announced he would unleash American industry to adapt and compete. He led a massive program of deregulation, broader than any the world had known since the dismemberment of the mercantile system some two hundred years before. Six industries were picked for deregulation: airlines, railroads, trucking, natural gas, banks, and utilities. Ford especially attacked "agencies which act as guardians of businesses they are supposed to regulate." Foremost among these were the agencies regulating, and preventing competition among, the nation's airlines.

Airlines all over the world were in desperate trouble. In the first six months of 1975 American domestic losses reached $43 million; international losses, $63 million. Round trips to Europe were down 37 percent. London's three airports had counted one million fewer passengers in 1974 than in 1973.

This change in air-travel habits was particularly embarrassing to the Canadian government in the autumn of 1975 as it prepared to open the world's largest (and costliest) airport at Mirabel, some forty miles north of Montreal. "We have an airport that will never be choked by urban sprawl," boasted the general manager at the October fourth opening. "Total Montreal traffic, including the suburban airport at Dorval, is forecast to grow from eight million in 1974 to twelve million by 1980, and seventeen million by 1985." That was a major miscalculation, and the effects remained to haunt the government: Besides the two-thirds of a billion dollars wasted, ninety thousand acres of farmland were destroyed, and ten thousand noisy and unhappy people displaced. Far worse, transatlantic passengers would henceforth go out of their way to avoid Montreal.

The Canadian planning fiasco at Mirabel was modest compared to the Concorde disaster. In 1975 the first Anglo-French supersonic jets were testing out their new routes. Americans, who had abandoned their Boeing 2707 project in 1971 after realizing the planes could never make money, were not anxious to have the celebrated and subsidized Concordes serving New York and Washington. The Concordes had cost the two European governments more than $2.5 billion and would never repay their investment, even with seats selling at twice the first-class fare. They used three times the fuel of a standard jet and carried only a fraction of the passenger load. All foreign orders for the Concorde had been canceled, but neither government could abando.: it. The jets were emblems of national pride as well as monuments to the failure of national planning.

Transportation had always been the customer for the great industrial age machines, and those machines had always been the symbols of national power. Now they were dinosaurs. Shipbuilders around the world laid down their tools, leaving unfinished supertankers to rust in their slips. Ocean liners, once proudly considered the Industrial Age equivalent of the cathedrals, ceased plying the North Atlantic in 1975. A few would become love boats, others floating hotels. An age was coming to its end.

The failure of planning was not confined to sensational disasters such as Mirabel and the Concorde. It was not the occasional planner who was wrong, but the whole profession. The failure was exemplified by the most important planners of all, the economists. *The Encyclopedia Britannica Book of the Year* for 1976, covering the previous years, sums it up:

> Both as a profession and as a science, economics lost considerable prestige during the recession of 1974–75. The crisis that seized the Western industrialized countries, including Japan, was of a character not to be found in economic textbooks. . . . The press seemed to delight in printing articles about the plight of the professional economists who had, by and large, failed to predict either the magnitude of the inflation or the depth of the recession, and who seemed unable to agree on what ought to be done.

The reason the economists could not explain what was happening was that the economy was no longer operating under Industrial Age rules. The past was no longer instructive and the present was baffling, and so the world turned to the futurists, who held their second convention in the summer of 1975 in Washington. Futurism was a new field, barely ten years old, and many regarded futurists as kooks. "This is a much more responsible group," announced World Future Society president Edward Cornish. "This time there are no astrologers and teacup readers."

The futurists' predictions at the conventions were picked up and sensationalized by the daily press, and these were followed by more serious reports in the weeklies and monthlies. "Suddenly the future had become big business," declared the *Village Voice*. The *Wall Street Journal* devoted a front-page article to "the Soothsayers." Even the distinguished weekly *Science* was impressed, reporting favorably on the new discipline and the growing role it was playing in government.

If the futurists managed to put on a happy public face in Washington, their private statements betrayed a fear that world changes were not good for the United States. Daniel Bell, a leading intellectual who had documented the postindustrial society in the early seventies, warned his fellow Americans of "the end of empire, the weakening of power, the loss of faith in the nation's future. . . . There are clear signs that America is being displaced as the paramount country, or that there will be a break-up, in the next few decades, of any single power hegemony in the world."

The year was characterized by fear. In addition to the fear of loss of leadership, of economic disaster, and of nuclear annihilation, there were fears that the ozone layer was being depleted and that we would be irradiated by ultraviolet beams from space and die of cancer. And there were fears that scientists experimenting with gene splicing would create a new strain of virus against which there was no defense.

The ozone layer, which protects us from skin cancer–causing solar radiation in the ultraviolet range, could be destroyed by supersonic aircraft and had already been harmed by fluorocarbons from millions of aerosol spray cans. Journalists and ecologists fanned the flames with sensational articles, until governments resolved the tension by banning the sprays.

The gene scare, too, was officially resolved that year. In the summer of 1974, concerned scientists had published their fears about the undisciplined rush to modify genes and requested a moratorium until safety rules could be approved. By the time the moratorium was lifted in June 1975, fear of the irresponsible scientist and the runaway mutant organism was a part of the national psyche, played on by TV program writers and the makers of horror films.

In contrast to the fears of change, perhaps complementing them, were new forms of awareness. The most widespread was the new role of women: Nineteen seventy-five was International Women's Year, and one of the fastest growing magazines was *Ms*. In the summer women of the world convened in Mexico City, and agreed to fight sexism and discrimination. A new stream of energy was being unleashed. Government planners, already struggling with problems raised by the arrival into the work force of the biggest generation in history, were faced with a wave of women insisting on their right and need to work. Unemployment figures headed for the sky.

Less threatening was the heightened attention to the human potential movement, then reaching its zenith. Many bookstores devoted large sections to "personal growth." New therapies were spreading: primal, est, behavior mod, biofeedback, gestalt, transcendental meditation, assertiveness training. The message was that we could take charge of our lives; we didn't have to live up to other people's expectations. All we had to do was find out who we were.

This was an important question in a world where structures were shifting, values changing, and career paths reaching dead ends. It was the opposite of the spirit of conformity that had so characterized the opening years of the revolution. It was a search for internal strengths when corporations were threatened, institutions helpless, governments swollen to counterproductive dimensions. America had been built to greatness by individuals, and now in its hour of weakness, individuals were searching again for their strengths.

Not everyone saw it that way, however. If to some the human potential movement was a rejection of the mechanical view of man and a realization that we must all assume responsibility for our own development and salvation, to humanists of the literary culture it represented a retreat from collective action, an abandonment of the values to which they were dedicated.

In the October, 1975, edition of *Harpers,* Peter Marin gave the first public expression to a view that would grow to a chorus and reach its crescendo with Christopher Lasch's book *The Culture of Narcissism.* Marin was deeply disturbed by "the ways in which selfishness and moral blindness now assert themselves in the larger culture as enlightenment and psychic health." For the humanists, the self-actualization movement was at best "a child's garden of absurdities, an impotent dream of power," and at worst, "a kind of pre-Nazi Germany or prerevolutionary Saint Petersburg."

While Marin was preparing his sermon, a distinguished Japanese computer scientist, Yoneji Masuda, was correcting the English in a statement of his economic philosophy to be published in an important American engineering journal. Masuda agreed with Marin that the individual had become self-centered, but in Masuda's view this quest for self-actualization was the force that drives society toward prosperity. If everyone realized his or her potential, society, too, would become actualized. In this great rush for self-actualization, the purchase and consumption of information, of lessons and training, of therapy, of art and entertainment turn these ethereal products into wealth. The production and distribution of information is the engine of economic growth in the information society.

Information that was given away in the Industrial Age—in the form of public education, broadcast programs, and libraries—becomes a commodity in the Information Age. Though libraries still exist, users increasingly turn to on-line information services for complete and convenient intelligence. Though broadcast networks still provide free programming, viewers increasingly turn to pay-TV and rented videocassettes. If this trend is fundamental, then commercial interactive learning materials on videodisc and in computer programs can be expected to replace free education with its thirty-student convoys crawling through curricula at the pace of the slowest learners.

Masuda also recognized the humanism underlying Marin's criticism of self-fulfillment. Humanism was the spirit of the Renaissance and became the value toward which classical economics was directed. It helped balance the excesses and social deprivations of the industrial economy. It inspired national governments in developing their social systems. That time, however, was gone.

In the information economy, Masuda wrote in 1975, humanism is superseded as guiding principle by globalism—not as an imposed idea but as a popular development. The ecology movement was not merely a grass-roots rejection of industrial pollution but an expression of global concern for the environment. Worldwide intolerance for even "limited" wars helped end the Vietnam War and continues to constrain national governments. Government attempts to limit access to global cultural products, such as film and television, rock music and blue jeans, are thwarted by piracy, by smuggling, and above all by the new technology, which disregards political boundaries. However strongly national governments deprecate globalism, global values are on the rise. Eventually these values will become the new political wisdom.

Assuming that the quest for self-actualization does indeed turn information into money by providing eager consumers, and assuming that the spirit of globalism does indeed define the extent of the market, one further pillar is still needed to support the economic edifice: information technology to generate, process, transmit, and store the new wealth. "The computer is thousands or hundreds of thousands of times superior to man's brain in information productivity," Masuda wrote in 1975. "The increase in material productivity made possible through the invention of steam engines and machinery in the Industrial Revolution was in the order of hundreds of multiplications at most. As compared with this, the increase in the scale of information productivity by means of computers is incomparably large.''

Not only can computers make information workers more productive, he suggested, they can generate information, knowledge, and visions of their own. Not only will computers provide us with free time, they will allow us to use this free time to develop ourselves, our nation, and the world.

While Yoneji Masuda was defining the basis of the new economy, American thinkers were looking more pragmatically at the changing structures. Daniel Bell had defined information as the central axis of the new system in his major work, *The Coming of Post-Industrial Society*. Fritz Machlup, Peter Drucker, and Edwin Parker had begun to measure the trade in information. But it was a student of Parker's at Stanford, Marc Uri Porat, who in 1975 recalculated the national accounts to determine the size, shape, and growth of the information sector.

Porat took the Standard Industrial Classification list of all jobs in the United States and examined each one for its information content. Some workers, such as writers, artists, and market researchers, were creators of information. Others processed information, or built and serviced information technology. Still others—such as those in the media or telecommunications—saw to its distribution. Many others wrote, typed, filed, retrieved, and carried documents. To some workers whose jobs had only partly to do with information (doctors, for instance) Porat assigned a percentage to each part of the job. Once every job had been rated, he counted up all the people in each job category, did his sums, and determined for the first time the role of information in the work place.

"We are now an information economy," he wrote in 1975. "Over half our wages and nearly half our GNP originate with the \ production, processing, and distribution of information goods and services. Over half of all labor income is now earned by workers whose tasks are predominantly informational." Economists throughout the West began restructuring their national accounts along Porat's lines.

In the old days, before 1975, we knew what wealth was: what the bank would accept as collateral on a loan. Information, in classical economics, was a cost of doing business. Masuda and Porat contend that from 1975 onward, information in the form of culture, data, learning, and know-how is becoming the real wealth, and material things are becoming the cost of doing business, the means to acquire what we value most. A television set is not a good in itself, but a means to receive programs, view cassettes, or act as a window into a computer. A car is an instrument to move us to new sources of information, not a good in itself. A kitchen is a place to prepare food so we can continue to create or process information. If creating and processing of information are becoming the dominant economic activities, then the materialistic world of yesterday is turning upside down.

Before we propose the year 1975 for canonization or knighthood, however, we must remember that gathering a mass of detailed, everyday evidence to prove a thesis is the modern historian's trick, and that few if any recognized what was happening at the time. The annual reviews at year's end missed all the important steps. It would be six years before the personal computer was smuggled into the office to challenge the arrogant authority of the data-processing departments. It would take six years before inflation peaked, confidence returned, and interest rates began to fall. If 1975 was the year the world changed, it was 1981 before the next phase of the Information Revolution would find the heart to begin.

Chapter 11
INFORMATION REVOLUTION

PHASE TWO: 1981–2006

During an economic revolution two great forces emerge to shape the ensuing age: an underlying set of values and a triggering technology.

In the Small-Business Revolution of the tenth to twelfth centuries, the new value system involved (1) a secularized Christianity and (2) independence from feudal service through craft skills and collaboration. The principal technologies were (1) mechanization (harnessing horse, wind, and water power), (2) specialization (trade, markets and fairs), and (3) incorporation. Wealth became defined as property, such as a shop or house, a farm or mill, or a horse and plow.

Thirteenth- to sixteenth-century Commercial Revolution values were worldly, historical, and humanistic, increasing the power of the state. The new wealth was created through trade and was represented by cargoes and gold. Technology was partly material (printing, guns, shipbuilding, and navigation), but mostly intangible (letters of credit, insurance, joint-stock companies, bills of lading and of exchange, science, maps) and dealt almost exclusively with distribution.

Industrial values of the nineteenth and twentieth centuries were democratic, materialistic, and mechanistic, advancing the idea of systems in the pursuit of a better living standard and more products for the common man. While industrial technology creates enormous wealth (represented by production facilities, stocks, bonds, and inventories) and affects all sectors of society, industry itself was seen as amoral. The state was responsible for its regulation and for the delivery of values (education, health, sanitation, welfare, justice, public morality, culture, parks, freedom, defense).

The Information Revolution, pushed by powerful new technologies, is currently in the process of restructuring the value system. The concept of wealth is also changing, along with the way of measuring it. These trends are discussed in detail in this chapter.

In general, the first half of the revolution is characterized by confusion and slither, as the old value system is rejected and a wild search ensues for the new. The new values and technologies emerge in their definitive form in the second half of the revolution, which ends as this metamorphosis is completed.

Value and technology shifts are accompanied by structural changes so vast they may remain unrecognized until the revolution is finished and the new age is well under way.

VALUES

At the heart of any economic system is a set of values. Because these values emerge out of the unrest and dissatisfaction of the first phase of the revolution, they seem to take the form of a reaction to the corrupted values of the previous age.

This rejection and re-creation of values produces a characteristic pendulum swing from age to age. The Feudal Age demanded a life of service on earth for spiritual rewards in heaven, while the Small-Business Age was concerned with ownership and production of craft goods, sacks of wool and flour, stone castles and churches, bridges and town walls—that is, material things. The Commercial Age, despite its new venality, worked with an ephemeral technology, letters of instruction and credit, insurance, bills of lading, share certificates, plays and books, honor and glory, philosophy and science. In rejecting this intellectual tyranny, the Industrial Revolution returned to materialism, with an emphasis on machinery, coal and steel, and an economic system that saw value exclusively in the production of tangible things. Intangibles such as nationhood, culture, religion, and basic science were kept pure and separate from the economic system.

Now, once again, we are abandoning the materialism of the previous age for intangible values. The basic tool is information; a growing part of our production takes the form of digital bits. Wealth is moved not in shipments of gold but in signals by satellite. Our most important physical goods are no longer automobiles but information processing machines such as video recorders or computers. Recreation takes the form of television watching, videogame playing, travel and tourism, and personal computing, while portable cassette players make music available even while we travel. Trade in these and other intangibles grows to rival and surpass material goods. Physical work is being turned over to automation, while information workers now number more than half of the labor force. Intellectual skills, knowledge and experience are highly valued. The number of university students approaches 50 percent of school graduates. Training and self-improvement become permanent needs.

The evolution of our value system, however, is not merely the endless swing from material to intangible and back again. To identify it as such ignores the ongoing gains made in individual freedoms, in the variety of opportunity and choice, and in the absolute numbers freed from subsistence life-styles, still dominant in civilizations at the commercial stage in their evolution.

In fact, little of value is lost in this cumulative process of growth. The monarchy is still held in awe, as it was in feudal times, and we display the most intense collective interest in royal weddings, coronations, or funerals. We still respect the values of the Small-Business Age, make tourist pilgrimages to their still-wondrous cathedrals, diligently attend their institutions, from universities to hospitals, even though the lecture system is a dull way to learn and the hospital is a dangerous place to go, especially when we're sick. We still keep our accounts and do business the way the Florentines taught us in the thirteenth century, and much of our time is spent, despite the appearance of more efficient media, with paper and printed books.

Though few of us still labor with our hands at the office or factory, we putter about with tools in our basement workshops, sail boats for recreation, as our ancestors did for pay or profit, and watch professional athletes perform their useless physical work with superb efficiency and skill. The eighteenth and nineteenth centuries are as close as our FM radio: the Commercial Age with Mozart and Bach, the Industrial Revolution with Beethoven and Brahms, the Industrial Age with Gershwin, Stravinsky, and all that jazz, or an old movie on TV. A tour of our home, our city, our office, will show the happy coexistence of systems, customs, and institutions from every age of our civilization. Among our acquaintances and friends are those whole values still reflect the various economic eras of the West. Everything about us and everything we can imagine has its origins in, and derives its character from, one or another economic age from our past.

VALUE SHIFTS: FROM QUANTITY TO QUALITY

When Adam Smith described the new economic system at the outset of the Industrial Age, there were few charts, tables, or figures in his book, and a great deal of moral philosophy and analysis. Quantification came later, much later. As the Industrial Age matured, the "numbers" people gradually took over, and our world was run by the arbitrageurs and econometricians and bean-counters with their inexorable yet often faulty math. Quality was squeezed from the product line to improve the balance sheet. Research was sacrificed to the clamor for instant profits. The company gradually fell behind and faltered because the comptroller had demonstrated, with the impeccable logic of a discounted cash-flow analysis, that modernization was an unjustifiable expense.

Why is it, asked Oswald Spengler a lifetime ago in *The Decline of the West,* that "the economic picture is reduced exclusively to quantities, whereas the important point about goods has been their quality?" At a time when Japanese versions of American products are outselling the originals in world markets on the basis of their quality, Spengler's question takes on new relevance. Meanwhile, many innovative American products are rejected in the Japanese marketplace because they are seen as shoddy, the ultimate nontariff barrier. How did this come to be? Japanese manufacturers work out of modernized–that is, information-controlled—factories, with collaborative management—labor relations. Their American competitors were operating under the confrontational rules of the Industrial Age, where alienated workers turned out "Monday" cars well on into the week, and inspection is passed on to the consumer in the form of warranties. So much higher is Japanese quality that American manufacturers regularly specify Japanese components and are rushing to introduce Japanese techniques into their own production lines. The conclusion is now widely accepted: World-class quality and low prices both come from the information-controlled factory. As Theodore Levitt put it in the *Harvard Business Review,* irresistible value is achieved through a combination of dependable world-standard products and aggressively low prices. Nothing less will survive in the global marketplace.

In the Small-Business Age, a shop was a workshop in which products were made by craftsmen aided by apprentices, under a master's eye. The shop faced the street, and the public's custom was sought for quality handmade products. The workers were literally part of the family, living together in the same premises, priding themselves in the quality of their work. Religious feeling was strong and universal, and the prosperity generated by the new economy was channeled into the great cathedrals. Masons and artisans, supported by peasants who volunteered their labor, worked with God in mind. The urge for quality was such that even the backs of sculptures mounted high on cathedral spires were finished with loving care.

The Commercial Era extended the craft tradition. Products were handmade for the wealthy classes. The manufactories of that era were owned by the state and devoted to quality products for king and court. Such quality can still be admired in the great chateaux of Europe, Sèvres and Meissen porcelain, the classic theater of Molière, the romantic theater of Shakespeare, the music of Bach and Mozart, the art of Michelangelo and Benvenuto Cellini, El Greco and Rembrandt. The great creations of the Commercial Age compare favorably to those of any previous civilization and have yet to be surpassed.

The Industrial Age ended this approach to quality. Machines, interchangeable parts, mass markets, and production lines all seemed so far superior and so much more democratic that the craftsman was swept out of the market, and the shop was torn down to make way for the factory. Of course, the craftsman lived on in the toolmaker, and the moonwalk was staged by a quality-minded team that makes a Metropolitan Opera production or a world's fair look both petty and careless by comparison. The triumphs of industrialism are immense.

On the other hand, its weaknesses are intolerable, as Ralph Nader pointed out so vividly. Quality control, introduced in the 1960s as the Industrial Era was waning, too often meant hiring an engineer to cheapen components to increase profits. Replacing a metal doorhandle with a plastic one, and similar acts of rationalization might better be described as controlled shoddiness. The customer was not fooled, and sought better-crafted products from abroad.

VALUES NATIONAL AND GLOBAL, WESTERN AND EASTERN

Before we can decide on what we should be doing about quality, or about jobs, or about competition, we have to make up our minds about who we are. As we of the West have seen, before the Commercial Age we were not so much Italians as Florentines, not so much French as Christians, and borders moved about with such frequency that they were all but meaningless. For the last half-millennium, however, nationality has been a growing concern, and love of country esteemed a great virtue and promoted by monarchs and statesmen alike.

In my country, Canada, as in many smaller nations, the way we perform German music, French or Russian ballet, British drama, or Italian Opera is considered a cornerstone of national identity. Culture (meaning the art forms of the Commercial Era) is so important to national governments that it has become a state religion. Artists, producers, publishers, and impressarios who wave the flag are patronized by the state, while those who create the global culture are deprecated as crass and unrooted. Political parties that fail to respect the nationalistic artistic community are hounded by this most vocal of minorities. Weakened through long-term subsidy, national cultural organizations are unable to create works strong enough to compete in the global cultural marketplace. Hard-pressed governments, unable to quantify culture's intangible benefits, seek in education or tourist development an economic rationale for supporting Commercial Age national culture. Or they withdraw its subsidies.

Global culture, on the other hand, is a powerful fact of life and a vigorous economic force. Jazz and jeans, rock 'n' roll and movies, McDonald's and Disneyland, athletics and sports, video-games and personal computing, newspaper stories and TV programs, science and data banks are all part of a shared global culture so powerful that if stopped at national borders, it is smuggled in en masse.

Behind the drive for global culture is an inescapable thrust toward global values. The spread of multinational corporations, brands, and services is unstoppable. Global transportation and telecommunications standards are irresistible. Popular global concerns over nuclear war, regional suffering, and the ecology are so powerful they can no longer be left to national governments or quasi-

154 THE INFORMATION REVOLUTION

governmental bodies like the United Nations to resolve; they have become the province of unofficial global institutions, increasingly able to challenge governments successfully.

Greenpeace, the Vancouver-based ecological movement, is a particularly successful example of this new class of unofficial global institutions, which includes the writers' global conscience, P.E.N., the Sierra Club, and Amnesty International. These organizations have assumed the right to criticize any government with regard to restraint of individual freedoms, torture, and ideological imprisonment, as well as ecological depredations. It makes little difference to their effectiveness that governments have not recognized their authority: It derives from their large and respected international membership, militant posture, and skill in using the press.

The modern global conscience is formed of elements chosen from a strange and wonderful grab bag—from *Star Wars* with its Buddhist "May the Force be with you," to Ronald McDonald. It is formed by concerts like Woodstock or Live Aid as well as by Shakespeare and Bach, still vigorously alive and performed somewhere daily. It is formed by news events with their full-color reality, plus "Roots" and "The Forsyte Saga", and by videotapes, records, and bluejeans smuggled past customs officers. It is the Oscars, franchised junk food, the World Cup and Olympics. It is Olga Korbut, Pavarotti, and J.R. It is emotion and experience shared.

These forces promote Western values the way the Church once did but no longer can. When billions from the Third World huddle about their Trinitrons to watch "Dynasty," "M*A*S*H," or "Bonanza" in its ninth rerun, a great leap forward, far more powerful than that forced on the Chinese by Chairman Mao, soon follows. But it is a two-way street. Take the case of the Japanese-American value exchange of the last decades, a globalizing value shift equal in importance to the crusades or the discovery of the New World.

EAST PLUS WEST EQUALS NORTH

(case history)

What is the fastest growing business in North America? Importer Young Choi of Toronto says it is martial arts. New schools are opening every day to teach judo, karate, kung fu, tae kwan do and ninja, and fortunately for Mr. Choi, they are stocking up on books, weapons, equipment, and magazines as fast as he can clear them through customs. Bruce Lee, with his scowl and tiger—scratched torso immortalized on film and videotape, is the new icon, a symbol of Eastern values infusing working-class Western youth.

Across Yonge Street from the Martial Arts Supply store on Toronto's Punk Strip, a video arcade serves a clientele just as avid, if perhaps more motley than our Western samurai. From "Space Invaders" to "Pac Man" to "Donkey Kong" (all designed by Japanese programmers) Western youths struggle against the Eastern fatalism that pervades the content of this multibillion-dollar segment of the information economy.

It is noon, and executives head for sushi and sake at one of Toronto's forty Japanese restaurants, the fastest growing branch of the new cuisine. On the way, they stop to scan the latest books on Japanese business methods from a rapidly growing selection. At lunch they debate whether their difficulty in selling to the Japanese is due to protectionism or their failure to scrute the inscrutable.

Heading home in their Hondas or Mazdas, they pass computer stores, camera and hi-fi stereo shops, all increasingly dominated by glistening, attractive Japanese products, including the ubiquitous videocassette recorders, now outselling Japanese cars in some markets. And everywhere, on the street, in the elevators, in cafeterias, Walkman headphones parenthesize blissful faces.

At home, their children are working on music lessons from the Suzuki or Yamaha school. Amateur photographers among them head for the Nikon seminars to improve their skills with Japanese cameras and film. Wherever they turn for the good life, the Japanese are there.

Since the Beatles dropped in on the Maharishi a generation ago, Western fascination with Asian religion and philosophy has grown with the speed once associated with Christianity. For those too shallow for Zen there are the Hare Krishnas or even the Moonies. For the serious-minded executive, there's TM, with its carefully documented scientific claims on the one hand and giggling promises of levitation on the other.

At every social level and in every age group, the West is Easternizing. On a scale of one to ten, we are probably somewhere around six. The process certainly isn't finished and may not even have crested. The Japanese haven't yet made their move in computers, although they're winning the war in semiconductors. The future holds the promise or threat of a massive invasion of Japanese robots, both household and industrial, and plans are relentlessly pursued for hand-held talking computers.

Japan has been Westernizing since the collapse of the shogun regime in the 1860s. By 1905 they had industrialized so successfully they could trounce the Russians, and in the forties, they nearly crushed the Americans and the British. Their samurai wear Western business suits and play the business game with the kind of all-out commitment Western nations reserve for war.

They drink Scotch whiskey, play golf, tennis, and squash, speak English, work in Western office buildings, listen to Bach and Beethoven played by Japanese classical symphony orchestras, watch more American movies than any other Western nation except the United States, and take Dancersize classes to get rid of weight gained eating American fast foods. They confidently expect their baseball teams to win a World Series, even though they know this may take several years.

Their kids are even more Westernized than their parents. They dance the same dances, play the same music and videogames, wear the same clothes, follow the same fads, and enjoy the same vices with the same ritual fervor. Following the enormous Japanese success with electronic leisure products, Japanese youngsters are exchanging the national work ethic for North American ideas of leisure and free time, and they are trading conformity for Western ideas of self-development and individuality, shattering centuries-old traditions with the abruptness of an atomic bomb. When they can afford it, they check themselves into a cosmetic clinic and have their eyes surgically Westernized.

The Japanese preoccupation with Western ideas and technology goes much beyond industrial intelligence and reading Western books, magazines, and Journals (seven hundred titles translated from English to Japanese for each Japanese title translated into English). It extends beyond mastery to conquest. That last citadel of Western superiority, its technical inventiveness, which it took centuries to achieve, is now under systematic, state-directed assault. "Thou shalt create" is now the official first commandment, with world leadership the prize.

If the Easternizing of the West is six on a scale of ten, then we must place the Westernizing of the East somewhat higher, perhaps seven or eight. In some fields it might even read off the scale, since the

Japans, Koreas, Taiwans, and Hong Kongs sell more Scotch whiskey, 64K RAMs, Swiss watches, European automobiles, and a host of other Western mechanical, electronic, and optical products, either licensed or copied and improved, than the nations of the West combined. Some American computer buffs even claim the best-quality Apple computers are the counterfeits from Japan.

So strong are the influences each civilization has on the other that a third culture is emerging from the courtship. For instance, Japanese business methods, borrowed from America, have been so modified and improved that they are now being borrowed back. What is emerging from this "boomerang" effect is a new way of doing business and producing goods; it erases the sharp line dividing the administration from the shop floor, and reduces both the undercurrent of sabotage characteristic of Western workers and the plague of defects infecting Western products.

The Japanese have also mastered the hypocritical Western approach to protectionism and free trade, and they have placed the search for global markets, so skillfully developed by American industrialists over the past century, on a new level of efficiency. By beating us at our own game, they have not only taunted us to a new level of bluster, but are provoking us to rethink our global marketing strategies. Out of these trade wars is emerging a new mercantile practice— neither Eastern nor Western, but Northern.

The Japanese have already begun to assume responsibility for Third World development. While still an underdeveloped country, Japan raised the art of copying to industrial proportions and offered it as an economic lever to struggling Asian nations in the form of counterfeit, forgery, and piracy. Thus Japan accomplished what the West has failed to do: to contribute substantially to the economic growth and consumerism of the Third World. Now, through massive investment in Third World plant development via its trading companies (among the wealthiest and most international corporations in the world), Japan is accomplishing far more than the traditional and ineffective aid schemes of the West.

As everyone recognizes, it is essential for Japan to develop markets for its exports if its economy is to grow. To its billion or so Western customers, Japan would add three billion from the underdeveloped world. Illiterate, agriculturally ignorant, commercially naive, industrially unsophisticated, lacking the infrastructure essential for growth, the Third World yearns for the Japanese miracle and for the products which Japan makes best. Japanese philosophers, economists, industrialists, and statesmen predict that the new supercivilization of the North will depend for its growth on the development of the South.

In the late fifties and early sixties, Sony transformed the world, and world markets, by incorporating American transistors, then used only in hearing aids, into transistor radios and selling them worldwide. Barefoot illiterates from the Third World scraped up a few dollars to have one of their own. They didn't have to know how to read to enjoy the Beatles or the news. Thanks to transistor radios, they could share their fellow earthlings' first footsteps on the moon. Farewell innocence; now they belonged to the world.

In the early eighties, the videogame, a truly Northern development incorporating features of both Eastern and Western technology and content, emptied the pockets of the world. Once again, a foretaste of the new Northern culture swept the globe and allowed illiterate and sophisticated alike to match wits and come to terms with intelligent machines.

Now the talking pocket computer is taking shape in the workshops of the North. Within the next decade, as computers learn to talk and listen and are programmed with appropriate content, and as the price continues to fall along the so-called "learning curve," they will follow the global trade routes blazed by Sony a generation ago. In their wake they could leave the Third World on the road to growth, no longer hampered by illiteracy and economic unsophistication. This is the mission of the new North, a challenge that could keep both East and West busy and prosperous throughout the information century ahead.

HUMAN CAPITAL

There is a growing awareness that people are the real capital, that their skills and talents, knowledge, courage, imagination, integrity, and entrepreneurial spirit and energy have become the basis of economic growth. Put the right team together, and mere monetary capital flows in abundantly.

In the Industrial Age, people were expendable. Big wheels or merely little cogs in the great machine, any or all could be replaced. An organization was a beautifully crafted system of job descriptions, each meticulously placed in the hierarchy, each with its predetermined career path and graduated emolument.

Creativity, the expression of individuality, was subservient to the rule book or policy manual, and suspect. When the organization needed creative people, it hired them on a temporary basis, from an ad agency, PR shop, design studio, or architect's firm, and once their creative task was done they were banished until needed again. All this became clear when social critic William Arthur White published *The Organization Man* in 1952, at the start of the Information Revolution, and launched the assault on hierarchical organization.

To succeed in an organization, the young executive was advised by White and his followers to lie on personnel tests, to become visible and get on the fast track, to take credit for success and delegate failure, and to manage subordinates in such a way as to keep them from becoming a threat. Of course, these Machiavellian tricks detracted from quality of product or service, while adding to its cost. They were the road to power but not fulfillment. Those prepared to pay the price deserved what they got.

Rewards based on performance encouraged "shortcuts," particularly in a decentralized system. "I don't want to know how you do it; just do it!" came the disembodied command. Executives kept two sets of books of ethics: one for the legal system and the public; another more practical set to get things done. Public relations firms were hired to explain the frequent lapses. A cynical press waited and watched for slips, then moved in to exploit the story. Catching executive crooks became a public entertainment, the equivalent of a public hanging.

If power corrupts, as was claimed by Lord Acton during the British Industrial Revolution, then the more powerful the executive, the more corrupt he was likely to become. This adage was confirmed in the dying days of the Industrial Age as the nation's two top executives, Nixon and Agnew, were both discovered to be crooks.

Corruption, however, was not confined to the powerful. On the factory floor, union rules forbade all effort on behalf of the firm outside narrow jurisdictional zones. Pick up a hammer in the aisle and the maintenance men walk out. All gains were won through bitter dispute, which cumulatively made hierarchical relations contestatorial and reinforced an outdated class system. The typical industrial worker was alienated, hostile, frequently absent, and inclined to negligence if not outright sabotage, a by-product of the confrontational system.

Now automation threatens the rising executive and the office clerk as it has the factory worker. Forced on the corporation by competitive forces from abroad with lower-priced, better-quality, more generously featured products and services, automation technology is replacing the rising executive and alienated worker as fast as it becomes available. Since the first days of the second phase of the revolution, in the early 1980s, downsizing through automation has become strategy one.

With growing structural "unemployment" and a tendency to turn to government to solve problems, there has been much talk of "retraining" and much research into tomorrow's "jobs." This is a holdover from the Industrial Age; it is inappropriate for the age to come, because we will automate all jobs out of existence, get rid of unemployment by getting rid of employment and making ourselves all entrepreneurs, or entrepreneur-trainees. The current idea that jobs—working for somebody else's interest—are noble, valuable, or good could go the way of feudal or domestic service if the small-business ethic prevails.

"Retraining" suggests moving people from one industrial or clerical or executive job to another. But since these kind of jobs are disappearing, what is required is reorientation to some other sector, not retraining. Most of the new growth is in services, and the need for services is inexhaustible. Many of these are franchised, with owner/managers drawn largely from the ranks of downsized managers or outplaced workers. Others become consultants, salesmen, agents, instructors, or servicemen, working with personal computers or other personal tools.

There will of course be some jobs in these franchises or service shops, but increasingly the employees will be entrepreneurial trainees, learning the business and preparing to become owners or partners. The rest will go to those psychologically incapable or unwilling to take responsibility for themselves. There should be no shortage of "jobs" in the expanding services sector for this diminishing minority.

What the new economy requires is growth-makers, people as able to provide for themselves in the outside world as an Indian brave. The skills required are economic: how to start a small business, raise funding, profit from failure, develop and maintain energy, attitude, and enthusiasm, identify niches and trends, manage growth, use consultants, choose associates, bring others along, and above all, develop one's personal human capital.

What growth-makers need is an environment geared for success, which welcomes failure as an essential learning experience and provides support and counseling as well as access to funding. Financially, society must be prepared to share the risk as it does the rewards.

Growth-makers need to know how to network and how to barter

favors, insights, and intelligence, often on a global scale. This means they must have a general culture designed to acquaint them with the viewpoints and customs in various parts of the world and with a variety of professions.

Growth-makers need to know smart technology and the philosophy on which it is based. This means smart work stations and expert systems and telecommunications technology. It means knowing how to take advantage of artificial intelligence to evaluate and process the intangibles that make up the bulk of information work. It means having a suite of personalized programs at hand. In the Information Age, growth-makers will be known by the programs they keep and can bring to bear on their clients' needs.

As the requirements for economic and institutional growth become known and understood, those responsible for keeping the national and global accounts will begin to measure not merely the volume of sales, but the cumulative human capital of a firm, a city, a region, a nation, a common market. Management and governance will be mainly concerned with developing this capital and putting it to work.

Paul Strassman, the information economist at Xerox, is one of the first to attempt to establish measures of human capital. It appreciates, he says in *Information Payoff,* through education and training and software development, as well as through successful innovative experiences. On the other hand, it depreciates through lack of R and D, a demoralized work force, a high rate of transfer, frequent reorganization, and temporary subsidies.

Strassman strongly suggests the responsibility lies with the corporation to bring along its employees and to identify and refrain from counterproductive tactics in pursuit of short-term gains. In conflict with this paternalistic approach, the corporation is also eager to automate and restructure, eliminating large numbers of employees entirely as fairly as possible, while encouraging those still employed to behave with confidence, trust, and the firm's best interests at heart. This contradictory situation will presumably apply until all possible jobs are automated out of existence and stability is at last achieved around a skeleton crew, sometime in the twenty-first century.

In Europe the problem is compounded by the remnants of an archaic class-consciousness—the feeling that those beneath the manager quite rightly belong there and should be encouraged to keep their place—which effectively denies the system the contribution this enormous group could make. This is combined with the feeling that government is responsible for education and culture (that is, indoctrination in nationalist and class values), as well as for retraining the dispossessed for other servile roles. These traditional views are in conflict with the idea of developing entrepreneurial behavior in the working classes.

The pawns in these games, the individuals concerned, are of several minds as to where to place their trust. After all, the question is of the utmost concern: life-style, growth, and retirement are all at stake. Psychological well-being is so wrapped up in work that to invest one's all in a career only to find it has been dead-ended by automation is to risk one's sanity.

Having survived the social and economic chaos of the first half of the revolution, the individual is at risk, now that the economy is restructuring, of losing his or her livelihood, of being trampled and abandoned by the onrushing economy. Church cannot help. Union cannot help. Government cannot help. The bank certainly won't help. The employer can offer only modest consolation for employment lost. The only one responsible and able to do anything to preserve and advance his or her interests is the individual concerned. Hence the trend to self-actualization, so deprecated by social critics and intellectuals.

Self-actualization takes the form of lessons or self-instruction; the acquisition or learning of new technology, skills, culture, appearance; the development of a marketable personality through therapy, assertiveness training, martial arts, or outplacement counseling arranged by the ex-employer. Most of this involves heavy investment of personal recreational time as well as considerable personal funds.

It is this explosive trend to self-actualization that is turning information, in the form of instruction, counseling, software, publications, and information technology (such as videocassette players and home computers), into wealth, into burgeoning industries. While corporate employee-training programs now equal state funding for education, the two of these together are more than matched by individual expenditures on self-development.

How does investment in human capital (unmeasured by classical economists) compare with the investment in capital goods? How do we account for deskilling, the depreciation of obsolescing skills? How do we measure or evaluate the tenacity of counterproductive industrial ideas and values? Or quantify the growth of entrepreneurial spirit and skills? How do we construct policies to increase this investment in human capital so that society will obtain the maximum benefit? Do we develop a national skills inventory? Do we include this in our statistical base, along with (or instead of) the increasingly meaningless GNP?

ECONOMICS

As we move into this closing phase of the Information Revolution, a change is taking place in the discipline of economics. Information products and services are now dominant, while industrial products and commodities, though growing in absolute terms, play a declining part in the rapidly expanding global market. We are passing from a material to a symbolic economy. Classical economics, with its emphasis on the production and distribution of tangible things, grows increasingly inadequate when it comes to assessing:

- human capital, with its education, culture, skills, attitudes, age, sophistication, and readiness to risk;
- intangible products like lessons and software, credit and know-how, tourism and entertainment;
- ephemeral arrangements like networks;
- ecological qualities such as clean air, fresh water, a safe and caring neighborhood, and a culturally rich environment;
- evanescent processes such as creativity, judgment, and learning;
- ethereal characteristics of works of art or entertainment, buildings or places, such as beauty, harmony, depth, variety, excitement, or serenity; or
- the quality of information as it is created, processed, distributed, and stored.

Business or government decisions based on classical economic factors and excluding all the qualities of information products and services, on the grounds that they are difficult to measure, are proving increasingly inadequate; but a massive change in economic science is under way. The development of computer judgment ("expert systems") in the eighties and early nineties is gradually placing handles on these intangibles. As social and economic values gradually merge, management becomes more of a science, good judgment less rare, investment in information products less risky, collaboration of man and computer more frequent, and productivity gains in the office increasingly powerful.

Information quality is a case in point. Business lives on information: that generated by contact with its clientele, that which describes its internal workings, its competitor's plans, changes in the regulatory environment, developments in the market, new technologies and techniques and so forth. The function of the office is to acquire, digest, process, store, evaluate, transmit, and eventually act on this information. Most of us spend most of our lives at these various tasks.

Unfortunately there is no objective measure of information quality to aid us in these tasks. Consequently, there is no measure of productivity in the office. Bureaucracies thrive in this trackless wasteland. The larger the bureaucracy, the greater the likelihood that critical information flows will be delayed, degraded, or stopped, thus giving rise to bad or untimely decisions—as an increasingly bureaucratic NASA was to discover when the shuttle Challenger blew up in its face.

By the mid-nineties, the quality of information will become the number-one concern of economists and senior management. The profusion of expert systems—in which the dissected judgment of leading specialists is embedded in software or silicon so that it may be applied by lesser talents to routine situations—is speeding up both the decision-making process and the economist's quest for quality quantifiables. The poet Shelley's search for the equivalence of truth and beauty during the latter phase of the Industrial Revolution finds its parallel in the Information Revolution's almost metaphysical pursuit of quality.

SMART TECHNOLOGY

The automation of work through the application of smart technology is the economic force driving the revolution. What began as "hard" automation in the first half of the revolution has now become CAD/CAM (computer-aided design and manufacturing), computer-integrated manufacturing (CIM), robotics, and flexible manufacturing systems (FMS) as we move into phase two.

Similarly, what was called computerization in phase one is expanding in the revolution's second half to include office automation, office of the future, or office integration. Along with the introduction of the personal computer in the home, electronic funds transfer and automatic teller machines at the banks, electronic diagnosis in health care, data bank searches at the laboratory, and educational software in the schools, much of the smart technology pervading our lives is a variety of automation. It allows us to do more for less, by making professional services available without paying a professional.

This move to productivity gains through automation is not about to end. It will accelerate throughout the rest of the revolutionary period and continue through the ensuing Information Age as its dominant characteristic. It will be our equivalent of mechanization in the Industrial Age, our driving technology.

The shape of automation in the coming decades will continue to evolve with startling rapidity, since each advance liberates the economy from mechanical labor, routine paperwork, and costly and too-often-hurried professional services. Not only is cost reduced and output increased, but, by decreasing the effect of human error, incompetence, ignorance, antagonism, drunkenness, or absenteeism, automation raises quality to a higher and more consistent level. This leaves people with one major concern (with a million minor ramifications): growth. Economic growth, personal growth, family growth, social, cultural, and artistic growth, people growth.

What expressions of automation are yet to come? Personal robots around the home and in service institutions such as nursing homes and hospitals. Factory robots integrated into a flexible manufacturing system and a network including designer, office, dealer, client, supplier, banker, and government agency. Expert systems replacing middle managers and other professionals through the exercise of judgment.

The design, development, manufacture, promotion, sale, installation, customizing, and maintenance of this smart technology will be our most important growth sector, providing many of tomorrow's new jobs. Training or reorienting people to its use could be a growth industry all by itself. Unless automated, of course: "This machine will self-instruct in five minutes."

AUTOMATION

The doors opened, automatically, on the Information Revolution in Dallas, in 1950, as the new Atlantic Refinery Building demonstrated its automatic Otis elevators. "No operator is needed in the new *Autotronics* elevators with their self-leveling and automatic dispatching," said a company press release. "In return for the operator's personal touch, Otis offers the 'electronic politeness' of its new safety-designed elevator door system." Within a generation, the elevator operator's job, known more for its up and downs than its prospects, was a thing of the past.

A few months later, Ford opened two automated plants near Cleveland to turn rough castings into six-cylinder engine blocks. Some five hundred operations were performed by automatic machines as the castings hustled along the quarter-mile line "untouched by human hands."

By 1955, the automation race had attracted the attention of the U.S. Congress. Representative Wright Patman chaired a well-publicized committee to look into the "problem." After listening to a number of experts, including labor leader Walter Reuther and automation guru John Diebold (writer of the first book on the topic in 1952), the legislators concluded that the new processes would only improve America's position of industrial leadership. New industries would arise; new products would be made possible by the new technology; new service functions would be required.

From 1955 onward, automation moved ahead on five fronts. Process control of oil, chemical, and electricity plants was becoming increasingly sophisticated. There was hard "Detroit" automation, typified by Ford's two engine-block plants near Cleveland. Numerical-control machines could be quickly reprogrammed for the kind of jobs small plants were called on to do. Printed circuit boards brought automation to the electronics industry. And finally there were the computers: A dozen of them in industry in 1955, over ten thousand by 1960, and the pace was quickening.

That year, a book by the American social activist Donald Michael blew the whistle on automation. *Cybernation, the Silent Conquest* carefully weighed the human costs of the productivity race. It warned that not only would unemployment continue to rise in industry, but management too would feel its bite; blacks would be stopped in their climb; and a generation of youth, the biggest in history, would be left to rot on the vine.

The avalanche of protest triggered by Michael's book soon reached hysterical proportions. Computing's elder statesman Norbert Weiner, in *The Human Use of Human Beings,* had warned of "an unemployment situation in comparison with which the depression of the thirties will seem a pleasant joke." The head of U.S. Industries, the country's leading robot manufacturer, told a Senate subcommittee in 1963 "that automation is a major factor in eliminating jobs in the United States at the rate of more than 40,000 a week. . . . It is entirely possible," he warned, "that we will have a permanent segment of our society unemployed, which will have to be provided for."

Horror stories poured forth in the press: 40,000 operators displaced by automatic elevators in New York; 28,000 meat packers unemployed through automation; 17,000 steelworkers dropped; autoworkers down 130,000 from 1955 to 1960; total manufacturing employment reduced by 1.5 million between 1955 and 1961. About that time, Wassily Leontieff predicted, "Human workers will go the way of the horse."

As the second phase of the Information Revolution opened around 1980, the standard scenario went something like this. The West would be forced out of heavy industry by developing countries with cheap labor and would concentrate on high-technology and service sectors of the economy. Even Japan, it was thought, would eventually get out of cars as wages and standard of living rose.

This was supposed to be in the West's best interests. Heavy industry was ruining the environment and making our world ugly. In yesterday's contrary paradigm, corporate executives were seen as conspiratorial villains restrained only by the most determined efforts of government. Labor was corrupt and counterproductive, seeking to featherbed and prevent change. Workers hated their jobs and their company and were inclined to sabotage. "Monday" cars were coming off the line all through the week. Five years before, smokestack industry was even losing money. It seemed the time had come to dump this white elephant onto the Third World.

Quite suddenly the picture changed. Chrysler's Lee Iacocca became an instant hero (even in Japan) for turning around an underdog car company that many had written off. His book has achieved a new record among best sellers, indicative of a profound change in the public mood: a sympathy to capitalistic enterprise and a willingness to concede that big may be beautiful too. There's even a waiting list for some of his cars.

Now, with surprising speed and some dazzling acquisitions,

GM's Roger Smith is turning around the number one industrial company, changing it into a high-tech firm, rebuilding morale and confidence. He's even creating public excitement again for his upcoming Saturn and Jupiter cars.

THE INFORMATIONIZATION OF GM

(case history)

The barriers seemed insuperable: wages in North American auto plants were running around $20.00 an hour, compared to $10.00 in Japan, and $2.00 in Korea's Hyundai Pony plants, contributing to a $2,000 price differential between comparable Japanese and North American cars. GM's answer: Make better, more interesting cars. Measure and reward quality. And diversify the company, building on strengths.

In 1983 Smith embarked on a multibillion-dollar program with four main thrusts: Introduce Japanese techniques in production and in labor relations; standardize automation technology; diversify through acquisition; and restructure the corporation from bottom to top. The whirlwind pace with which Smith is tackling these changes has raised the corporation's excitement level to wartime pitch.

First, GM had to admit that Japanese methods of making cars were superior. Joint ventures with Suzuki and Isuzu paved the way for the Toyota venture: The jointly owned NUMMI (New United Motor Manufacturing, Inc.) opened in November, 1984 in a plant in Fremont, California, which GM had closed two years earlier because of insurmountable labor problems. In order to learn Japanese production methods, GM and the auto union began implanting Toyota's techniques in smokestack America.

Fremont's workers were as tough and as antimanagement as any in the world, and Toyota reluctantly agreed that they would be given first crack at the twenty-five hundred jobs. About 150 were sent in stages to Toyota City to work alongside Japanese workers and spread the word about how the system works and feels. Management and UAW officials negotiated deals to abandon traditional make–work rules and to allow teamwork which meant each worker could do everyone's job: American productivity nearly doubled in actual assembly.

White-collar cadres were also reduced from seven to five levels of management, with fewer managers in each. Managers eat in the same cafeteria and share the same parking privileges as the workers. Health maintenance organizations reduce fringe benefit costs, and pensions have been made portable, since the American government has limited the life of the venture to twelve years.

The plant was stripped out, machinery from Japan (including 170 robots) installed, and Just-In-Time inventory control methods initiated, where suppliers delivered parts and materials as and when required. About half the components, including the engines, are imported from Japan. Production speed is 200,000 Novas per year.

GM plant managers and engineers from all over North America are making the pilgrimage to Fremont (next door to Silicon Valley) to see for themselves how the Japanese methods work under North American conditions. They were surprised by the eagerness the tough union workers bring to the new approach. If these Japanese methods spread through North American industry as expected, then the reopening of the GM Fremont plant at the end of 1984 was an historic date in the economic future of the West.

Another significant GM innovation is the imposition of MAP (for Machine Automation Protocol) on the automation industry. GM's size gives it the clout to impose an interconnection standard on the industry. Since GM expects to buy some ten thousand robots by 1990 and to spend some $40 billion to automate its two hundred plants, vendors wishing to sell computers, robots, or automation equipment to GM will have to make them conform to MAP.

Beginning in 1983, GM has been running workshops on MAP and has persuaded some of the heavies to come on board. IBM, Honeywell, DEC, and Hewlett-Packard paved the way for at least a hundred suppliers who have accepted the standard, and it's beginning to look like any automation supplier who goes his own way won't be going anywhere at all.

The third arrow in Roger Smith's quiver is code-named Star Trek: a policy of restructuring through acquisition that will transform the company into a diversified high-tech giant with perhaps a third of its income from nonautomotive sources by the 1990s. GM began in 1908 as a trust of industry leaders, and grew over the decades by acquiring its competition. (It even tried to get Ford to come on board.) It was once a leading name in refrigerators (Frigidaire) and defense, and was twice indicted by the American government for strong-arming its way to the top in diesel locomotives and buses. ("If your railroad won't buy our locomotives, then we won't let you ship our cars.") And so industry watchers have one eyebrow raised at Smith's new acquisitions.

Some of these are merely look-see positions in a host of high-tech companies (five of them are machine-vision firms that help robots see what they are doing), but the acquisitions also include top-drawer consulting groups such as Ed Feigenbaum's artificial intelligence company, Teknowledge, and Philip Crosby Associates, leaders in quality control. The usual tactic is to take a 10 percent interest for a few million dollars.

The big money has gone into Ross Perot's high-flying computer service bureau, EDS, which Smith bought outright for $2.5 billion in the summer of 1984. A year later, Hughes Aircraft was acquired for $5 billion. In both of these instances, a new class of shares was issued to preserve a measure of autonomy and independence for the resulting entities, while integrating some of their activities with those of the giant parent.

The $500-million-per-year Electronic Data Systems acquisition, when combined with GM's $6-billion internal data processing budget, could put EDS in close competition with GE's computer service bureau, the current industry leader. Smith expects EDS will help General Motors Acceptance Corporation manage its $53 billion in assets, as well as its policies issued through the corporation's 10,500 dealers. It will also help headquarters reduce health care costs, an important component of its wage–benefits package.

It is expected that GM will eventually acquire a bank, so that it can offer a Sears-type basket of financial services. Meanwhile, when EDS and GM's own financial services are integrated into a world voice-data-video network, GM should be able to sell excess capacity, while moving ahead with its needs for office management, communications, and data processing.

GM has been playing in the defense game for years, but perhaps because of its adversarial role with government, this side of its business has been stuck at the billion-dollar level. With its acquisition of Hughes Aircraft (ninth among defense contractors) it is in a position to work alongside government in such programs as Star Wars (in fact it was Theodore Maiman, working at Hughes Labs, who first perfected the laser in 1960). Not only will GM acquire a top position in defense and benefit from the U.S. government's research initiatives, it should have the best brains in electronics to help give its new cars, such as the Saturn, a spectacular edge in tomorrow's marketplace.

Finally, Smith has begun to reshape GM's organization chart. Where there were five auto production companies, there are two: the heavy-duty Buick-Oldsmobile-Cadillac group, and the more sporty Chevrolet-Pontiac-Canada group. Divisions (there are nine) are more competitive: competing with outsiders to sell within the corporation; competing too for outside business.

No one believes the changes are over. Smith has promised more major acquisitions, more "lulu" projects like Saturn, more moves into high-tech and factory automation, a stronger presence in financial services, and perhaps a move into health care. Roger Smith is bringing new life to smokestack America, and a new dimension to the information economy.

FACTORY OF THE FUTURE

Let us push these changes ahead to the year 2000. Factories tend to be smaller and have fewer windows, fewer offices, and fewer parking spaces filled with more expensive cars. In harsher climates, some are built underground to reduce energy costs. Those we can see are more sculptural than their Industrial Age predecessors, and more welcoming, with parkland and day-care playgrounds.

Inside there are cells of robots and machines linked by conveyers and tended by unmanned carts. Floors are spotless. The occasional white-coated orderly moves among the brightly painted machines with test equipment. Another is upgrading a robot's vision system. A small group of students and visitors follows a doctor of engineering making his morning rounds.

Looking down over the factory from a glassed-in second-floor gallery is a row of engineers working at design terminals. Behind them blinks a bank of small computers, printers, and communications consoles. For this is an integrated factory, and designers are directly linked with their clients, their suppliers, their office and sales department, and each of the machines on the floor.

When designing a component, the engineer works in consultation with his client. The part to be made and assembled is described to the computer in terms of coordinates, materials, and surfaces. Then the computer casts a picture of the piece upon the screen, either in the form of a "blueprint" with all its fine lines and dimensions, or in three-dimensional form with colors and textures richly shown and finely detailed in appealing superrealism.

At any stage in the work, the computer can create a bill of materials and determine their cost and availability. It can indicate the machines to be used and show the bottom line both in cost and in time. Change a parameter in the design and the cost comes down; fine-tune another and production time is reduced.

When designer and client agree to proceed with a test, sample materials are procured, the test run scheduled, and the work cells programmed with particular instructions for each step of the manufacturing process, all automatically. In most cases, the test run only briefly interrupts the flow of work through the shop, and if materials are on hand and the design is not flawed, finished samples are soon sped to the client's test-bench.

One of the interesting things about the new "smart" components of the flexible manufacturing system of the 1990s is that they are constantly being improved by new sensors, new manipulators, new software. Its value also increases as other automatic equipment is installed around it. In other words, while older machine tools depreciate and have to be replaced, these machines *appreciate* as the system becomes more integrated. They acquire greater capabilities, are used in more powerful and more productive ways.

Turnkey general factories, such as the one described above, are beginning to appear in all population centers in the Third as well as First and Second worlds as the 1990s unfold. By reducing the cost advantage of labor and minimizing the impact of rising protectionist barriers and transportation costs, these highly flexible minifactories produce for the local or regional market at much the same cost in Pennsylvania as Tegucigalpa.

Arrangements between plants are becoming standardized. A plant may be licensed in Seoul or Bombay to turn out samples and short runs for a product designed in Toronto for a new market niche; the instructions for making it are sent by satellite. A teleconference may be all that is required to explain the product's qualities and market approach. Sales could even be made by teleconference to South America, and the product, once completed, made under license and instructions by a local plant.

As flexible manufacturing develops in the nineties, trade, in the sense of import and export, and of costly long-distance transport of manufactured goods, is bound to decline.

OFFICE AUTOMATION

In the fall of 1981, the Japanese announced their project to create an intelligent, fifth-generation (5G) computer that could talk with humans in everyday language, answer their questions, and solve problems with the aid of expert rules. Since then, the great nations of the world have buzzed with a single concern: not to get left behind in the rush.

Galvanized by the fear of massive transfer payments to the Japanese for office automation equipment, the European Economic Community, and separately the British, French, and Germans all set up industrial plans to master the technology of intelligence, move it into their offices, and sell it all over the world. The idea of bottling and selling intelligence, at first stunning, soon became challenging and promising. For aging governments it was the fountain of youth. Austerity be damned. Open the coffers. Full speed ahead.

American policy advisers were somewhat taken aback, somewhat fearful, and not a little amused by the Japanese announcement. The idea of a government setting the imitation of intelligence as a national goal is similar to promising a cure for cancer. Boldly announcing a prototype for a mere hundred months hence was vaguely ridiculous, even though the American government (by way of the Pentagon) had been pouring billions into research of similar chimera. In the American mythology of the eighties, the U.S. private sector (mother of invention and father of the personal computer), with research budgets larger than the rest of the world combined, would develop the 5G computer in its own good time and see to its deployment around the non-Communist world.

Nevertheless, the challenge of a research consortium of leading Japanese companies, operating out of a collectively financed lab, in pursuit of a technology as significant to world leadership as the atom bomb, could not be ignored. Within months, a similar American consortium was formed under an ex-leader of the intelligence community, deeply funded and guaranteed immunity from antitrust prosecution.

Each in their own way, the Japanese, Americans, and Europeans embarked on the pursuit of artificial intelligence, the Holy Grail of the Information Age. When the chips were wired, the methods and structures each used were very much the same, for it is difficult to keep secrets in an age which believes that freedom from global destruction and foreign exploitation hangs on the slim thread of espionage.

What happens if we push current 5G research to its logical conclusion in the near-trillion-dollar office-automation marketplace? In the nineties, fallout from the 5G projects will grow from a trickle to a flood. As the various projects mature, smarter technology will move into the office to shorten the channels of information as well as the chains of command. Investors will find a new outlet, manufacturers a new market, as office managers integrate their equipment, downsize their operations, outplace their clerks and middle managers, flatten their hierarchies, and automate their bureaucracies. The race to debloat will suddenly become the key to competitive survival in the global marketplace. The collapse of white collar work will follow the pattern set by blue-collar decimation, hard on the heels of farm automation. If 2 percent of the population could feed all the rest, why should it take another 60 percent just to send them the bill?

TRIGGERING TECHNOLOGY NO. 1: ELECTRONIC MEMORY

Three technologies will help unleash the office restructuring process in the nineties. Placing files in *electronic memory* cuts the cord between the worker and the office, as files and other corporate data can then be accessed from anywhere in the world. Since most written material is in electronic form at some point in the creative process, transfer to electronic files will be automatic. Software can automate both indexing and retrieval. In theory, nothing need ever be lost or misfiled again; in practice, the cost associated with filing (clerks, cabinets, office space, commuting to a central office) is cut by orders of magnitude. Material in electronic files becomes part of the corporate data base, to be used in answer to larger questions; it becomes a whole new and precious resource.

Electronic publishing is just beginning the rush to optical disc and CD-ROM. Within the next ten years, back issues of commercial and technical periodicals will be distributed on compact disc and can be searched and replayed with simple equipment in the office, lab, or home. Costs associated with the library, with storage, centralization, employees, will all but disappear. Material will be kept by its most frequent user, and others may access it, often automatically, by making an electronic request along the corporate network.

TRIGGERING TECHNOLOGY NO. 2:
VOICE PROCESSING

Voice processing is one of the three main technologies that will restructure office work in the nineties. By making it possible to deal directly with the electronic corporation without need for a keyboard and terminal, business can be concluded anywhere, anytime. Files can be accessed en route to a meeting, points of fact clarified, minutes kept automatically, and agreements (attested by voiceprints on inerasable discs) concluded without further paperwork.

Voice processing requires that the system understand what is spoken into it, and this means real-time translation can be part of the dynamics of a conversation between two people who don't know each other's language, and that records can be kept in both languages. In the nineties, pocket translators will make foreign travel a pleasure, foreign culture easier to understand, and foreign business less difficult to conclude.

Voice processing is also a prime feature of portable 5G computers the Japanese plan to sell in the Third World during the late 1990s. Following paths pioneered by Sony's founder Akio Morita with the transistor radio in the fifties and the Walkman in the eighties, the portable 5G computer, when programmed in a native language with information and instruction about health and economic growth, works like an economic bootstrap in these least-developed parts of the world. The social and economic power of this technology will do much to lift Japan to the status of a world leader among those who tire of the strings attached to superpower aid. It will also help Japan maintain both its access to resources and its high rate of growth.

TRIGGERING TECHNOLOGY NO. 3:
EXPERT SYSTEMS

Smart programs are the third technological trigger behind structural change in the office in the nineties. It is not enough that they speak, these fine machines must have something to say. The transformation of data into information, information into knowledge, knowledge into expertise, judgment, and wisdom are human skills of a very high order. Their painstaking translation into computer rules and strategies is perhaps the central marvel of the Information Revolution—and the most disturbing: the imitation of life at a level attained by only the best professionals at the top of their performance.

It is significant that these technologies are being pursued not only by the corporate world with its academic connections, but also by the small entrepreneur working independently or in collaboration with the personal-computer makers. Most of the major innovations in computing, going back to the original ENIAC in 1948, have come not from the corporate establishment, but from the solitary entrepreneur (the equivalent of the Victorian artist struggling in a garret), or in California mythology, "two guys in a garage."

It also should be noted by the serious-minded that the often frivolous consumer electronic market, so often ignored by corporate and government planners, has been behind much of the push to perfect smart technology.

NETWORKS

Networks are the Roman roads of our time, stretching our empires across cities, continents, oceans. Our banks have networks of correspondents from Geneva to Singapore. Our brokers electronically shop world markets for the best price on a stock before signaling our order. Like celestial spiders, each new satellite spins more webs, catching more of us every day.

Yesterday's highways, roads, canals, or railroads are hard-wired networks. You went where they took you, at convoy speed. Then you got off and finished your trip. Today's software-controlled networks are flexible, fast, and dynamic, carrying data and voice, facsimile and video, often mixed together in digital packets, wherever you want them to go.

When the phone companies had it all their own way, the cost of networking was so high only large corporations could afford it. It was often cheaper to put a reel of tape on a plane than to send it over the phone. Now that alternatives are multiplying, phone companies are sharpening their pencils, and costs are starting to fall. Forecasters see videoconferencing calls anywhere down to a dollar a minute in the nineties. Planes can't compete with that.

Satellite transmission costs are falling almost as fast as those of computer memory. In the nineties, great space platforms will carry signals from here to anywhere for a tiny fraction of yesterday's costs. Charges for long-distance calls disappear since it costs no more to speak to Melbourne, London, or Tokyo than to the next town. At first, governments are afraid of the consequences; but as private satellites begin linking continents with competitive services, governments can't keep their national enterprises at a disadvantage and will agree to let rates fall.

Many new office buildings are wired to bypass the local phone companies, offering even the most modest tenant a choice of shared-services, high-speed lines if and when required, least-cost routing, and a host of other features only available in the past to the largest corporate users. Some of these new buildings are connected by microwave or optical fiber to teleports, huge private antenna farms offering direct access to domestic and transcontinental satellites at wholesale prices.

In the 1990s, every office desk is expected to have a voice-data work station linked to the corporate computer grid as well as to an outside world full of integrated services. The last important barriers will have fallen. Once, we dreamed that all computers and terminals would be standardized, communicating at the same speed and with the same internal codes. This meant that since the network was lacking intelligence, the machines would have to be smart. Now that telephone companies have to compete, the network is smartening up. Superswitches connect computers and terminals with different speeds and protocols, mixing and matching voice and data, still images and video signals. The network is becoming intelligent.

Communications and computer networks are by no means the end of the story. The electrical power grid, a network par excellence, ties together private and public companies for the exchange of power in either direction, depending on demand. Thus the grid becomes the marketplace automatically trading reserves, automatically settling accounts.

During the eighties, the idea of networks began working its way through society. Computer hackers "networked" together, exchanging ideas and tricks via their burgeoning bulletin boards, much like the good buddies of CB radio. Clubs of all sorts blossomed as the cost of communications networks fell, and proximity was no longer a criteria for companionship or common purpose. That some of this activity was "underground" only added to its appeal.

This networking of common minds at a distance could first be seen in the invisible colleges of scientists. Many of them were linked by that first great computer network, the ARPAnet of the Advanced Research Projects Agency of the U.S. Department of Defense, which back in the seventies first tied North American scientific interest groups together and linked them to their overseas counterparts.

The network model of corporate structure is not a new idea to the Japanese. Their general trading companies, or sogoshosha, date from the Japanese Industrial Revolution and consisted of a world network of commodity buyers and traders linked by telegraph. In addition to finding the best prices on commodities and the best markets for silk, they acted as a secret service of market intelligence for the government and their clients and were critical in technology transfer. One of the first acts of the Allied Occupation Forces in the 1940s was to disband these giant octupuses.

By 1947, permission was given by the Allies to reestablish the sogoshosha. Since Japan was almost totally without resources and had to export to pay for them, the sogoshosha quickly became the principal arm of government economic policy. Soon the general trading companies were operating computer-controlled telex networks around their global empires, and the two largest, Mitsubishi Corporation and Mutsui and Company, moved up into the top ten of world companies. The combined sales of the sogoshosha amount to over a third of Japan's GNP.

Since the second phase of the global Information Revolution, the Japanese economy has been undergoing a radical restructuring away from materials-intensive industries like shipbuilding, and toward high-tech components like VTRs, computer chips, and memories. And the sogoshosha are undergoing similar changes. The emphasis shifts from commodity trade to the service sector, financing, consulting, project management, and engineering consulting. They are becoming increasingly active in joint ventures throughout the north. Sogoshosha trade is moving rapidly from Japanese import-export to third-party or offshore trade, which has tripled in recent years.

During this second phase of the revolution, the sogoshosha are following a social strategy, seeking their interests by serving the social goals of their world host countries. In developed countries, they are transforming themselves into autonomous local companies, setting up plants, creating jobs and exports. They are also offering small- and medium-sized companies access to global markets through their network. In the Third World they are increasingly active in technology transfer, arranging the financing, engineering, and capital equipment for factories and agricultural projects and agreeing to accept the project's output as repayment.

As the sogoshosha become world service traders, the network style of global organization is appearing among Information Age industrial concerns in the United States. The new network industrialist is little more than a switchboard, commissioning design and engineering from one source, prototypes and production from others, marketing and sales from another group, and the factoring of receivables from yet another.

Network production, in the sense of a small office commissioning its various services from independent shops, traces its origins to the putting-out system of the Italian merchant bankers. Since the end of the studio system of film production, it has been the style of independent film and television producers all over the world. Most book publishers have little to do with the physical product they produce. They operate as networks and are engaged in symbolic trade. What is novel is its appearance in industrial production. What is interesting is that most of these network industrials are "manufacturing" products with a high symbolic content, such as toys, computers, clothing, and sporting goods.

AUTOMATING THE HOME

"A person's home is his or her castle" reads a clumsy modernized version of an age-old principle. Yet more than the wording has changed. The major characteristic of the closing phase of the Information Revolution may well be the massive shift of employment from the big-business to the small-business sector, triggered by low-cost personal computing and network technology. Employees whose jobs are collapsing are contracting to perform the reduced work load from their homes, then marketing their remaining time. They are no longer employees, but independent business persons or consultants, and their home is their office.

Throughout most of Western history, families worked out of their homes. In successive ages, peasants and farmers, guildsmen and shopkeepers, bankers and landlords lived and worked in the same place. Since the Commercial Revolution, merchants put out wool or flax to be spun and woven into cloth by families living and working together in their cottages, the father at the loom, wife and children making thread and loading the shuttle. Just as much of today's new technology was developed and first manufactured at home in a basement or garage, writers and artists for centuries labored at notepad, canvas, typewriter, or word-processor in a quiet corner of their own home.

It is only during the Industrial Age that we have trudged in such numbers to office and factory to sell our time by the hour or the year, and turned to unions to speak for us and to governments to set or change the rules. It was an interesting experiment, turning people into the wheels or cogs of the industrial machine, but it didn't outlast the Industrial Age. Now that smart technology is beginning to liberate industry and business from their armies of clerks and workers, with their unions and government rules, the rush is on. *And the more employees are replaced, the stronger grows the firm.*

As Westerners discovered in the tenth and eleventh centuries, going into small business may be severe in its demands, but the rewards are rich and deeply satisfying. Working from one's home thinned one's social contacts while strengthening the family. If the employee is expendable, the small businessperson is an economic force, so the social and political as well as the economic structure of society is strengthened as the great migration unfolds.

The entrepreneur's electronic castle will not be the same thing as a residential home. There is a strong need to enrich the environment in which one spends so much time. In the eighties the big import from Japan is not only the compact automobile but also the videocassette recorder. Telephones blossom in every room. Personal computers proliferate. Cable and dish antennas offer a widening spectrum of signals and information. Optical discs are providing impeccable music and will soon offer immense data bases, with encyclopedias and directories, complete back issues of technical magazines, courses and seminars in specialized subjects, or a client's corporate files. Satellites and teleconferencing facilities provide increasing access to clients and prospects, teachers and data anywhere in the shrinking world. Subcontracting work to low-wage colleagues in India or Jamaica will be as easy as dialing a call.

The money invested in turning one's home or apartment into an electronic castle suitable for work and learning as well as living is one of the engines driving the revolution. The demand will prove endless. Smart appliances. Intelligent robots with entertaining (or comforting) personalities. Talking liquor cabinets with an unlimited repertoire of jokes. Wide-screen wall-sized television with stereo sound to enjoy the music videos, films, interactive graphics, sports and games from all over the world, with a built-in real-time translator to make it available in English (or Spanish, or Japanese).

ROBOTS IN THE HOME

It was the glory of great writers to create memorable characters with extraordinary characteristics. Tevye in Fiddler on the Roof. Hamlet. Ulysses. Faust. Don Giovanni. Antigone. Falstaff. Tartuffe. Rhett Butler. ET. Jane Eyre. Fanny Hill. Many, perhaps most, were created during, and expressed the central conflicts of, an economic revolution. The writers of the Information Revolution have a new medium in which to express their understandings of the deeper workings of the human mind. It is not enough that a computer program contain the wisdom and political expertise of a Martin Luther King; to be truly successful and respected, it must speak with his voice. And so the creation of human personality within the computer, of compassion, feeling, loving, nurturing, humor, conviction, will become the ultimate distinction of the programmer's art.

There is work here for lifetimes, for generations of programmers, and for an enormous industry. Here are the patient and knowing teachers, the caring robots, the playful companions, the faithful servants, the thoughtful advisers, the careful accountants, the skillful diagnosticians, the wise judges, the gifted negotiators, and the kindly and constructive critics to help us on with our work and our lives. Pygmalion's dream, to create a beautiful work and then have it come to life, is about to be realized.

THE INFRASTRUCTURE INDUSTRY

The great industry of the Small-Business Era was building the tens of thousands of towns of the West, with their walls and bridges, churches and homes, shops and market squares. Then there were the hundreds of thousands of new farms drained from the marshes, cut out of the forests, built up on the hills. In short, the town and the farm formed the infrastructure that let the Small-Business Age occur. Putting that infrastructure solidly in place was the major source of new wealth of the age.

The infrastructure of the Commercial Age was the ships and shipyards, ports and canals, warehouses, stock exchanges, and financial establishments of the new economy, together with the great houses of the newly rich. Paralleling their development were the palaces, armories, mints, furniture and ceramics factories, and customs houses of the royal court. Building this infrastructure was the main business of the age.

The Industrial Age was preoccupied with constructing its own infrastructure: merchant marine, railroads and highways, factories and machinery, communications systems, government buildings, educational systems, health systems, cultural systems, power systems, and so on. Putting the industrial infrastructure in place took up much of the capital and energy of the day.

Now, once again, the West (or North, as we should be calling it) is building a new infrastructure: office-, factory-, and home-automation equipment, networks with their microwave towers, fiber optic cables, electronic switches, satellites and computers, together with high-tech factories, clean rooms, and laboratories required to design and build them.

As we have seen, these infrastructures are cumulative, each age adding its own layer, and transformative, each age restructuring the infrastructure of the previous ages in its own image.

Chapter 12
PHASE TWO: STRUCTURAL SHIFTS

1981–2006

With the new interest in Information Age values and human capital, and in smart technology and networks, comes a series of structural changes in the economy. Although we are only at the beginning of the second phase of the Information Revolution, we can already discern a number of these fundamental shifts, which will continue into the Information Age.

- From hierarchical to network organization. Aided by smart technology, the number of management levels in the organization is reduced until it is flattened from a pyramid to a network.
- Repealing Parkinson's Law. Government and institutional bureaucracy will be simplified in the shift to network organization. Some of the money previously absorbed by salaries will be freed for programs, some will go to reduce the deficit, and some to cut taxes.
- Privatization. Many functions of government can be performed profitably by the private sector, cutting government expenses and adding to the tax base.
- Corporate downsizing. The corporation is peeling away unrelated subsidiaries acquired during the conglomeration era, and is "outplacing" unneeded managers.
- The growth of franchising. Small business is growing as "outplaced" managers leave the big business sector. Many go into franchising with its ready-made rules and high rate of success.
- Transformation of the West to the North. Collaboration is

replacing competition between nations and national corporations, tying Europe, North America and Japan into a northern coalition.

These changes should all be in place in twenty years' time, as the Information Revolution draws to a close. The structure of the Information Age will then be as different from that of the Industrial Age as the latter was from the Commercial Age before the French Revolution.

FROM HIERARCHICAL TO NETWORK ORGANIZATION

It was inevitable that the network concept should infiltrate the corporate establishment. Executives all have their well-furnished networks of cronies, gossips, schoolmates, and relatives with whom information and favors are regularly exchanged, traded, or bartered, to be repaid in kind.

The late seventies saw an invasion of word processors, followed in the early eighties by personal computers, often smuggled in behind the backs of data processing priests. The late eighties is witnessing the spread of smart networks (superswitches and local area networks) and the executive work station with color-graphics screens. Electronic filing will come onstream as optical memory disks become widespread in the nineties. With voice actuation you can consult your electronic files from your car phone and check your facts as you drive to a meeting.

The integration of these elements into a single global system is assured by an international master plan called the Integrated Services Digital Network, or ISDN, four letters which will soon become as well known as RSVP. The ISDN is a series of conventions and standards that accomplishes for business communications what the international direct-dialing system did for the telephone. All equipment with communicating capability will soon be built to this standard. Telephone and transmission companies are modifying their systems and their planning to conform to its vision.

Each time a blank is filled in in the Great ISDN, a portion of the industrial office system collapses: a clerk here, a manager there, some typists from the pool. Automatic translation cuts a few more. Teleconferencing saves on travel, telecommuting on office space and maintenance. Eventually the personnel department becomes too large for the smaller staff. Accounting gets pared back. The company moves to a smaller building.

Not everyone agrees that the office hierarchy will collapse as the new technology is introduced. Networks will let us do better work (so the argument goes). We may do newer kinds of work, but the interaction between office employees is too complex and too little understood to be automated like a factory floor or a chemical plant. Government regulations and reporting requirements would never permit it, the opponents proclaimed. Generally accepted accounting principles, it is believed, are a necessary barrier against shortcuts, holding chaos at bay.

At first, equipment salesmen supported this cautious approach. "Our devices will help you do your job" was their claim. They learned never to say, "Our system will eliminate jobs." This taboo is powerful. Industrial Age executives who loudly proclaimed that government has grown too big refused even to consider that business administration is equally bloated. "Me, give up my secretary? No way. You're out of line, mister."

By the nineties lines will be drawn between hierarchy people (the *ancien régime*) and the network crowd (revolutionaries). The latter proclaim their vision of an interconnected world in which routine work is computerized and dispersed executives are joined in global purpose. Governments will compete for their business by accommodating their laws and requirements (as Nevada did for divorce). Networking becomes their banner; low prices, high quality, flexibility, and speed, their arms. Joint-ventured global consortia battle large and inflexible industrial conglomerates. In the nineties, when the first fifth-generation computers appear with their built-in intelligence, a major crisis will develop: The *ancien régime* surrenders and networking prevails.

If we look deeper into the Information Revolution, we notice that one of its characteristics is the creation of more and more individualized products and services, both information and industrial. This suggests that the creation of small specialized networks over a widely dispersed area will become typical. We are already seeing the first minitransnationals or "network companies" operating with limited personnel in various parts of the world. In an information environment, small businesses need not be confined geographically; nor need these minicorporations grow to great size to justify their continuing existence, as long as they can continue to provide their specialized service to their particular clientele at a competitive price. Since economies of scale would not apply, such corporations could be stable and free from challenge by larger organizations.

Partnership, that Small-Business Age form of business association, where trust and responsibility are extended to the group, may once more become an appropriate form of incorporation under information technology. Traditionally, partnerships have been geographically focused, but there is no reason why they may not be widely dispersed and generally effective in the global marketplace. The example of the large international accounting firms will serve.

Other forms of brotherhood could be based on religion, on psychogroups such as est or gestalt, on minorities such as native clans—in fact, on any grouping where loyalties are strong enough to break through local intolerance and the limited responsibilities of hierarchical corporate life, and the members are able to take full advantage of information technology. This form of social-industrial cohesion by which an ethnic or religious group grows to dominate a business sector, is as old as commerce itself.

Whether global, national, or local, the drive for renewal, to escape from hierarchical bureaucracy and operate as a brotherhood along network rules, has a dual appeal. It is more economical, powerful, and responsible, so its appeal to clients is very real. It is also much more psychologically rewarding, with a deep challenge, a joyous feeling of strength, a sharing of power and a direct participation in the rewards of growth. The satisfaction arising from network organization will be one of the forces behind the reorganization and renewal of the nineties.

REPEALING PARKINSON'S LAW

Government bureaucrats will be torn between the drive for renewal, arising from network organization, and the safety and sure rewards associated with hierarchical organization under Parkinson's Law. Given their unionized structure, their immense numbers, their power over elected officials through their enormous voting size and through their control of the policymaking apparatus, civil servants have it all their own way. On the other hand, their huge salary bill is bumping the ceiling of a competitive society's ability to pay, and as a result, money is borrowed from programs to pay their bloated wages. Constraint programs prevent travel, modernization, and the purchase of new equipment, and so the bureaucrats are increasingly limited, in Parkinson's acid-etched words, to reading each other's memoranda.

Yet there is so much to be done. As the new age unfolds and

government begins to glimpse its import and direction, the urge to be part of the new thrust for growth leads people and teams within it to move voluntarily to network organization, simply because the hierarchy constrains them from activity.

Government, too, feels threatened by the new globalism. Citizens' values become more global and less national. Chauvinism declines. National borders are more of a nuisance than a protection; national politics of less interest than global economics. Where global institutions such as Greenpeace, Amnesty International, and Live Aid are moral and credible, governments have lost their credibility and, with it, their constituency. Fewer people bother to vote.

Governments are called on less to constrain business than to help it grow. This means fewer national regulators and more global nurturers. Both of these trends will demand more use of network technology. Foreign offices and missions will grow in importance as centers of market and industrial intelligence, and at home, government information departments will become better organized in the automatic gathering of information and its rapid analysis and feedback to competitive businesses at home.

Deregulation, a feature of maturing economic revolutions, got under way in 1975 in America under President Ford, and has been forced by increasingly global competition to grow in pace around the world. The greatest growth in government bureaucracy took place in the sixties, in response to violent criticism of the industrial system by the baby-boom generation. In the same way, the great slimming down of the bureaucracy will occur in the late eighties and early nineties in response to the growing pace of deregulation.

How will the move from hierarchical to network organization occur? It has, in fact, already begun. The introduction of work stations on executive desks is well under way. As programming, network capability, and on-line resources improve, executives will learn to use them, and work stations will proliferate. Access to real-time information from the automated real world will short-cut the clerical process, freeing up person–years for more urgent tasks. Power will gradually accrue to those with terminals and software and with fewer underlings to administer. More time can go to real work when less is wasted in solving personnel quarrels and personal problems. Those whose salaries are based on larger empires will be competing on unfavorable terms with those who are networked, lean, and clean of unproductive effort. There will be intense pressure to revise the salary structure, basing it on quality-of-output instead of quantity-of-people-administered.

Government, bloated with middle management, will be most

affected by the automation of judgment arising from the development of smart programs. One by one, job categories will be automated, freeing personnel for more vital tasks. Expense accounts will be automatically monitored by computers, with exceptions flagged for human attention. Clerks will be "outplaced" during budget cuts. Young turks in the administration will tie their new program proposals to network organization, miniscule personpower requirements, and the consequent modest costs.

PRIVATIZATION

The immediate postwar period in Britain and throughout Europe and the British Commonwealth saw the creation of a number of national companies, and the nationalization of many others. The Labour government of Britain, in power from 1945 to 1951, nationalized coal, gas, electricity, the railways, and the Bank of England, and created the National Health Service as well. British public corporations were responsible for less than 1 percent of the GNP when the process began, and more than 10 percent when it finished. Then followed nearly thirty years of alternating Tory and Labour governments. Finally, in 1979, the Thatcher government set about the denationalizing or privatizing of government services.

If the Thatcher government achieves its goals before its term expires in mid-1988, it will have denationalized twenty state companies, sold off nearly a million state-owned dwellings to their tenants, and transferred some 600,000 jobs from the public to private sector, reducing the public sector GNP from 10.5 to 6.5 percent, according to a detailed midterm report card published in *The Economist* in October 1985.

While the sale of these assets has brought over £20 billion to the treasury, the Thatcher government sees another benefit: increased competition and efficiency for the industries concerned. In addition, as the *Economist* puts it, "The government believes wider share ownership is, in itself, a good thing, encouraging more people to be interested in the success of commerce and industry." The enormously successful sale of half the shares of British Telecom in the spring of 1985 reached two million shareholders, most of them first time investors.

Whether the privatization trend represents the end of the "mixed economy" or not is another question. Canada's Brian Mulroney, while pursuing a privatization program, has assured the nation that the state-owned Canadian Broacasting Corporation and Air Canada are not for sale, and President Reagan's attempts to find buyers for the U.S. Weather Service were, perhaps, premature.

Nevertheless, if we look at the West as a whole, rather than as a series of national governments, we can see that the trend is to privatization in the interests of efficiency, flexibility, choice, competition, reduction of national debt, increase in the tax base, and escape from union control in public service.

Paralleling the sale of national companies to the private sector, there is the rush to privatize services, particularly in the United States. Developments in this area of massive restructuring come as a series of surprises, so deeply entrenched are our ideas of the role of the nation state (and of regional and local government) in our "public sector" institutions.

Of course the city collects the garbage. Of course it looks after sewage and water treatment plants. Running the jails is a natural function of government, just as it runs the schools and the hospitals, the army and the airports, provides assistance to other countries, maintains the art galleries and museums and parks, and looks after the justice system. Tax assessment is about as pure a government activity as one can imagine. Yet, one after another, all of these "services" or functions have in some measure become privatized, contracted out to the private sector. And that measure is increasing, particularly during this second phase of the revolution.

In a remarkable and neglected piece of social history, San Diego journalist Richard Louv toured his country and in 1983 published his account of *America II*, which he sees as a separate society forming in the bosom of the older America I. It's composed of rural sophisticates, the world of walled cities with private police, fire, and garbage departments—and private governments. "Public services all over the nation are being decimated by budget cuts and replaced by private services for those who can afford them," he states of the new America. Soon, every other new house in America will be a condo. By 1980 there were more private enclaves with their own minigovernments than there are small town governments. In 1982, nearly ten million Americans were members of community associations. By 1990, a federal government agency estimates, some $20 billion in assessments (the equivalent of taxes) will be taken in.

"They already collect more revenue than the nation's small towns and may soon come to represent more financial power than all elected local governments in the U.S. combined," according to Luov, who adds:

The range of goods and services bought by these associations is impressive. Fancy electronic surveillance systems, private police, telephone answering services, central utilities, and home-owners' insurance are all purchased with the leverage of group buying power. This communal approach is quite attractive to the service provider; instead of an insurance agent dealing with 300 to 400 individual consumers for private coverage, he or she deals only with the community association. As a result, the cost of such coverage is often reduced by as much as 60 percent. Some community associations are even buying group vacations.

Much of the experimenting in the privatization of civic services is taking place in the sun belt, and California is a bellwether state. According to *Fortune* magazine in the spring of 1985:

At the southern end of Los Angeles County, Rolling Hills Estate broke off a contract it had with the county prosecutor to handle all its cases, mostly involving violations of building and other town codes. City Manager Harry R. Peacock says the service was totally inadequate. Rolling Hills Estates now pays a private law firm to act as town prosecutor. Rancho Palos Verdes, next door, closed its public works department and turned over the care of parks, buildings, and roads to an engineering company.

Some states have more convicted criminals than jail cells and are under court orders not to jail convicts until places become available. Under these circumstances, it is not surprising that they are turning over the building and operating of jails to private contractors. *Fortune* reported:

The Nashville-based Corrections Corp. of America operates five facilities [as of May, 1985] including detention centers built for the Immigration and Naturalization Service in Houston and Laredo Texas. At Houston in 1984, the company charged the INS $23.84 a day per detainee, compared with the U.S. average of $26.45 a day it costs the INS to run its own services—and Correction Corp.'s figures include capital costs, while the INS's cover only operating costs.

The operation of hospitals has usually been associated with government. After all, there are numerous responsibilities that go with hospitals, such as care of the indigent and researching new techniques, which are usually not associated with private enterprise "out to make a buck." Nevertheless, the private hospital business has been growing and it has a surprisingly good record of handling the poor and the needy, while public hospitals have long since hit the ceiling government trustees will tolerate. One industry leader, the Humana Corporation, has caught the public's attention and perhaps changed its attitude by allocating $100 million to perfecting its artificial-heart transplant program over the decade.

The problems of state-controlled education are legion: students who can't read or understand documents and manuals; students trained for career paths that ended with the Industrial Age; shortage of mathematically trained and science-oriented college entrants; teachers intimidated by classroom bullies; and perhaps worst of all, a curriculum and faculty that are essentially socialistic in outlook, stressing government and downplaying or disparaging the private sector, and unable to turn out entrepreneurs.

Early in 1981, the outspoken president of Boston University, John R. Silber, suggested the city turn over the schools to the university, which would raise the academic standards and shave more than 15 percent from the budget. The schools were in an economic mess, with no controls over the budget process and no way of knowing what had been spent. In the seventies the school board more than doubled the teaching and maintenance staffs in the city's schools while student population fell by a third.

The universities, however, are not without problems or free from antigrowth biases, and so since the earliest days of the Information Revolution, industry has been developing its own training and academic programs. General Motors University teaches those particular skills needed to run a multinational motor company, while McDonald's runs its own program with degrees in hamburgerology. Private-sector higher-education budgets surpassed those of the public sector sometime in the mid-seventies, and collaboration between universities and private industry is the front line of new financing in the sector. The state is becoming but one sponsor among many.

The problems the private sector will undertake are without limit. In some respects, the global ecology yields more to the privately funded and staffed Greenpeace Foundation than to government action. Live Aid's global concert and rationalized aid measures for the famine victims of Ethiopia jostle the efforts of governments and are far more effective in raising the consciousness of the young. More important, they have shown that government is not the only—and not necessarily the best, most moral, or most efficient—vehicle for international action. The mystique of the importance of national governments, so carefully established over the past five centuries, is coming apart.

So far, these various privatization projects have only grazed the enormous budgets posted for such services as defense, health, education, welfare, and justice, which are forcing Western countries so heavily into deficit. Although considerable gains have been realized in efficiency and budget cutting, there are moral issues to be resolved. And while the campaign to privatize government services has some of the characteristics of a religious crusade against the bureaucracy, it lacks the cohesion of an economic movement. This is yet to come.

CORPORATE DOWNSIZING

In the dying phase of the Industrial Age (that is, before 1975), many industrial firms became divisions of conglomerates and passed into the financial sector. New firms which had successfully weathered the entrepreneurial phase and passed into the hands of professional managers quite easily slithered from industry-trained managers to accountants, comptrollers, and other members of the financial sector who knew or cared nothing for the industry they controlled other than the bottom line.

This conglomeration movement was the result of government antitrust legislation dating back to the American Industrial Revolution and of government attempts to prevent corporations from controlling the market. In the last days of the Industrial Age it created some of the most disheartening monstrosities in corporate history.

The second phase of the revolution is concerned with the birth of the new economy, just as the first was devoted to the death throes of the old. And so a great *dance macabre* is under way, a dance in which huge elements of the old system are dismembered and redistributed, often from one sector to another.

This rationalization or restructuring comes with its own jargon: "Downsizing" and "divestiture" are synonyms for the hiving–off of divisions that have nothing in common with their "parents" and could be better managed by those familiar with the industry concerned. The chosen instrument for this is leveraged buy-outs, in which the managers and employees of the company concerned borrow on the assets of the company to acquire it from the accountants in charge of the conglomerate. In fact, what is happening is the transfer of the company from the financial sector, where it has no business, back to the industrial sector.

Downsizing has a second meaning: the internal restructuring of an organization to get rid of redundant staff. "Redundant staff" refers to employees whose jobs are being eliminated and who will not be replaced. Legalistic definitions are necessary because of political concern over jobs, and consequent government interference in the labor market. Redundancy arises from restructuring; it is usually the result of automation of the shop floor or office, rendered necessary by competition from more productive firms abroad, over which the government has little or no control. Each nation handles the jobs/competition/productivity problem differently, but the general tendency is to allow market forces to rule.

Since industry is contracting, many "downsized," "dehired," or "outplaced" industrial workers have moved into the small-business sector, with many of those joining the underground economy. Statistics are particularly weak in this area. In general, the underground economy employment figure is close to the difference between the participation rate and 100 percent, minus those in jails, hospitals, or mental homes, plus illegal immigrants. The official unemployment rate is a political fiction and the source of much misguided activity and misspent public funds. This situation will deteriorate as factory automation gathers speed.

Very few redundant industrial workers will find their way into the high-tech sector. Employers, anxious to avoid the inflexibilities of unionization and the deep-seated antagonisms of two hundred years of industrialism, have kept them off their production lines.

Other ways of speeding the outplacement of unions are being forced on industrial corporations by the new competition from firms abroad and deregulation at home. In one technique, called "leasing out," the company closes down a unionized, labor-intensive division and hires a nonunionized outside firm to provide the service under contract or lease, as frequently occurs in the airline industry. Often the outside firm hires the former employees back at a more competitive rate. The new team, free of union restrictions, is usually able to increase productivity and take on additional work.

(One by-product of this hiving-off of service departments is an apparent increase in GNP: the total of all goods and services sold in a country. If a large company sets up its own printing department and stops buying printing services from outside sources, the GNP appears to contract by this much. If it contracts out for services once performed in-house, the GNP expands accordingly. When these trends begin on a massive scale, the GNP growth rate appears to contract or expand.)

When American firms are particularly hard-pressed by competition from the outside and inflexible union arrangements from within, they sometimes seek protection under Chapter XI of the bankruptcy laws, which allows them to abrogate unrealistic union contracts and renegotiate a more competitive deal with their employees. Thus generations of labor legislation inherited from the Industrial Age are being rewritten not on the floor of the Congress, Commons, or National Assembly, where they are politically too hot to handle, but in the rough and tumble of the global labor marketplace.

A similar transformation of the office is just getting under way. Office automation, coupled with a better understanding and control of information quality, is following the course of factory automation. As it progresses, the replacement of office workers, managers, and professionals by electronic systems will create further massive transfers of people and investment from the financial, government, and industrial sectors to the small-business sector.

"Outplacement" of redundant middle managers is a rapidly growing field. Of the ten million executives estimated by *Business Week* to be employed in America, perhaps half are at risk of losing their jobs in the next decade, as network replaces hierarchy and productivity gains are compounded by smart technology. Some will take advantage of early retirement; others will accept voluntary separations with special conditions; some will simply be dismissed. In almost all cases, there is some sizable financial package involved, as well as the services of outplacement counselors. The cost of getting rid of these redundant managers during the revolution's closing phase will be in the hundreds of billions of dollars, perhaps as much as a trillion dollars.

A sizable portion of this money will go to set up the manager in a small business of his own. Some become consultants; some set up shop in a hobby or sideline; and many become managers of franchise operations. Thus one of the major effects of the Information Revolution is the massive transfer of capital from the industrial and financial sectors to the small-business sector.

Some of these outplaced executives leave with more than a cash settlement: They continue to serve their old firm under contract.

The pioneer in this field is Rank Xerox of Great Britain. According to a September, 1984 issue of *The Economist*:

> Rank Xerox is pleased when executives want to leave it to form their own companies, and then sell their services back to Rank Xerox and others. It has 48 so-called networkers working from home, including two former directors of the company. Most are specialists such as pension managers and tax lawyers. Rank Xerox wants to increase the number of networkers to 150. It reckons that for each £10,000 of full-time labour costs in central London it must add another £17,000 for non-wage over-heads. Savings come in other ways: it has sold an office building that housed 50 people and cost £330,000 a year to run.

Often the trauma of separation, with its blow to the ego, leaves its victim bruised, surprised, and feeling deceived. Outplacement counselors are becoming skilled at ego rebuilding, and the search for marketable skills, deeper interests, and psychological needs sometimes leads the outplaced executive into quieter streams, a craft business or service based on a hobby or pastime. Thus the basement workshop becomes the basis for a small custom furniture business, while the yachtsman becomes the owner of a marina. According to outplacement counselors, such second careers are happening at an earlier point in people's lives. If it was fifty-five before, currently it's forty-five, and in the future it will be even younger. The counselors also report that executives who have given up or lost their jobs are generally happier, more productive, and often much better off financially building a business for themselves.

Because the well-defined responsibilities and the well-structured environment of the corporate manager are so far removed from those of the entrepreneur, the problems of adaptation into the sink-or-swim of the small-business marketplace are considerable. Managerial skills are only part of the armory needed for survival in the entrepreneurial world. For this reason the franchise, with its structured rule book, prebuilt reputation, and well-tried business plan is the popular solution for the outplaced middle manager.

THE GROWTH OF FRANCHISING

In this second phase of the Information Revolution, franchising has been growing more than five times faster than the GNP. In 1975 sales by franchised companies accounted for 9 percent of GNP, doubling to 18 percent in 1985. They could double again by the end of the revolution—and spread across the world as well. Already McDonalds and Kentucky Fried Chicken are well known in Japan; PepsiCola in Russia; and Honda in North America and Europe. They are but the edges of the wedges as this powerful globalizing force sweeps the world.

The executive who buys an established franchise has a number of things going for him. There is a proven business plan, one that the banks are familiar with and have confidence in. The success rate in franchising is high: Nine out of ten succeed, compared with a less than even chance for independent small businesses.

Most franchisors are looking for company men to run their franchised operations. They are familiar with operations manuals and with following each step faithfully, and will train their staff in the same virtues. They are neither creative nor entrepreneurial, qualities franchisors seek to avoid. They have the money and are credit-worthy, and they are used to managing. It is an almost ideal match.

Middle managers are pleased to be in a business that is easy to sell. In many cases the parent company is willing to buy back the franchise as it matures, say ten years down the road, in order to create a wholly owned chain. In the ideal scenario, the outplaced middle manager invests his $50,000 compensation in the franchise, works on it for ten years, and then sells it back to the franchisor for a million dollars. This executive is much more richly rewarded in every sense than if he (or in 9 percent of the cases, she) had stuck it out in the corporate hierarchy or had joined another large firm. He's created work, not consumed it. The economy is restructured and strengthened, and he's at the center.

The forces we have described are likely to speed the move to franchising in this closing phase of the Information Revolution. Downsized executives could have as much as a trillion dollars to invest over the next twenty years. New demands for service will develop as the population ages and life care becomes their priority, and the private sector will take over those services the government can no longer afford to provide.

Because he is risking his own capital, the franchise owner tends to work harder and smarter than he did as a corporate executive. Behind him are the collective resources and experience of the global concern, and the name brand of the franchise is a global attribute in a marketplace dominated by increasingly difficult choices for the consumer.

As the share of goods and services operating under franchise grows, the financial sector will move in and perform its integrating function. This will permit the franchising of larger and more ambitious parts of the economy. Education, health, and tourism are prime sectors. As an example of the scale franchising can reach, the Disneyland franchises in Japan and France run to hundreds of millions of dollars per unit.

There is an alternative to the conglomeration of franchises: The owners could decide to increase the scale and scope of their operation by federation. In either case, the result will be a number of "general services corporations," which we may expect to appear and evolve during this closing phase of the revolution.

THE GENERAL SERVICES CORPORATION

(fictive case history)

The first of the general services corporations will come into being in the conglomeration movement of the 1990s. Diversified conglomerates of the sixties, because of American anti-trust legislation, were made up of businesses in unrelated fields. This meant there was no overriding sense to the corporate family, nothing with which the public could identify, nothing which would engender loyalty or direction in the staff (which often found its company traded like a baseball player), nothing other than the bottom line on which senior management could focus. To the accountant in charge of these monstrosities, nothing matters but figures. Not quality, not continuity, not tradition, not craftsmanship, not innovation, not creativity, not employees, not customers, not clean air, not a rich environment, not a happy community, not a growing economy. Just figures.

The GSC is the opposite of the sixties conglomerate. Its various firms will form what the Japanese call a harmonious family of companies. Each will serve a major human requirement: education (from prekindergarten to postgraduate); health (mental and physical); life care (security, retirement, pension); entrepreneurial support (training, credit, and advice); and life-style (entertainment, recreation, culture, and tourism). Together, they offer responsible and coordinated cradle-to-grave service all around the world. Many of its clients are in for a lifetime, as are practically all of its staff or partners.

For people to devote their lives or even much of their business to a single corporate entity, they must see it as superior: that is, ethical, quality conscious, perhaps even beneficent. They must be able to believe in its growth and continuance. They must be convinced that it is a force for the good in the lives of its clients and staff and for the regions in which it operates. And they must see it as offering a rich and fulfilling life before they will choose it as their global family.

During the eighties the industrial corporation began taking on a hybrid Western-Eastern structure with a blurring of the distinction between management and labor and an end to confrontational relationships, a greatly reduced bureaucracy, and a shared corporate pride in world-class quality products. The services corporation of the nineties will follow a parallel path. Modelled as much on longstanding Western institutions as on the Japanese harmonious family of companies, the general services corporation will be neither Eastern nor Western, but a new third-stream culture appealing to the deepest in peoples of all the races and cultures it serves. While the old multinationals were primarily national companies with branch plants or offices abroad, the GSC will be a truly global entitity, with no overriding national loyalty.

Eventually the GSC will train its own personnel (or partners) in its own schools, but in the formative years, as it assembles its critical mass of firms, it will acquire the staff and management of existing service organizations (financial, tourism, health care, education and training, etc). In order to turn staff into partners, a process of renewal is required, where payment and bonuses include training grants in entrepreneurial skills. When qualified, most employees become partners, contracting to provide services to member companies or to the public, in some cases taking on franchises, in others creating new types of businesses. In this way, the GSC will become an extended family, or network of small businesses backed, supported, and half-owned by the conglomerate. It might eventually be made up of tens of thousands of employees and entrepreneurial trainees, and hundreds of thousands of partners all over the world.

Because of the strength of its education/training system, which prepares its graduates for entrepreneurial activity and orients them to growth, Third World countries will be prepared to contract with the GSC for regional economic development. In turn they will provide attractive land for tourist, training, or retirement-home centers under long-term lease. The development of this global network of centers will enhance the appeal of the GSC to clients and staff.

The GSC will not be the only general services enterprise in the field, although by far the biggest, due to the wide appeal of its middle-of-the-road value system. In competition will be "life-style" service conglomerates offering a wide choice of value systems. At one extreme, there could be the Love Insurance Corporation of the Bahamas (or Love-In), which will appeal to a young clientele through its entertainment and tourism sectors, although its financial services and retirement groups are weak. At the other extreme, there will be a variety of service collectives, representing racial, social, and religious minorities, labor unions, and political parties. None of these will grow very large, as they will be unable to obtain government contracts for education and other general services.

The transition of power will not be easy. Education, health, life care and security were once considered, for historical reasons no longer relevant, government responsibilities. Yet, burdened with debt payments, hierarchical bureaucracies, and intransigent unions, governments will be unable to compete with the GSC in the content, orientation, structure, and cost of services. The marketplace will decide. Customers will choose the GSC for the quality of its services. As these services pass from government to the private sector, the tax base will grow, tax rates will fall, and government debt will be retired.

It will be one of the ironies of the information economy that the withering away of the state, first envisioned in the 1840s by Karl Marx as the outgrowth of socialism, will actually begin 150 years later in the 1990s through private enterprise and the entrepreneurial system.

TRANSFORMATION OF THE WEST INTO THE NORTH

The first half of the Information Revolution saw the restructuring of Western Europe from a handful of competing and autonomous countries into a Common Market, with a European government and bureaucracy and with common goals, institutions, strategies, and policies. Under the leadership of brandy-merchant and statesman Jean Monnet, the Eurocrats managed to accomplish by consensus in one generation what generals, kings, and popes had failed to do by coercion over more than a thousand years.

The European Community was not born fully formed. It was painstakingly constructed through continuous negotiations, the creation of common institutions, and the responses to developing problems, threats and opportunities. The first great act was the creation among "les six" of a European Steel and Coal Community in 1951, and the sentences of the preamble ring with a constitutional sound:

[Germany, France and Italy, Holland, Belgium and Luxembourg,]

CONSIDERING that world peace can be safeguarded only by creative efforts commensurate with the dangers that threaten it,

CONVINCED that the contribution which an organized and vital Europe can make to civilization is indispensable to the maintenance of peaceful relations,

RECOGNIZING that Europe can be built only through practical achievements which first create de facto solidarity, and through the establishment of common bases for economic development,

ANXIOUS to help, by expanding their basic production, to raise the standard of living and further the works of peace,

RESOLVED to substitute for age-old rivalries the merging of their essential interests; to create, by establishing an economic community, the basis for a broader and deeper community among peoples long divided by bloody conflicts; and to lay the foundations for institutions which will give direction to a destiny henceforward shared,

HAVE DECIDED to create a European Coal and Steel Community.

Pushed by the closing of the Suez Canal and fears of dependence on Arab oil, the Eurocrats added the twin institutions of Euratom and the Common Market in 1957. All that was needed to build a Europe strong enough to become an equal partner with America was Britain's entry. For much of the sixties, however, a long winter of French greatness under President de Gaulle kept

France's ancient foe out of the community and effectively stopped the community's growth. Happily, de Gaulle resigned in April 1969, and by June 1975 the British people voted overwhelmingly to join the Market. Soon Europe would be a power, like America. The West was reborn.

As these plans were developing, no one had envisaged a Japan of equal magnitude, but in the second phase of the revolution, as Europe moved to consolidate and expand its scope and power, the partnership of America and Europe was becoming a triad. Without formal agreement, the West was becoming the North. The instrument of change this time was not the bureaucracy or political process but a striking new form of economic association pulled together by joint agreement among consenting corporations.

The multinational enterprise (MNE) with its national ownership and distributed subsidiaries, first appeared during the American Industrial Revolution. It reached its zenith in the first stage of the Information Revolution, which is, as we have seen, also the closing phase of the Industrial Age. A successful MNE produces in all the countries of the world a similar product, which it frequently manufactures locally to avoid tariff barriers and to take advantage of local incentives. No matter how hard it tries to be a good corporate citizen, its interests are primarily those of its home nation, in whose favor the inevitable conflicts are usually resolved.

During the first phase of the Information Revolution, MNEs from America, Europe, and Japan dominated the marketplace. They competed among each other viciously. According to industrial economic theory, this competition served all our interests. The harder they competed, the better we all were served.

Because of the fierceness of competition, some multinationals so dominated the world marketplace that nations turned to protectionist policies and national strategies to protect domestic jobs and industries. This distorted the marketplace and drove up prices, defeating the advantages of competition. Americans, who had often been accused by smaller nations of playing the economic bully in the years following World War II, began to scream against unfair practices by the Japanese multinationals and their collusive government. Charges of economic warfare were muttered but rarely proven. Nationalist feelings on both sides threatened economic growth.

In phase two of the Information Revolution, a collaborative model began to replace the competitive one. In new industries, as well as those newly reborn along information lines, Japanese firms, American firms, and European firms share technology, financing, productions, and markets in joint ventures. International competitors join forces to become global collaborators.

Kenichi Ohmae, a McKinsey & Company consultant based in Japan, has documented the new corporative industrial structure in his book *Triad Power*. "Traditional multinationals" he writes, "have tried to do everything on their own as they entered each market. They can't do that any more because the skills and products required to compete worldwide have increased greatly. . . . Old frameworks designed for, at the most, 200 million people, have become obsolete in the Triad's new and dynamic markets of 600 million people." And he concludes, "The future key factor for success for multinationals will be their ability to develop and enhance company-to-company relationships, particularly across national and cultural boundaries."

Ohmae unravels the complex interrelationships that tie the four major American auto manufacturers to the Japanese big nine and the fourteen leading European firms. An even more complex network joins eighteen American, eighteen Japanese and thirty-two European robot manufacturers into consortia, technical partners, or mutual sales agents. Similar consortia are forming in such high-tech areas as biotechnology, carbon fibers, airplane engines, silicon wafers, computers, and chips.

Each of the partners in the triad, Ohmae suggests, has access to a major geographical market: America to the rest of the Western hemisphere, Europe to Africa and the Middle East, Japan to the ASEAN (Association of Southeast Asian Nations). What Jean Monnet has done for Europe in phase one of the revolution, the corporate community is beginning to accomplish for the North during this second phase. The last word should go to Jean Monnet, who, perhaps more than he realized, started the process. This is how he concluded his life's work, and his *Memoirs*, in 1975, as the first phase of our revolution came to its end:

> Have I said clearly enough that the Community we have created is not an end in itself? It is a process of change, continuing that same process which in an earlier period of history produced our national forms of life. Like our provinces in the past, our nations today must learn to live together under common rules and institutions freely arrived at. The sovereign nations of the past can no longer solve the problems of the present; they cannot ensure their own progress or control their own future. And the Community itself is only a stage on the way to the organized world of tomorrow.

Chapter 13
THE
INFORMATION AGE

2006–2060

In order to use what we have learned for long-term fore-casting, we begin with the form of economic revolution. Then we set the time frame: the pace and rhythm of change. Only then can we speculate about actual content.

Historically, an economic age begins when its revolution ends. It is marked by a slowing of technological innovation and entrepreneurship. The pace of creation of new industries falls off. There is a speed up in social innovation and in the creation of government programs.

At the transition, two forces are in conflict. The economic liberals want the corporation to remain free to innovate and create wealth (for growth continues even though the phase of innovation is ending). The forces of reaction want the old values restored, and the corporations restrained in their immoral behavior. They want to channel the wealth generated by the private sector into socially useful programs. At the end of the British Industrial Revolution liberalism was at its height, but the forces of reaction managed to control it through legislation and social ostracism. At the end of the American Industrial Revolution, antitrust forces strove to prevent what they deemed corporate conspiracy, and when the market failed in 1929, social programs dominated the economy. We may expect a similar situation to prevail following the Information Revolution, sometime during the first decade of the next century.

Following the first economic revolution of each cycle, a second wave of economic revolution takes place. The fifteenth and sixteenth centuries saw the spread of the Commercial Revolution throughout Europe some centuries after its first appearance in Italy. Forty years after the end of the British Industrial Revolution, America, Japan and Germany began their own Industrial Revolutions. If this pattern holds, we might expect to see a second wave of Information, or High-Tech, Revolution in the mid-twenty-first century.

And after that second wave is completed? Our historic pattern suggests that the technology behind the next revolution is already here in embryonic form. Mechanized factory production was developing throughout the Commercial Era, but no one was able to open it up to its potential at the time. Telecommunications was developing throughout the Industrial Age: The telegraph came into widespread use in the 1850s, the undersea cable in the 1870s, the telephone in the 1890s, broadcasting in the 1920s. Their explosive potential was not realized in practice until the 1950s and the Information Revolution. This would strongly suggest that the technology behind the next revolution is already in place. We have already identified this as a Space Revolution.

THE REVOLUTION ENDS, THE AGE BEGINS

THE PRIVATE SECTOR

Throughout the Information Revolution, the agent of change and innovation has been the corporation, aided by government in the form of grants and subsidies (in the United States, these overwhelmingly take the form of defense contracts and quasi-military programs such as NASA), nontariff barriers, infrastructure development, and education. As the Information Age opens, there will be three major types of private-sector corporations: the traditional nation-based MNEs (multinational enterprises), the Northern-based triad alliances, and the global-based GSCs (general service corporations).

The MNE is an anachronism in the increasingly global economy and is on the decline. Since the MNE is headquartered in one of the leading nations and operates subsidiaries elsewhere, it is a foreigner in most of its markets. While it tries to be a good corporate citizen, its outlook, ethic, and interests are primarily those of the home country, and these inevitably conflict with the goals, needs, and regional styles of most of its markets. Despite MNE claims that its subsidiaries are autonomous, its policies and strategies are handed down the hierarchy from the head office, which increasingly is in some foreign country.

Many MNEs in the industrial and high-tech sectors have become triad alliances: great family groupings equally based in the EEC, Japan and North America, with each serving its continent to the south. These are dominated by the four automobile alliances (represented in North America by Ford, GM, Chrysler, and American Motors), the largest corporate groupings in the world. Other alliances in aerospace transport, robotics, factory and office automation, and home electronics dominate their industries in all three market areas.

Triad alliances (TAs) have no head office—or they have three head offices, which amounts to the same thing. Decisions are reached by consensus. In most cases, control has passed from professional managers with an accounting background to engineers with management skills *and* a lifetime commitment to the industry.

TA employees expect to spend their entire working life in the TA, as there is sufficient variety of opportunity to allow for personal growth, which TA human capital policy encourages by a variety of means. Skill acquisition is rewarded, particularly when it is crosscultural. Management is open, with the decision process recorded in the computer and available on-line. Decision analysis is fostered and promotions are based in part on the quality of critiques and decisions.

The TA intelligence system is particularly strong in market and industry information. Some of this information is shared with competitors and suppliers, which helps promote the industry and develop standards. Some is shared with academia, where future employees are identified and research is promoted. Some is shared with government, so that global trends can be identified while they are fresh enough to be acted upon.

TAs look to the development of the markets for which they are responsible, since any improvement in standard of living and sophistication soon results in increased consumption of TA products. Regional factories are installed as soon as possible in developing parts of the world in order to boost that development and assure the TA's presence. Nevertheless, their policy toward developing areas is essentially patronizing and, as it represents the privileged and hatred North, subject to radical attack.

Whereas MNEs represent their individual nations and the TAs represent the North, the GSCs are more democratic and global. Much of their operation is in the developing world, and as global traders in services, they are among its principal instruments of development.

Since the GSCs are democratic federations of small businesses and franchises, the number of employees is comparatively small. Moreover, many of these are entrepreneur-trainees or students paying for and acquiring their education by working.

Many GSC services are in the life-style and life-care area, offering cradle-to-grave support to their clientele. Services begin with fertility and obstetrics. They pass through nursery and day-care, education, and recreation. They progress to career guidance, training and placement, tourism and culture, investment guidance, and health care. They end with retirement, nursing, and burial. This immense range of services is continually expanding.

Like the trading companies of old, GSCs are constantly on the lookout for bargains and variety—and synergistic arrangements. Much of their business comes from looking after the needs of fellow members. More comes from regular clients, who pile up credits by increasing their business with the federation. The balance comes from the general public.

Now that they are reaching maturity, GSCs are beginning to take on government services: education and training, tourism and housing development, and infrastructure creation and management, all of which have great appeal to Third World countries. Tourist facilities established by the GSCs in the Third World are recycled into retirement properties and eventually into training facilities. Locals are absorbed into the GSC system not as employees but as entrepreneurial trainees, as everyone else. The GSCs don't provide jobs, they provide opportunities. They're out to abolish jobs.

What the private sector seemed to understand, and what the GSCs have proved able to teach and foster, is the secret of economic growth. Before, it was thought that only a few unique people had the talent and drive to make things happen and prosper, and they would manifest themselves no matter what, strengthened by adversity. Now we know that entrepreneurial skill and support can be fostered throughout the community.

Government, which had been responsible for education, had been inclined to teach conservative cultural values, good citizenship, respect for one's betters, and job skills. Most teachers spent their lives trained and paid by the state, and they communicated their belief that public service was somehow natural, noble, and desirable, while private enterprise was the opposite.

From an economic point of view, the general services corporation is a creator of wealth par excellence. In Paul Strassman's view of the next economy, "Wealth is extracted from high value-added benefits in the delivery of high-quality services on a global scale. The accumulated wealth should be sufficient to secure for everyone a decent standard of life. There should be no economic adversity. The only threat to survival might come from political breakdowns." As he states in *Information Payoff*:

> All of the institutions of a service society are shaped by questions of the ownership and control of knowledge and by the attempts to share equitably the opportunities such knowledge provides. Individual enterprises attain their position by superior competitive performance in serving customer needs and not by government franchise. The autonomous, market-driven service-oriented form of enterprise is the most stable organizational structure for managing kowledge workers. Individuals are members of enterprises in which they have a direct, gain-sharing interest. . . . A service society may generate $40,000 to $100,000 per capita because limitations on the physical consumption of scarce resources have largely been removed. The amount of knowledge that can be created and the services are, for all practical purposes, infinite.

As Strassman says, however, the dangers will be political. The corporation, heretofore amoral, nondemocratic, and controlled by national laws, becomes increasingly moral, constitutional, and responsible as it moves beyond national boundaries. It seeks a global rather than national clientele and continues to take over and commercialize the functions of the state.

For almost a thousand years, the church controlled the affairs of men. For the past five hundred years they have been controlled by the state. In the next millennium, control will pass into the hands of global corporations, if, as, and when they prove themselves worthy of trust. This is already happening today at the grass-roots level: Citizens organized into private communities contract to put their affairs into the hands of a corporation, as they did once before, a thousand years ago, at the time of the Small-Business Revolution. Global government could, a step at a time, pass into the hands of corporate councils.

THE PUBLIC SECTOR

As stated, two forces will be at work in forming government policy during the early stages of the Information Age. One is based on the premise that prosperity and growth are dependent on privatizing government activity to the utmost and encouraging the private sector in every possible way. The other is based on the notion that morality and profit are mutually exclusive; that enterprise is a conspiracy to rob the consumer and can only be tolerated if strictly regulated and heavily taxed, much as a cow is fenced in and milked.

All those in the antibusiness camp attack the MNEs. The triads are criticized by the South as a Northern conspiracy, and by Northern radicals because they make enormous profits which escape national control and taxation. Only the globals (the GSCs) are grudgingly admired, although their strategy of locking in consumers and partners with lifelong rewards is criticized as deprivation of freedom.

In 2006, though, the forces of minimal government are in the ascendency. According to neoliberal theory, the government's main function is to develop policy and standards. All programs devolve to the private sector. Although this will take a long time to accomplish, by 2006 many government employees have already joined private corporations to develop and carry out these programs. Others have banded together and invested their "outplacement" payments into firms that provide their services by contract.

Meanwhile, the process of devolving government programs to the private sector makes heavy demands on lawyers and administrators, and is under constant examination in the press. It is also subject to driving criticism and dire warnings of disaster from the opposition and the traditionalists.

Devolutionists believe not merely that the private sector is more efficient than the public, but that programs must be restructured so efficiency is rewarded and inefficiency punished. The privatized health-insurance system is the classic example. Doctors are no longer forced to order unneeded tests. Hospitals now lose rather than make money on unnecessary surgery and overlong stays. When the proper structure is found, developing checks and balances is a relatively simple matter. In every case, though, debate remains intense, and the decision and implementation processes of program devolution are long.

One area where government bureaucracy will be expanding is in the Northern Council, located in Montreal, where members of triad governments meet to deal with common problems. Transfer of personnel across borders is an early example of the kind of problem dealt with by the council. Migration from one sector to another and compensation for the investment in education, health, and training of migrants are variations on that theme.

The council is also becoming the central authority for establishing measures of the new economics, validating judicial and economic computer programs and expert systems, and establishing quality standards for Northern products. It provides a court with authority over triad alliances, MNEs and general service corporations. It maintains data banks on Northern and global markets and services, and a development bank for investment in the South. The whole focus of the council is the measurement and development of economic growth. It has no social programs: These remain the concerns of national governments.

The council is becoming a new level of government, to which Brussels (the capital of the European community), Tokyo, and Washington have transferred some sovereignty. In fact, however, this authority is not surrendered. The council is a private organization under contract to the three national governments to assume some of their responsibilities that can be better carried out in common. Should the council exceed its authority in a particular area, that contract can be rescinded and authority returned to the national governments.

Most of the functions of the Northern Council are informational and are carried out by networking with individual governments, research organizations, and transnational companies. Great emphasis is placed on the confidentiality of information, with the result that governments, research organizations, and corporations all have access to up-to-the-minute information about the global marketplace. This information speeds and improves the decision making process at all levels, public and private.

It is expected that developing countries will apply for membership in the Northern Council as they move toward its economic objectives. Thus the move to world government is gradual, consensual, and cooperative, not coercive.

INSTITUTIONS

As the revolution ends and the age begins, innovation will turn from the development of new industries and technologies to social change. This finds its expression in the making and transforming of institutions. At no time since the Small-Business Revolution has a more profound transformation of our institutional structure been undertaken.

Three major transformations will occur at the transition to the Information Age. A new type of institution appears, without physical presence: the not-for-profit network. A second change is the explosive growth of the self-sustaining community, or commune, providing a safety valve for an increasingly economized society. And a social institution, the home, is transformed as it becomes the locus of work and entertainment which once took place away from home in specialized buildings.

The decentralization of information work is the factor that most provokes change in the Information Age. Many office buildings are converted to condominiums, as filing cabinets, desks, and office dividers are thrown out. Many of these are occupied by executives, who need intimate access to colleagues to explore and consummate deals. Urbanists are delighted with the trend, as this humanizes the downtown area. Rush hours diminish. Social services and facilities grow.

Most information workers labor at home. The cost of going to work (the time wasted in traffic, in office politicking, and in looking for misfiled documents), and the cost of providing office space and facilities translate into enormous savings for the company and less expense and more free time for the worker. For those whose companies are global, the work may spread out over twenty-four hours, placing the information worker on call, like a doctor or fireman.

Once work is freed from the forty-hour week, various members of the family may work for periods ranging from a few hours to long stretches. Taking care of children can alternate with time at the work station and can be shared with family members. School children have their own stations, and much of school is on-line.

To some, this is a return to the worst periods of cottage industry, where families labored late into the night spinning and weaving, stopping only for sleep and food. To others the electronic cottage is more of a castle, with many rooms in the mansion and many pleasures to be shared. In either case, the transformation of family life and life-style will be dramatic, the impact on values immense, and the revitalization of the countryside as great as any since the arrival of the automobile.

NETWORK INSTITUTIONS

In general, Information Age institutions will tend to be networks rather than buildings, global rather than national or regional, and user-funded rather than financed (and influenced or controlled) by the state. Networking, which by 2006 has transformed the business world, will have an equally dramatic effect on our social life.

Those who work at home at an on-line terminal will tend to use the device for social purposes in their spare time. Clubs and associations will meet on-line. Lobbies and political-pressure groups will be relatively easy to form and very difficult to ignore. Geographic limitations will decline as telecommunications costs fall. The strength of professional associations will increase. Consumer groups will be quick to respond to changes in prices, service, and quality. Electronic bulletin boards will inform every conceivable interest. Used articles will find a quick market. Spare time will be easily sold. And as real-time language translators become available, the sense of community will widen to include the world.

In such a network world, there is little place for schools. The ideas on which they are based—collective learning, the "socializing" of children, the convoy classroom, and the lengthy exposure to national and social propaganda—may go rapidly out of fashion. Schools will be deemed counterproductive in an age based on creativity and entrepreneurial behavior, inappropriate when computerized learning is so much more efficient, and inconvenient when the electronic castle is located in a small community or off in the wilderness.

Those schools that remain are likely to be private. They will be run by corporations (such as the GSC) which have established their trustworthiness, efficiency, and global-mindedness, and which are oriented to growth, capable of turning out entrepreneurs, and likely to offer lifetime careers to graduates. These schools will largely be found in developing countries that have contracted with the GSC for bootstrap education.

Universities, hardly changed since their beginnings as professional schools a thousand years ago, will be shattered by innovation. Some will become largely on-line organizations, marketing courses and certifying intellectual accomplishment. Others will identify with industry and develop training programs to suit their special needs. Still others will focus on the preparation and sale of courses in software stores and through the library system. Professional schools may assume a responsibility for keeping their graduates up-to-date on changing knowledge and skills. Faculty members will increasingly make their income from on-line consulting, while consultants increasingly teach.

The market for packaged courses (which includes the right to sit for an accreditation exam) will prove extremely competitive. Popular professors, whose classes were limited by geography, language, and size of classroom, will reach enormous audiences around the world and be well rewarded with royalties. Smaller universities, with lower-rated faculty, will become resellers of top-rated courses, or trade schools. Many will close their doors.

As human capital grows in importance, specialized combinations of skills, knowledge, and experience will become more marketable through the network, and the business of accreditation will grow in importance. The big accounting firms will stress this remunerative side of their auditing business and issue carefully documented and tested résumés under their name to candidates and employers. As measures of quality improve, firms which were merely bean-counters to the Industrial Age will become judges of excellence. Once measured, human capital may then be invested, rewarded, and recorded in the balance sheet, alongside its financial counterpart.

Hospitals, saturated with technology, will become less important as network consultation and preventive medicine spread, but they will always be needed for the isolation and treatment of new diseases and for the repair of victims of accident, crime, and war. These two functions, treatment and repair, are likely to be separated physically to check the spread of infectious diseases, which inevitably appear faster than they can be controlled.

Another group of global institutions benefiting from network connections with the on-line community are those which have established moral positions and can serve as global forces where governments fail—like the activist Greenpeace Foundation, the impartial Amnesty International, and the quietist Red Cross. The growth, success, and moral power of these private organizations will stand as a silent criticism of the failure of national governments to maintain moral or even military authority.

SELF-SUSTAINING INSTITUTIONS

There will be many to whom this electronic networking of commerce, schooling, employment, and social contacts is grossly dehumanizing. They will bend every effort to restore human contact and values as they once knew them to be. Their instrument of preservation is the self-sustaining institution.

In some cases, self-sustaining means well endowed, like a great university with enormous sums invested in blue-chip stocks and real estate. As experience teaches, however, the financial marketplace can betray even the staunchest endowment over the years. The only truly self-sustaining institution is one which houses its staff, grows its own food, makes its own power, and produces sufficient goods or services to trade for what it can't provide.

In the Information Revolution, North American communes stabilized at a tenth of one percent of the population. Because of the prevalence and variety of robots and other forms of office and factory automation, the number of jobs or opportunities will continue to hover below the number of people seeking fulfillment in work. Those not inclined to entrepreneurial activity and those not in sympathy with the new corporate global society will have a number of courses open to them. They can join the humanist underground, the neonationalists who seek a return to a package of political divisions, Commercial Age culture, collective education and state-funded services. They can find work in one of the global institutions seeking to promote social objectives, or they can join a collective. By 2006 the share of population in self-sustaining communities may have grown tenfold, numbering tens of millions across the three Northern continents. Many of these will have joined a new monastery.

The new monastery, based on an economic model fifteen hundred years old in the West, (and millenia more in the East), is a classic institution that usually finds renewal at the start of each economic age. During the five dark centuries between the fall of Rome and the Small-Business Revolution, monasteries kept the arts and crafts alive, and stored and copied manuscripts not only of Christian texts but of other civilizations and cultures as well.

By 2006 there will be those who see the new Northern civilization as a threat to humanist culture and arts, and who will dedicate themselves to their preservation through secular, Buddhist or Christian monasteries. Monasteries could help keep alive the crafts of the pre-electronic as well as the preindustrial world. They could offer refuge and sustenance to scholars while they researched and composed books too costly for the information marketplace. They could keep alive the communities of scholars abandoned by the closing of smaller universities under the new regime.

The new monasteries could devote themselves to rehabilitation of criminals and the habilitation of the urban underprivileged and untrained. They might look after teenage mothers determined to have and keep their babies, and set them on the road to economic survival. For these socially useful services they might be reimbursed by the state or concerned corporations.

By these or similar acts of renewal, monasteries, one of the first great institutions of the West, could last another fifteen hundred years. Their great secret is what they offer: an economic way of escaping the demands of the economy, a life of spiritual development in the company of like-minded souls, and a level of human activity that is unquestionably good. They are also ahead of their time: They are preparing the basis for human relationships in a closed environment, essential for a space colony or interplanetary spaceship.

THE REVOLUTION'S SECOND WAVE

2025 to ?

Hardly had the Information Age settled down to sort out its problems and come to terms with its new modes of production, when a second Information Revolution erupted. Where will it happen? And on what technology shall it be based?

It won't likely happen in Japan or its Asian imitators, or in North America or Western Europe, for these triad economies will be quietly digesting fifty years of revolution and twenty of stable economic growth. Africa, South America, and Southeast Asia will be growing smoothly under the wings of their triad partners. India,

China, and the Soviet bloc, however, will follow socialist paths to independent economic growth. From America they will have learned much about developing and unleashing human capital; and from Europe and Japan about running a mixed economy. Let us set the Second Information Revolution in the second triad.

For their technological breakthroughs, we shall give them fusion power, portable nuclear packs, biotechnology, and a collective will to make tourism, already the world's largest industry, their private domain.

India will have long since passed China as the most populous country in the world. Together, the second triad will account for nearly three billion people, compared to one billion in the North. Their collective history extends back through time to periods of glorious splendor, which they have boldly recreated and packaged to appeal to travelers and globalists from around the world.

While the Soviet historical legacy is poor when compared to its partners, Soviet space hotels and space hospitals will be enormously attractive and very profitable, as will their space factories. These developments will be funded in part by returns from their fusion reactors—a complex technology they will be the first to master and which avoids the dangers and costs of Northern nuclear plants.

In our scenario, the Soviets will also be the first to master the safe packaging of portable nuclear reactors, small enough to be carried by one person, powerful enough to provide a house, truck, or small ship with power for a number of years, and to run an automobile for its lifetime. At first, the North will refuse to license the technology on the grounds of safety, but the second triad market will be sufficient to support economies of scale. Years of operation will prove the technology safe, and eventually, as the West begins to master the technology, licensing will be allowed. The Soviet's lead, however, will keep it ahead of its rivals in this massive new industry.

Collaboration between the two triads will become essential as the oceans rise from melting polar ice caps. By the 2020s, the greenhouse effect, so long feared, will threaten to inundate the coastal cities of the world, and in the face of this common danger a global plan will be needed. To cool the arctic, the Soviets and the North Americans will at last undertake their long-planned redirection of rivers emptying north. Needless to say, there will be ample use for this water in the parched farmlands in the Soviet south and the American South West.

DECLINE OF THE INFORMATION AGE

The traditional causes of decline of economic ages, we have seen, are overtaxation and overregulation, structural rigidity that prevents innovation, institutional corruption, lack of belief in the economic system, hopelessness of the young, moral failure of leaders, tyranny of officials, arbitrary confiscation, counterproductive government measures, and a stagnant economy. As the Information Age wears on, all of these factors will begin to grind down the cutting edge of the economy, and the spirit of innovation. The networks will turn into caste systems whose effect is more to exclude pushy opportunists than foster economic growth. Innovation centers and laboratories can only be accessed by those with the proper connections who can afford the huge budgets now needed to innovate.

Here is how economist Paul Strassman, writing in *Information Payoff*, foresees the end of the Information Age:

> It is already possible to speculate about the outlines of a social order to follow once the service society reaches its own limits of development.
>
> If a service society is successful, it may overinvest in supporting unproductive individuals for political purposes, it may misdirect its educational system to increase the power of the state over mental development of individuals, it may misapply the talents of its workforce to destructive forms of enjoyment, it may create costly totalitarian institutions to compensate for societal malfunctions, and it may consume any remaining surplus in the attempt to preclude further evolutionary changes through further development of knowledge. If a successful service society pushes its development beyond the productive limits of its managerial capabilities, its prosperity will decline.
>
> What may happen when a successful civilization starts its decline is anybody's guess. This possibility is many decades away, not just a few years, as futurists have suggested. Orwell's 1984 was, after all, too early a date for the creation of a society completely monitored and directed by a computer-aided dictatorship.

Once the corporate regime is established, in the second half of the next century, taxation will pass from the government to the corporation, through the setting of prices. At first, this will be restrained by the fear of government action and by competitive pressures; but as certain products and services become dominated by particular globals (the market for safe nuclear power units, for instance, is owned by one group), prices will tend to rise, threatening the stability of the system. Although the globals grow by encouraging creativity and innovation, if they decide not to support a new product or service, there may be no other alternatives. Regulations established by the two increasingly powerful triad councils become oppressive. Critics of the system have no way to flee official displeasure of the council. No way, that is, but out.

PART FOUR

REVOLUTIONS FUTURE

Chapter 14
THE SPACE REVOLUTION
AND BEYOND

2055 ONWARD

"To every action there is always opposed an equal reaction."
> —Isaac Newton,
> *Principia Mathematica,* 1687.

"To set foot on the soil of the asteroids, to lift by hand a rock from the Moon, to place travelling stations in space, to form living rings around the Earth, Moon and Sun, to observe Mars at distances of several tens of kilometers, and to land on its satellite or even on its surface, what could be more mind-dazzling!"
> —Konstantin Tsiolkovsky,
> *Exploring Universal Expanses With Jet Instruments,* 1902.

First recorded use of rockets: 994 A.D., the siege of the city of Tzu T'ung.
> —Wu-ching Tsung-yoa,
> *Complete Compendium of Military Classics,* 1054.

Most of what was demonstrated by the 1969 flight to the moon had been known by the thirties, and developed by the V2 team at Peĕnemünde. Their great accomplishment, however, was not the technology of the rocket, but convincing the severely challenged Nazi political machine to fund it. The decision by President Kennedy in May 1961 to put a man on the moon before the decade was out was also largely political: an attempt to recoup the prestige first lost by the Eisenhower administration following the 1957 Sputnik incident, and again following the April 1961 orbital flight of Yuri Gagarin. In a speech to Congress on May 25, 1961, President Kennedy set the tone:

I believe that this nation should commit itself to achieving the goal, before this decade is out, of landing a man on the moon and returning him safely to earth. No single space project in this period will be more exciting, or more impressive to mankind, or more important for the long-range exploration of space; and none will be so difficult or expensive to accomplish. In a very real sense, it will not be one man going to the moon—we make this judgment affirmatively—it will be an entire nation. For all of us must work to put him there.

Because of the importance of political considerations, the timetable for space development during the closing years of the Information Revolution and the half century of the Information Age requires much more than a forecast of technological capability. The standard guess places events in the next three or four generations as follows:

1990s—the construction of a permanently manned space station in the low earth orbit, with material imported from earth;

2000s—lunar station, supplied from earth;

2010s—lunar colony, with material manufactured on the moon;

2020s—construction of a hotel in low orbit. Beginnings of tourism, shuttle trips and brief holidays in low-orbital space stations, visits to the moon colony;

2030s—solar power station in geostationary orbit, with material supplied from the moon;

2040s—partially self-sustaining colony at LaGrange point (gravity null point, where the pull of the sun, moon, and earth cancel each other out), supplied from the moon and manufacturing materials for other space colonies;

2050s—self-sustaining space colony for 10,000;

2060s—more and larger space colonies, the beginning of emigration from earth, and of intercolony trade.

This standard scenario, which many space enthusiasts would dismiss as overly conservative, supposes the gradual transfer of responsibility from the public to private sectors. Space promoters doubt the early practicality of commercial manufacture of space products for use on earth on any large scale. They suggest that the first major commercial use of space will be solar power stations, large arrays of solar panels in geostationary orbit whose energy is beamed to massive earth antennas in the form of microwaves and sold to power grids. Its development could be hurried by a strong ecological attack on earth-based power as demand escalates, or slowed by the prospect of low-cost and pollution-free fusion power.

The economics of space are as different from information economics as these are from the classic economics of the Industrial Age. In space, energy is free and environmental pollution is easily managed. Manufacturing has many benefits conferred by plentiful materials and energy, a perfect vacuum, and controlled weightlessness. Transportation between space stations is easy and inexpensive, and materials may be moved from low-gravity bodies, such as the moon and the almost zero-gravity asteroids, at far less cost than from the high-gravity earth.

Industrial projects of enormous size, such as the construction of self-contained space colonies and tourist facilities, are expected to be well within the investment and technical capabilities of twenty-first-century firms. A ten-thousand-person, free-floating space colony, for instance, should require about the same amount of structural materials as a large ocean liner, about a hundred thousand tons, according to the leading Western proponent of space colonies, Princeton physicist Gerard O'Neill.

In O'Neill's highly regarded scenario, outlined in *The High Frontier*, the first colony, known as Island One, will be "a sphere one mile in circumference, with sunshine brought inside through windows. If the sphere rotates twice per minute, it will provide Earth-normal gravity at its equator, near which most apartment areas can be located. . . . In such an environment each family of five people can enjoy a private apartment as large as a spacious house."

> Island One will be small, though far less crowded than many Earth cities, and it can be attractive to live in. The inhabitants can have apartments which will be palatial by the standards of most of the world. Each apartment will have a private garden, bathed every day in sunshine at an angle which will correspond to late morning. Even within the limits of Island One and its water supply the colonists can have beaches and a river, quite large enough for swimming and canoeing.
>
> Even within Island One the new options of human-powered flight and of low-gravity swimming and diving will be possible, and the general impression one will receive from a village will be of greenery, trees, and

luxuriant flowers, enhanced if the village chooses to run
with the climate and plantlife of Hawaii. Heavy industry
can be located outside but nearby, so that no vehicle
faster than a bicycle will be needed throughout the
community.

Trailing the living sphere in toruslike tubes, (shaped like a tire's
inner tube) are the factories and farms of Island One. Farming is
carried out in narrow fields running around the individual tubes.
Manufacturing is more varied: Some requires escape from gravity,
some is better performed in a vacuum. Raw materials, sent from
the moon, are stored "outside," as are finished building materials
waiting to be sent to future islands.

It will be rather easy to separate the sphere visually into
three "villages." That arrangement will permit making
the day-length and time of day of each village independent of all the others. . . . In order to get the most out of
machines, chemical processing plants, and other industrial facilities, they should be run full time. . . . In
Island One, three villages can run at time zones separated by intervals of eight hours, so that industries can be
run full time while everyone remains on his own "day
shift."

O'Neill calculates that a space crew will work for some years to
complete Island One. During that time, it will have to be provis-
ioned from the earth and supplied with building materials from the
moon. Once the sphere is completed, the workers will be able to
live in the houses they build, with their life-style gradually improving. More and more permanent workers will be brought to the
colony as living conditions permit, and they will have the creation
of farms and the landscaping of the sphere's interior as their responsibility. As the colony grows self-sufficient, the factories and
farms will be manned, and the colony will grow to its ultimate
population of ten thousand. Work will then be directed at creating
building materials for the next colonies. The process from start to
"ignition point" (where other colonies are launched) could take a
decade and would cost its investors hundreds of billions of dollars.
But from then on, the venture should be self-sustaining and very
profitable, as additional investment will come from the savings of
future colonists.

Why would anyone want to go and live in a space colony?

Crowding: "On Earth," O'Neill writes, "even with the assumed success of population control programs, the total population will rise to at least 10 billion some time in the next century. On the average we should assume that population densities here will just about triple, until substantial emigration to space communities takes place. Crowding, already severe in some areas on Earth, can be expected to get worse."

Paradise: The earth will have long since ceased to be a natural environment. Pollution has made air unbreathable, water undrinkable, allergies endemic. By contrast, the unnatural environment of a space colony may be kept pure. There is no cause for pollution, no need for heavy industry within the atmosphere of the colony. It is an idyllic environment, where even the effects of aging are slowed.

Work: While physical and office tasks have been largely automated on earth and meaningful jobs are scarce, a colony offers a lifetime of richly satisfying work, free from the fear of poverty, rejection, and helplessness that haunts earth's citizens. Like the poor but genteel Hidalgo who settled Spain's American colonies in the sixteenth century, the underutilized middle class of the Information Economy will seek adventure and fortune in the New World.

Slither: The decay of growth in the Information Age will bring about all the anguish of the end of an economic era. The temporary institutions of slither—inflation, overregulation, overtaxation, stagflation, crime, terrorism, the collapse of values, cynicism, eroticism, and neonationalism—create an oppressive climate against which the clean, simple life of the colony offers a meaningful and highly appealing alternative.

Freedom: The spread of global culture, at first a great adventure, will become oppressive to those with belief systems incompatible with the Information Economy. And so, like the pilgrims who first settled North America, some colonies will be settled by religious factions unable to coexist and flourish in the sophisticated global economy.

Assuming that the output of space colonies is other space colonies, growth of population and land area, slow at first, would accelerate geometrically. Though the first colonies on the Island One model have room for an eventual maxiumum of 10,000 souls, later Island Two models would be designed for an order of magnitude more: 100,000 to 140,000 each. These could be cylinders a mile in diameter, over three in circumference. O'Neill imagines that space population could be around 300,000 by the end of the first decade, 9 million by the end of the second, and 600 million by the end of the third. By then, population emigration would be on the order of 200 million per year. O'Neill tells us:

> The round-trip travel time for a large ship . . . could be as little as twelve days, with the outbound trip taking only three-and-a-half days—less time than is required by the fastest ocean liner for the Atlantic crossing. If each ship were to carry 6000 passengers, then about eleven hundred ships in all would be needed. That's comparable to the number of large ocean vessels that now sail the waters of the Earth. . . . Ticket costs . . . would be about $4500 per person in [1975] dollars, comparable to the present cost of a round-the-world trip, and equivalent to only a few month's earnings under conditions prevailing in the communities.

THE TRIGGER

CIRCA 2055 A.D.

It is not the commercial development of space that triggers the first phase of the Space Revolution. At first, space is but one of many high-tech industries that are generating profits and growth in the Information Age. Some order-of-magnitude improvement in its potential will occur, some synergistic completing of the economic picture. It could be a technology that will allow a major improvement in the cost-benefit ratio—perhaps a new propulsion system that will dramatically reduce the cost of getting out of earth's gravitational pull and speed the trip to the incredibly rich resources in the Asteroid Belt. Or it could be competition from a newly developed nation—China, India, or the Soviet bloc—whose exuberance carries it past the financial limitations holding back investment in the development of space colonies. What at first appears bravado and old-fashioned national chauvinism may, in twenty years, trigger profits on a scale hitherto unknown.

While the trigger is being prepared, there is an accompanying slowing in the pace of innovation that has characterized the Information Age. Opportunity, which had been spiraling open, collapses. Dissension grips the triad manufacturers. Advancement is thwarted. Real innovation dissolves into cosmetic model changes in personal robots and vehicles. Global federated corporations, led by the GSCs, stumble in their forward motion: A crisis in leadership, an inherent weakness in their constitution, an economic slowdown in the world, an increase in the failure rate of small businesses which are at the heart of the GSC formula, and growth slows.

As the opportunity to start new business closes, the service sector, floating on a sea of confidence, begins to dry. This sets the tone of an economic revolution, and unleashes the emotional aspects of slither. Cynicism, despair, eroticism, loss of belief in the system, trust only in one's feelings, and an accompanying return to drugs, romanticism, mysticism, historicism, irrationalism, antiintellectualism, and neonationalism are in the ascendant. Terrorism erupts. Crime explodes. The underground flourishes. Piracy and counterfeit challenge the legitimate economy, which is plagued by absenteeism and sabotage. Private security forces grow corrupt. No home or business is safe from thieves. None of this is new. We've seen it all before. We're going through it now.

And so it is that the self-sustaining space colony is the trigger, and that it will take twenty-five years from start of construction in 2050 before a critical mass is reached and the colonies become economically viable. This covers the emotionally destabilizing first phase of the revolution. The investment required is enormous, and the payoff is delayed for more than a generation. Even the largest globals, with their trillion-dollar annual sales, cannot match the trillion-dollar investment the new program requires before returns may be expected to cover ongoing investments. Perhaps a consortium of globals contract a joint venture with a nation still in its exuberant phase, as it moves away from socialism and into entrepreneurial growth. As we have suggested, India, China, and the Soviet bloc are likely prospects.

THE SPACE REVOLUTION
PHASE TWO: CIRCA 2080–2100

Exhausted by the ravages of slither, tired of cynicism, anxious for concrete achievement after a century of the abstract products of the information economy, intrigued by the new economics of space, the second half of the Space Revolution is a time of building. The space people are building a new philosophy, a new hope for a rational earth—and a growing belief that the space economy will prove viable and can operate on a scale which will soon cause it to exceed the earth in population and wealth production.

Inflation subsides. The market for counterfeits dwindles. Corruption is no longer tolerated. Eroticism pales, and the idea of family returns. The attack on poverty resumes. Trade with the colonies produces its rewards. Manufacturing moves into space. The ecology improves. Massive emigration begins to reduce the population. Tourism finds a new dimension with so many worlds to visit.

THE SPACE AGE
2100–2500

Each new age brings a new form of economic organization, and in the Space Age it is the colony. At first, there are many variations, as in the city-states of commercial Italy. Once our space colonies become productive and selfsustaining, once they begin profiting from intercolony trade, once they become responsible for a growing proportion of earth's consumption, they will revolt. They will no longer accept control by the consortium or the nation state that gave them being. They will reorganize their structure to suit themselves. As history is our guide, they will federate.

The power of myth is overwhelming. The proud and supercapable space teams that build the colonies of the third millennium are the masons who built the cathedrals and towns which launched the second. The Commercial Era's Westward expansion to the New World which occurred precisely halfway through the millennium—the founding of colonies, the pioneering push, the break for freedom, and the great nation-building that followed—has its direct parallel in the colonizing and humanizing of space. In many ways, the first five hundred years of the new millennium, beginning with Yuri Gagarin's flight on April 12, 1961, are the repeat of the preceding five hundred, beginning with Cristoforo Colombo's setting sail from Palos on Friday, August 3, 1492.

During the first five hundred years of this new age, the population of space continues to grow, while that of earth continues to decline. Yet it remains by far the largest of our habitats, the richest in variety, and despite problems of weather, climate, earthquake, and volcanic eruption, its ecology rapidly improves. With its historical sites reconstructed, earth is the preferred vacation for generations born on colonies, the preferred choice for sabbatical and study, the preferred headquarters for the giant space corporations and federations, the councils of which guide, without dominating, the humanization of space.

AFTER SPACE

2500 ONWARD

Is it possible that our solar system will seem crowded, that the closeting of human ambition within the confines of the largest colonies will send men looking beyond our system for expansion into the universe? And where will the quadrillions of dollars needed to mount such expeditions be found, when returns could not be imagined for generations, perhaps centuries?

We must believe it will happen. Growth is the one constant of life which defeats death. Through incorporation, we have learned to grow and make wealth, to triumph over folly, error, war, bureaucracy, rigidities, cynicism, and despair, and to accomplish miracles. This secret, almost lost with the fall of Rome, was kept alive for half a millennium in the bowels of church and monastery, for five hundred years more in our postfeudal towns, guilds, hospitals and universities, and for five hundred more in the state, it passed to the global corporation as the third millennium dawned. Such is the spirit of growth that will, before this new millennium ends, humanize the universe.

PART FIVE

STRATEGIC
INITIATIVES

Chapter 15
SUMMARY

ABOUT ECONOMIC REVOLUTIONS

Economic revolutions have much in common; their historical pattern seems to repeat. For instance, most economic revolutions are two-phased events, approximately twenty-five years each, usually but not necessarily consecutive.

It may take centuries for a revolution to work its way around the civilization, as nation after nation imitates the success of the pioneer. Some have revolutions of their own, which usually add a new dimension to the economy. Yet growth does not come only from revolution. Assimilation is another possible route into the new economy. Most progress in France came from assimilation, not economic revolution.

Each revolution adds another economic class to society, while modifying the older economic classes. Thus the established groups persist, as the economy grows more sophisticated and integrated, and things which were free become economized.

Economic institutions peculiar to the revolution are called slither. Considered wrong in normal times, slither is tolerated because it greases the transitions. Typical forms of slither include administrative bloat, inflation, smuggling, piracy and counterfeit, underground economic activity, crime, terrorism, and espionage (or "industrial intelligence").

The new economic era comes as a surprise, from an unexpected class and region. It is usually accompanied by at least one new communications medium, such as printing, theatre, recordings, television; as well as artistic ferment, new values, new institutions, new structures, and most characteristic of all, a flood of innovation.

The old age ends as the economy grows tired and innovation becomes increasingly difficult to achieve. Barriers to entry rise higher. Regulations proliferate, taxes multiply. Social classes grow rigid. Young people revolt, refuse to join the "rat race," attack older values and compromises, and rail against corruption. They seek new values, often in mysticism and romantic returns to the past, and search for truth in feelings because intellect seems sterile.

SPECIFIC REVOLUTIONS

The feudal economy established the West's religious and military aristocracy, as well as its administrative style. Everything descended from the king (or the pope). Warlords and knights received land in exchange for military and administrative service. The rest were serfs who worked and produced, had few rights, were not free, and owned nothing. The economy was not monetized. Priests were most often paid in kind.

The Small-Business Revolution saw serfs leave the manor to farm for themselves, selling to and buying from the town. Newly incorporated, the town included craftsmen, shopkeepers, and merchants who were themselves incorporated into guilds. Businesses were private property or partnerships, and all belonged to the small-business class. The Small-Business Revolution began in Italy in the tenth century, spread across Europe reaching England in the twelfth.

The Commercial Revolution began in Venice around 1200. Its distinctive features were long-distance trade and an empire of colonies that provided raw materials and exotic foods and consumed products and administrators from the motherland.

Around 1275 The Commercial Revolution passed to Florence, which developed banking, commerce, and the putting-out stystem of manufacture, as well as long-distance trade. Commercial technology included letters of credit, insurance, bills of lading, warehouses, ocean-going ships and navigation. Also the first big businesses appeared: limited joint-stock companies and holding companies.

The Commercial Revolution moved to Portugal, then Germany and Spain, and opened up new worlds to colonization, development, and plunder. They were in turn subject to piracy from the Dutch and English. England had a partial Commercial Revolution in the sixteenth century, not completed until the end of the seventeenth, when modern financial institutions were introduced. Holland's Commercial Revolution, perhaps the most complete and successful in Western history, brought her great wealth and world leadership for over a century.

England's Industrial Revolution soon followed a century after her Commercial Revolution and brought steam, factories, railroads, and immense power and empire. Everything became "systematized": trains, electricity, sewers, hospitals, education, libraries, police, and other services.

America, Germany, and Japan all had Industrial Revolutions a century after England's, beginning around 1870 and ending with the First World War. The Americans had widely imitated Britain's inventiveness and systematic approach since the 1800s, but their own Industrial Revolution had to await the unification of the country in the Civil War, the linking of both coasts by railroad lines, and the development of commerce. It produced a flood of industries, mass production, and modern management.

The Japanese passed from the Feudal to the Industrial age in one sudden burst when faced with the threat of Western domination. Under the direction of the warrior (samurai) class, massive government intervention, wholesale copying of superior Western technology, and a war every decade made Japan a modern military and economic power by revolution's end.

Atomic energy, the computer, the satellite, the transistor, the laser, the jet aircraft, the space rocket, the credit card and automation ushered in the Information Age almost simultaneously in parts of Western Europe, Japan, and the United States in the late fifties. Thus the Information Revolution is much more widespread than its predecessors, occurring in several centers simultaneously. It is now beginning its closing phase, which may last another twenty years.

In the Commercial Age, everything became commercialized. In the Industrial Age, everything was industrialized. Now everything is becoming informationized: Industrial plants, banking, government, and our institutions, even our homes become linked in a vast electronic network.

New information industries grow from basic science reduced to fundamentals: elementary particles, chemical elements, electrons, photons, quarks, ions, genes, bits and bytes are used to write or compose new products. There may well be a second round to the Information Revolution, occurring perhaps in the Soviet bloc, India, or China.

A major revolution ahead of us in the twenty-first century will make space our new home and go beyond earth's limited resources and energy.

NEW BUSINESS

The closing years of the Information Revolution may be expected to bring a number of fundamental or structural changes. Based on the model of economic revolutions we have developed, we might expect these to be:

1. *Human capital will predominate.* The desire for self-development is one of the forces driving the information economy. Financial management will no longer be an end in itself, as automation reaches the office and wipes out clerks and managers. Flexibility returns to the work place. Industrial firms will be returned to industrialists. Small businesses will be run by entrepreneurs, people who care about quality, innovation, service, fulfillment, and growth above short-term gains.
2. *Values shift from quantity to quality.* Economists who emphasize industrial production and quantitative measures are now dealing with only a fraction of economy. "Expert system" software deals with intangibles, which are becoming the bulk of the economy and

engender all the growth. Christianity, once its principal instrument of expansion, no longer constrains Western growth, which now includes Asians. "East plus West equals North" is the formula for the new civilization and determines its goal: a global civilization.

3. *Smart technology* handles routine work, leaving people free to innovate, adapt, humanize, and create. Productivity gains stem from microelectronics, a million times cheaper than a transistor or vacuum tube, with all the circuits thrown in free. Robotics and flexible manufacturing systems free factories from old constraints; office automation frees us from heavyhanded and inflexible management. Unlike the old mechanical technology which depreciates with age and use, the new technology appreciates with integration and software.

4. *Dynamic networks* replace inflexible hierarchical systems and allow kindred souls, minds, and businesses to communicate around the globe. They also permit a skeleton crew of motivated owners to run entire businesses. Network organization replaces the old hierarchical management structure. Administration, finance, industry, information, and small-business sectors are plugged in to each other and create wealth with each transaction. In this way, networks integrate the economy.

5. *New structures* emerge from new forces. Management is "outplaced" from industrial commercial and government sectors, transferring human and financial capital to the small-business sector. Small businesses integrate into federations. Many of the services once provided "free" by government are economized by "value corporations," which are widely seen as beneficial to, rather than conspiracies against, society. Privatization takes services out of the inefficient tax-consuming category, and makes them efficient as well as tax and wealth creating.

These trends are exemplified in the *general services corporation,* a federation of franchises and small businesses dedicated to growing new entrepreneurs and new businesses. The GSC "constitution" assures limits on managements's power, pursuit of quality, human values, and growth. The GSC integrates services, looks after clients from cradle to grave, and offers services once provided at enormous expense by government. The GSC proposes to make everyone an owner, ending employment except for trainees. It is also postnational, dedicated to the growth and development of regions in which it operates. The GSC is not in conflict with national or regional governments, but in their service.

More traditional industrial products, such as automobiles and personal robots, are made and distributed throughout the North by triad alliances, extremely wealthy groupings of industrial companies in Asia, North America, and the European Community.

As the Information Age matures, as the innovative revolutionary period ends, social innovation begins. The big three Northern governments transfer some authority to a Northern Council. This may be matched, in the second round of the Information Revolution, by a second triad, made up of India, China, and the Soviet bloc, which have managed to develop a lead in some major technology, such as fusion power.

The Information Age ends as all its predecessors, with increasingly oppressive taxes and regulations. Innovation becomes too expensive. Society becomes rigid. Advancement is denied. The forces of slither return, like the four horsemen, to ravage the economy.

To escape from these problems, one need only sign up for a space colony. Each colony makes its living by becoming self-sufficient and building and providing for others. Emigration from Earth speeds up. When a critical mass of colonies is reached, they federate, freeing themselves from earth's control. Thus begins the humanization of space.

Chapter 16
STRATEGIC
INITIATIVES

Given the historic facts and resultant hypothesis, what strategies should we pursue to maximize our interests, those of our country, our new Northern civilization, and the world? This depends in large part on the sector of the economy in which we function, or toward which we are heading, in the case of sectoral change.

The classical division of the economy into primary, secondary, and tertiary sectors is a product of the late Industrial Age. This system of keeping the national accounts, developed by the Australian economist Colin Clark in the late thirties, was not generally adopted until after World War II as the Industrial Era was coming to its end. Shortly thereafter, the primary and secondary sectors (roughly resources and manufacturing) went into decline, and the services sector (everything else) began its prodigious expansion.

The classical system was well suited to tallying costs and benefits of the processing, production and sale of physical things, but quite unsuited to measuring the intangibles of the tertiary sector: finance, transportation, government, education, health, tourism, entertainment, and other services.

Our historical division of the economy would place resources and manufacturing in our industrial sector, with some of each falling into the small-business and high-tech sectors. We would divide the various tertiary sector services among our commercial, administrative, information/technology, and small-business sectors.

In developing our list of strategic initiatives and opportunities for winning the future, we will use the historical division system as outlined in this book.

INDUSTRY

To find its rightful role in the new economy, industry must

1. informationize its operations, that is automate, integrate, decentralize, and globalize;
2. reduce costs while improving product quality;
3. free itself from its financial bosses and return control to industrialists who know and care about production and product; and
4. see to the growth of the markets it exploits, the people with whom it works, and the regions in which it sets its facilities.

At each revolution, the old economy is vilified for problems real and imaginary. Today, industry stands accused of despoiling the environment, of neglecting the safety, quality, and maintenance of its products, of colluding to raise prices and lower quality, of failing to contribute to the growth and development of the markets and resource areas it exploits, of favoring the home country over the host country, of failing to develop its human capital, of corrupting the authorities, and of manipulating public opinion to hide these things. The Industrial Era press is structured to provide evidence of these crimes. Many journalists believe their duty is to expose this "true face" of industry beneath its carefully groomed disguise. Scholarly researchers often seek to strengthen these convictions. Industrial Age public servants believe their mandate is to develop regulations to keep an otherwise irresponsible industry in line.

The multinational firm in particular is believed to incline to irresponsible behavior. Since the number of foreign multinationals is rapidly growing, the level of suspicion is rising and may very well lead to protectionist policies which, economists warn, could bring on worldwide depression.

Ahead lies a generation of restructuring. As we have stressed, the industrial corporation will be forced by global competitive pressure to modernize, to informationize, to automate its shop and its office, and to integrate its information flows forward to the client, backward to the supplier, upstairs to the office, downstairs to the shop floor, and horizontally to government, bankers, joint venturers, and the academic and scientific community.

At the same time, and responding to the same pressures, the corporation will be forced to automate its management in the manner we have outlined: that is, replace clerks, specialists, and middle managers with smart systems that can assure the immediate and faithful processing, generation, storing and retrieval, and evaluation of information. As this process progresses over the next generation, the firm will change from a hierarchical to a network form of organization. The transformation will be painful, And if flexibility is lost in the process, the firm may well go under.

It is one of the great synergies of our time that automating the production process should both reduce costs and improve quality. The same may well be true of the office automation process, since human strengths are maximized and human weaknesses minimized.

By careful management of the downsizing process, by in-depth training and skillful planning and investment, the industrial firm can strengthen its alliances with the small business sector and grow a family of loyal and sympathetic suppliers, while building morale and developing rather than abandoning its no-longer-needed staff. Outplacement need not be a dirty word. Used intelligently, it can be a creative and integrative act, tying together the various sectors of the information economy.

Since innovation grows harder as firms grow larger, industry could become more closely associated with small high-tech firms, providing financing and services in exchange for innovation. This will reduce the disproportionate risk born by entrepreneurs, while refreshing older firms.

Internal restructuring is not an end in itself or a sufficient answer to its critics. We need a larger view of the industrial corporation and its role in the new economy. The holiest concept in classical economics is competition. National wisdom suggests competition at home, collaboration abroad. Pursuit of these policies handicaps domestic firms, while markets gradually become dominated by foreign multinationals. This path usually leads to protectionism and economic war.

The success of Japanese industrial strategy is forcing the West to rethink the role of competition in the domestic and global market. Industry-wide collaboration, in the form of joint research ventures, was impossible under Industrial Age rules. Joint ventures with foreign firms leads to a rational partition of world markets and to a reduction of foreign control of domestic markets. A new kind of venture could appear: a triad alliance, with major partners in North America, Japan, and the European Economic Community. With triad alliances in the ascendant, the dangers of protectionism and economic war subside.

If we explore this collaborative trend further, it becomes evident that a sharing of Third World markets and responsibilities among the partners of the triad alliance is advantageous: North American triad partners look after Central and South American market development; Japanese partners concentrate on Asia, and EEC partners on North Africa and the Middle East.

As domestic markets become saturated, *growth will depend on the speed with which the developing countries improve their economies*. As the triad system matures, North American firms in various industries could collaborate in developing the economies of their adopted countries. Collaboration with government could integrate this development and assure its maximum effect. Collaboration of the triad governments would further enhance development.

The capitalization of industry is another field ripe for restructuring. As human capital moves onto the balance sheet, the overbearing role of financial capital can be reduced. Many jobs will disappear as factory and office automation mature in the next decade. Much of the remaining work can be contracted out. The remaining jobs can be capitalized, paid in shares against which advances may be drawn.

The more human capital is recognized, the less the equity market controls decisions. The time has come to take industry out of the hands of investors who are solely interested in short-term returns, and give it back to the engineers and industrialists whose interests are quality, innovation, and long-term growth.

COMMERCE

It is the function of the commercial community to integrate the economy, by

1. making and linking markets;
2. rationalizing industries;
3. providing the great services such as transportation, communications, energy, information, banking, finance, insurance, capital, warehousing, real estate, tourism, entertainment, education, life care.

Commerce is busily involved in the rationalizing, the "deconglomeration'' of industry, a problem of its own making. The current merger mania, says *Business Week*, is equaled only by that of the tycoons of the American Industrial Revolution. Surprisingly, some recent corporate takeovers have been concluded at a price many times book value. Philip Morris acquired General Foods for three and a half times times the sum of its component parts. And GM paid five times what the accountants said Hughes Aircraft was worth.

Obviously, when accountants can only measure 17 to 28 percent of a corporate giant's worth, a new method is needed. Unquantifiables such as quality, reliability, reputation, brand-name recognition, service and maintenance, corporate policy, employee pride or morale, investment in the long-term, innovation, community service, and responsible treatment of problems and crises all contribute more to value than material assets, and this ratio appears to be rising.

A major portion of this vast treasure house of unaccountable goodwill is composed of human capital. Scientists and engineers, designers and decision makers, marketers and salespersons, toolmakers and inspectors all contribute to the intangible value of a company and should share in its profits and selling price along with the holders of shares.

Various systems of token rewards to productive personnel merely postpone a rational solution to the problem. The secret to unlocking the productive power of human capital lies in measuring and suitably rewarding its value. This is particularly true and even more difficult in service companies, which account for more than half of measured GNP and over 60 percent of the labor force in Northern economies.

The commercial community cannot trade effectively in an information economy until it develops and masters information economics. This is problem number one. It must get its own house in order before it can effectively integrate the other sectors of the economy. Fortunately it already has some of the components.

Accounting firms, which measure tangible assets, could profitably undertake the auditing of human capital. Some measures may be borrowed from insurance companies, which insure a firm against loss of a key employee. But an even longer tradition of measuring human worth comes from the visual and performing arts and the world of print, where the price of a pound of a superstar's flesh or a square meter of a celebrity painter's canvas has been the subject of negotiation and contract since the time of Michelangelo and Shakespeare.

Even more fundamental is some measure of information quality, since the value of an information worker is directly related to the quality of information produced. (Again, we have five hundred years' experience in evaluating information in the arts.) The value of an office or branch, or of an entire organization, also depends on the quality of its output.

If we are going to measure the intangibles that make up the bulk of a company's value, and incorporate these into our management techniques, the most likely instrument is artificial intelligence. The expert system based on a superb broker's judgment may succeed where the econometrician fails.

The integration of global markets is the second great problem facing the commercial community. In the Industrial Age, these were prerogatives of large corporations that were successful at home and were seeking new worlds to conquer, new places for their capital. Now, however, new specialized services and products must begin in the global market if they are to find a sufficient client base to operate at all. Global market information defines these new businesses. Global networks make joint ventures possible.

Global traders are no longer dealing merely with spices and handicrafts, commodities and manufactures, but with intangible products such as tourism, culture and entertainment, software, high technology, information and business services, most of which can be transported by satellite rather than ship or plane. By making and linking these markets, the commercial community greatly expands the choice of product and service, as well as the opportunity for innovative people to create wealth and share in its rewards. It also enlarges its own business in the process.

The trade in intangibles depends on reputation, and this is particularly difficult to establish at a distance. One of the reasons for the enormous success of franchise operations is the guarantee of quality implied by the name over a decentralized and sometimes global market (e.g., Disney, McDonald's, Honda). The formation of general services corporations is a way of rationalizing the growth of the service sector, uniting the franchise community, expanding the often limited career paths offered, and undertaking service projects of larger scope (such as life care, tourism, and education). This is the kind of structural change for which the commercial sector is superbly and uniquely equipped.

There are several ways to create a general service corporation. Sears and American Express are seeking to do it by acquisition, the Industrial Age tradition in which companies are bought, sold, and traded like properties on a Monopoly board. But as Prince

Henry the Navigator learned when he "acquired" the trading port of Ceuta from the Arabs, the service sector depends on people, and if they move on, there is little of value left.

A more promising route lies in the federation of franchisors. Once the crucial role of human capital in the service sector is taken into consideration, a GSC that is entrepreneurial-based should outperform one that is entirely owned by shareholders and dependent on (under) paid employees. And a GSC that is dedicated to global growth and values may have wider appeal than one that is nationally based and esteems only the bottom line.

ADMINISTRATION

In a global information economy, the function of government is to

1. see to the safety, welfare, and prosperity of the people within its administration, and to cooperate with other governments to these ends, while refraining from belligerence;
2. see to the provision of an efficient infrastructure and accurate, up-to-date statistics;
3. set ground rules that encourage business and industry to create and share wealth, while acting responsibly; and in particular, to encourage entrepreneurial behaviour; and
4. perform these functions in the most efficient yet flexible manner possible, interfering as little as possible with income, liberty, and creativity, and turning its functions over to the private, wealth-making sector wherever possible.

At the end of every age there are always too many policemen, customs officers, inspectors, tax collectors, courtiers, and minor officials. Parkinson's Law could apply equally to the feudal church and the warlord's manor, the proliferation of guilds and guildsmen as the Small-Business Age drew to a close, the courts of the great kings and queens at the end of the Commercial Age, and the bloated bureaucracies of Industrial Age public service.

As Parkinson demonstrated, everything conspires to increase public bloat. Politicians get elected by buying votes with the taxpayers' money, promising programs without regard to cost. Public dissatisfaction results in regulations, with staffs exploding to design and police the action. Increased taxes to pay for expanded government encourage smuggling, piracy, and an underground economy, and require yet more policymakers, inspectors, and tax collectors. Public service rules and job descriptions seek fairness but encourage proliferation. Attempts to resolve problems inevitably mean more, not less, personnel.

The early eighties saw a taxpayers' revolt. Conservative governments were elected on the promise to cut back the public service and reduce taxes. The bureaucrats dug in their heels, threw up smoke screens, obfuscated, but the tide of battle is turning against them. While most public servants believe in their right to a job and career advancement and to unstrained working conditions with ample holidays and indexed pensions, they are operating under such stringent cutbacks that few actually accomplish any meaningful work, and everyone ends up writing policy that cannot be enacted for lack of funds.

For meaningful work to be accomplished, there is the private sector, and "contracting out." This has the dual advantage of reducing the cost to the taxpayer and adding to the tax base. It also brings flexibility to programs which, under public service rules, must be fair for everyone and thus not flexible at all.

Meanwhile there is much for government to do. By collaborating with industry instead of riding herd, it can help it with long-term research, simplified rules, foreign connections and leverage, intelligence and powers of negotiation, lowered infrastructure costs, and business opportunities through privatization.

Operating under constraint, Young Turks in government will turn to information technology and integrated office automation to accomplish meaningful results with limited resources. The old Parkinsonian system will collapse over the next generation and be replaced by dynamic networks of public servants dedicated to growth.

Superfluous government executives and specialists could be trained and encouraged to set up businesses, a practice that would move capital from the public sector to the private, and forge bonds with industry, academia, commerce, and high technology. This outplacement process need not be embarrassing to officials or officialdom. Properly conceived it can be both creative and integrating.

A key function of government is the gathering, interpreting, and sharing of information, but because of politicking, bureaucratic inefficiency, and bloat, this information comes to be so doctored and delayed that it is of little commercial value. The integration of the government's information flows with those of industry and commerce could provide real-time information about the state of the economy, its prospects, resources, and markets. This will have a direct and positive impact on business activity and improve the nation's competitive position and standard of living.

SMALL BUSINESS

The franchised or independent businessmen or women develops the economy, by

1. starting businesses and creating jobs, absorbing downsized labor from other sectors;
2. locating resources, discovering new industries, finding and filling niches, innovating in ingenious ways;
3. providing and developing services;
4. assembling capital and absorbing losses, making the economy flexible; and
5. federating into general service corporations.

Because of automation and downsizing, there has been and will continue to be a massive transfer of talent and capital from the industrial to the small-business sector. Soon we expect to see a similar transfer of administrators and clerks out of the public sector, and many of these will go into business for themselves, using their separation pay as capital. The fact is, today's entrepreneurs create jobs. All the jobs. And tomorrow's entrepreneurs will create all the work opportunities. Policies that help the small-business sector expand will enlarge the tax base and GNP. They should be the first priority of a growth-minded people, for without revenue and growth, nothing else is possible.

We can only eat so much food, live in so many rooms, drive so many cars. But the need for services is infinite. Materialists who mock the idea of a people prospering by taking in each other's washing are using the wrong economics: The storyteller, priest, king, and warrior prosper in even the most primitive economy, and most of today's celebrities, from entertainers and chefs to politicians and sports heroes, deal in symbolic products.

The failure rate of small businesses is high, partly because the entrepreneur is ignorant of the thousand things and tricks needed for success. This is because he or she is not trained in growing a business—and this is a mistake. Our whole education system is geared to training people for those jobs that will be eliminated as automation proceeds. Some suggest we change the government education system. Most teachers in the public system, however, know nothing about growing businesses; their whole training and orientation is toward hierarchical structures, conventional wisdom, and social if not socialist values. Pupils of the public school system don't know what to do if they can't find a job. And so a marvelous opportunity exists for developing an educational system within the private sector, using the new technology, and aimed at creating a generation of growth-makers able to find an opportunity, create a business, and express themselves economically. A privatized educational system would reduce our tax bill and contribute to the tax base, while graduating "growth-makers" able to thrive in and build the new economy.

Starting a business summons up all our resources and energies. We find the capital from somewhere: out of savings, a mortgage, from friends. Ingenuity and innovation run high. We work, not as a duty, but as though inspired. The challenge is all consuming, and it produces growth, strength, knowledge, experience, and perhaps even success (although, on the average, success comes from the third venture). Compare this to the energy level of a bureaucrat, clerk, or factory worker, and you can see why an education system dedicated to producing growth-makers, and an economic system designed to help them on their way and share the risk are priorities.

Most small business is in the service sector, which is little understood or appreciated by economists or government. By its nature, it is fragile and lacks the strength to impose its views. Strength and staying power come from franchising. But real power awaits the development of federations of franchises, the general service corporations, which combine the energy of the entrepreneur and the clout and recognition of the global firm.

INFORMATION/TECHNOLOGY

Most, but not all, small business is destined to remain small. The professional's practice, the garage or store, the restaurant, advertising agency, film company, or architect's firm each have a size beyond which they grow clumsy. Many are franchises that grow big while their individual units stay small, but some are destined to become new businesses or even new industries, and perhaps even entire economic systems. These innovative entrepreneurial enterprises often begin with "two guys in a garage [or a loft]." Apple's Jobs and Wozniak, Univac's Eckert and Mauchly, or Sony's Morita and Ibuka, are the Information Age equivalent of America's Wright brothers, or England's Watt and Boulton, or the Alberti brothers of Florence. They are doing more than starting a business, they are laying the groundwork for a new economy by

1. spinning off from well-established high-tech companies and creating new products or services, speeding innovation;
2. spinning off from universities and think tanks and other centers of higher learning, thereby converting scientific and technical knowledge to wealth;
3. developing new information products and services;
4. developing software that makes technology and networks more flexible, powerful, and integrated;
5. helping bring government services into the private sector;
6. helping other sectors of the economy and other parts of the world informationize;
7. making decentralized and global operations viable;
8. creating consumer technology that will make the home self-contained and extend the individual's earning power, network, safety, life span, comfort, pleasure, and development.

It comes as a shock to many to learn that high technology is not creating all the new jobs and that once a high-tech unit finds its market, automation quickly follows, and employment usually falls. In addition, high technology is creating the robots, automation devices, networks and software that are eliminating millions of jobs in the shop and office. In fact, high-tech is not the revolution. It is the trigger releasing the revolution.

It would be a mistake to equate high-tech's job-eliminating proclivities with a negative economic force. The IEEE, or Institute of Electrical and Electronic Engineers, with its quarter-million membership, claims to be the largest professional association in the world. IBM, a pure high-tech company, expects soon to pass its industrial rivals to become the world's largest company in terms of sales. And with the Pentagon pouring billions into high-tech-weapons procurement and research, probably equaling or even surpassing high-tech subsidies in Europe and Japan, growth in Western high technology is bound to continue at a forced pace for years to come.

Because of our materialistic heritage, we tend to think of the new sector as a branch of manufacturing. After all, a videocassette recorder has wheels; it is a machine; it is made on an assembly line like a vacuum cleaner. Even the most dedicated hackers speak of their computers as machines. This, though, is temporary. The wheels and mechanical components have gone from the calculator and the watch, and some lap-top personal computers now use solid-state memories instead of mechanical drives. Before the end of the revolution, recordings will be chips or cards that no longer require motors to play. No part of life will be spared from informationization. Energy beams could replace bullets and shells, as Star Wars research proceeds. Spaceships are already propelled by motorless chemical engines and may one day be driven by ions. Space electricity comes not from rotary generators but solar panels.

A similar move beyond mechanics is happening through bio-technology. Biological soups quietly leach metals from their ores, replacing giant crushers. Energy-intensive chemical plants yield to biologically active fermenters. As the Information Age proceeds, medicine will become more of a process of genetic control and repair, with less of the brutal mechanical and surgical intervention of Industrial Age medicine. And the time is approaching when the answer to spinal injury is nerve-growth genetics, rather than mo-torized wheelchairs. Already computers are bypassing spinal breaks to activate atrophied limbs.

To most, high-tech is magic. Hence the problem integrating it into the economy, into our plans, into our investment portfolios, into our lives. The shocks that we have experienced because of high tech are intimations of earthquakes to come, as artificial intelligence comes on-line, memory costs fall, expert systems bring professional advice and instruction, and work structures flatten. Gene-splicing programs will curl or uncurl our hair, even before we are born. As the imitation of life takes on soul-shaking dimensions, traditional ways will collapse, beloved institutions become redundant, and human potential explode. Interpreting this change will be as important as the change itself.

CORPORATE CONSTITUTIONS

When we contemplate all the changes taking place in the private sector, the new responsibilities it assumes from government, and the potential size and global extent of its operations, we come to realize that we are changing the way we run our civilization.

Industrial firms are starting to restructure into triads and could carry high-tech firms with them as part of the family. Commerce is beginning to restructure into general service corporations and could integrate the small-business sector into these wide-ranging global ventures. When they reach a certain size and take over social services, they become political forces. Their constitution is no longer a private matter, but one that concerns us all.

The creating of corporate constitutions will become the most important work of the next generation, defining the shape and the spirit of the next millennium. The rights, development, opportunities, freedoms, and wealth of the members of the North, and ultimately of the world, will find their first expression within the next twenty years. The generation now taking power will be remembered, along with that of Elizabeth I, of the Medici, of the French and American Revolutions, as the founder's of the new age.

PERSONAL INITIATIVES

Quite apart from the institutional strategies already described, what can the individual do to win the future? Strategies fall into four categories. The first group deals with values: understanding and developing measures of quality in a quantitative world. The second group deals with direction: integrating toward a postnational, or global, economy and culture. Thirdly, there is the question of means: understanding and using information technology. Finally, there is the question of putting all this to use: strategies for action; making what you believe in happen.

VALUES

As the emphasis shifts from monetary to human capital, we have a dual responsibility. The first is to ourselves: to develop or individuate our personality and understanding until they become clear, effective, and in tune with the times. The second is toward others: to help them do the same. This drive for self-development and self-reliance is fueled by the volatility of the economy, the restructuring of the corporation, and the instability of employment. The more turbulence threatens, the greater the need for strength. Many are buffeted about and uprooted, brain-damaged by their education and professional experience, frightened by the new. Others grow stronger as they see their strategies work; or strengthened by failure, they set out to try again, carrying others with them and helping make them strong. In an economic revolution, a region thrives in proportion to the number and strength of "growth-makers" it contains.

After two centuries of quantification, as more and more corners of our existence yielded to arithmetic evaluation, the emphasis now shifts to qualitization, onto those with the skill to make judgments about intangibles, and to smart programs, or "expert systems," that can evaluate the unquantifiable. As the search for quality spreads, those who understand the rules upon which judgements are based, and who have the wit to apply them, will be increasingly called on to make decisions and will receive above-average rewards. As these smart programs move through society, transforming its basic structures, the creation and application of expert systems will become our most strategic skills.

The organizational world is confronted by those who question its values. Government, corporation, and institution are endowed with Industrial Age objectives that may no longer be valid, or in our interests, or in those of the new Northern civilization or the world. It is our task to question organizations whose purpose is to push a narrow set of interests against the greater good. It is our task to debate and develop these new values, be they ecological, developmental, economic, organizational, or humane.

This will require courage and depth and energy. Particularly since the frightened forces of reaction are speaking out through conservatism (cut back *all* government growth except armaments), fundamentalism (a narrow and exclusive Christianity at a time when the North needs to reach beyond religion to find common ground with non-Christians), and nationalism (jobs and growth here at the expense of those of our customers and friends in the rest of the North or the world).

When everything is changing, it is time to redefine "motherhood" values. Corporations are good to the extent they bring growth, variety, and quality to their markets, as well as fulfillment to those who labor on their behalf. Governments are good to the extent they protect and see to the growth of their human and corporate citizens, as well as that of the rest of the world, in the fairest, least restrictive, and most flexible way. Institutions are good to the extent that they protect or enrich society and foster growth, variety, and integration. Technology is good to the extent it helps people, corporations, governments, and institutions carry out these goals efficiently and effectively.

In general, the old industrial society was based on complex sets of rules: boxes within boxes, all carefully and painstakingly coordinated. The organizational world, the bureaucracy, does not tolerate flexibility, unless, of course, there is a rule to cover it. Exceptions soon become precedents. It's one vast and interlocking machine, quite inappropriate to a revolutionary period marked by rapid and accelerating expansion, integration, and change.

In such a period, flexibility becomes a virtue rather than a weakness. The rule book and the decision-making hierarchy are handicaps to growth. More and more situations become exceptional. Computers are designed for "fuzzy logic" instead of rigid rules. Businesses that can grow to meet unforeseen demands rather than always saying "No" or "Wait and see" move ahead of their less flexible rivals. Government programs, set out in rigid detail, usually miss the really innovative and exceptional cases they should be helping, and are plundered by the loop-holers who don't need (but know how to qualify for) aid that should reasonably be refused. The challenge before us is to soften the rule book, to fight rigidity as a form of stupidity, and make flexibility a cardinal virtue at least until the new age has found its course.

DIRECTION

As the West struggles to become the North and to integrate profoundly different value systems, all elements of society are challenged. Quebec has decided to integrate with Canada, which is trying to decide to integrate with the United States. The members of the European Community are seeking deeper integration despite their nostalgia for national greatness and autonomy. China is seeking to Northernize, that is, to integrate itself into the Northern civilization and marketplace. If successful, it could regain or at least share the world leadership it lost in the fifteenth century. Marxism, which sought to unify the industrial world, is outdistanced by the rapid integration and growth of the information economy as it spreads across the North.

A lifetime ago, Oswald Spengler saw the decline of the West in its cultural sterility. He failed to foresee that a popular industrial culture would integrate and unify the West and carry it beyond its Christian shores. Fifty years ago, world historian Arnold Toynbee warned that outside barbarians would soon tear our Western civilization apart as our leaders and goals grew weak. Before he died in 1975, though, he concluded that, just perhaps, we might integrate with the barbarians, whom he recognized as Asians, and start the cycle anew.

The overwhelming goal of the Information Age is the integration of the world economy. Global corporations push global products into global niches. Global culture, seen by Marxists as the Coca-Colonization of the world, has made Charlie and Mickey, Lucy, Luciano Pavarotti, Elvis, J.R., Princess Di, Pope John and PacMan into global celebrities. The saintly Beatle John Lennon may not be as famous as Jesus Christ, as was once contended, but he is perhaps as well known, loved and deeply mourned as his Russian namesake, Vladimir Ilyich Lenin. A generation from now, a mass-produced conversational robot endowed with an appropriate personality and better suited for sharing affection than washing dishes could eclipse them all. Global culture may seem shallow and vulgar to the elite, but it is not sterile, it is of our time, it transcends religion and politics, and it is just getting started in building a common heritage.

Integration through the consumption of global culture is a relatively passive activity, however active it may seem to a participant in a Live Aid rock concert, but it has another dimension. For companies of two nations to venture together, they must strive for a consensus. No marriage-maker can force them together; no act of Parliament of Congress can mandate their collaboration. Striving for a consensus means adapting, changing oneself to move toward an understanding. This voluntary self-transformation, this growth toward a common ideal in pursuit of a common prosperity, is changing our world like a geological force.

Integration is the direction the North has chosen. Business leaders in Europe, North America, and Japan have set out a global agenda. Much hope is placed on the power of upcoming technology to bring about the development and integration of the world. Fifth-generation computing will soon begin to break down barriers of illiteracy, rigid hierarchies, and technological backwardness. Politics, traditional culture, and religion are becoming the forces of darkness opposing growth. In the end the grandson of the transistor radio, the son of Walkman will prevail: the hand-held conversational computer, with its endless fund of know-how, its patient willingness to explain, and its caring personality.

Integration as a direction is by no means confined to the global stage. Everywhere we work, play, converse, learn, or interact, it will be our beacon. It will break down barriers and borders, languages and customs, taboos and prejudices, antagonisms and confrontations. It will help overcome the errors of inexperience, the delays of bureaucracy, the shortsightedness of politicians, the ignorance of teachers, the exclusiveness of the professional, the pride of birth, and the hobbles of race and nationality.

We will team up to grow a company, make a film, change a law, right a wrong, build a house, do some science, play a sport, and, as Marshall McLuhan once called it, learn a living. All this is like our parents' barn-raisings, town meetings, and social clubs. But the difference is this: Our teams need not be in the same place. Some of our teams will be networks rather than gangs, computer conferences rather than meetings, spread halfway around the world.

MEANS

For us to express the values of flexibility, quality, individuation, and customization, and to work toward integration, we must both understand and use information technology and smart networks. Our objectives and values can only be pursued if we are freed from energy wasted in machine work. Automation is not just a way of cutting expenses and building quality. It is way of giving rote work to machines and robots and concentrating on what is creative, growth-building, and fulfilling.

Creating and using networks is not just a way to short-circuit the bureaucracy. It is a way of organizing our life, work, and society that augments our reach, amplifies our knowledge, and multiplies our effectiveness. It is a way of organizing our thought, so we see the new connections and escape from the hard-wired systems of industrial thinking and from the aristocratic goals of the Commercial Age.

By thinking economically and using the technology wisely and imaginatively, we can turn problems into opportunities, expenses into profits, burdens into challenges. Gordon Moore, one of the pioneers of the microchip, recently boasted that his industry is selling million-circuit microchips for far less than individual transistors sold for a generation ago, "with the connecting circuits given away free." That's a millionfold gain in productivity, and the end is nowhere in sight. There has never been anything like it before in a comparable span of time. The challenge is to put it to use for what we see to be the good. This can only be done if we understand it and have some creative idea of where we should be going. If not we, who? What else should we be doing that could have such a powerful effect?

ACTION

Once we've established our values (understanding and developing measures of quality in a quantitative world) and direction (integrating toward a postnational, or global, economy and culture) and are comfortable with the means (understanding and using information technology), we are ready to put all this to use: to develop strategies for action; making what we believe in happen.

Strategies grow out of our understanding of society's goals and of where we are in the path toward their realization. Naturally, each of us sees these goals in terms of our individual talents and skills. Our vision, however, is influenced by our childhood conditioning, by our reading and viewing, and by direct observation and experience. The problem is that much of this conditioning belongs to another age, and to other people's dreams, and is wrong for our time and for us. We must take the time to sort this out for ourselves. Until we do this, our lives remain accidental.

The initiation of the young Indian brave through isolation in the wilderness is a vital element missing in our society. We hurry from school to job without pause. We are buffeted by chance. Then one day, sooner or later, we are spit out of the system, rejected. This is usually when we start to think. Fortunately it is not too late. It is never too late.

The technique for defining goals and actions that I am describing is "dualizing," creating a duality of the ideal and the actual. Everyone will have a different and personal view of what that ideal should be. For the student it will be different from the young manager's, or from that of the long-time employee caught in the existential awareness that his or her life, so far, has been wasted. It is the very variety of visions which makes society rich, and their common elements which make it move.

The other side of the duality, the current reality in relation to the ideal, depends a lot on where we are. The economic revolution usually begins somewhere else, in a relatively small region. Then it spreads in waves to small pockets in each region, and then out from these pockets. Those regions that were slowest to adapt to the industrial wave may be fast off the mark in the Information Revolution, as the sudden rise of the sun-belt states of America suggests. Meanwhile the industrial and commercial Northeast was still clinging to earlier dreams. In a generation, backward South Korea leaped from per-capita income of eighty-two dollars to one accelerating through the thousands-per-year in a generation.

One place this continuum from actual to ideal can be seen and exploited is in the shift from urban to small-town America that began, the demographers tell us, in 1975. Here, the rush to open high-technology service businesses is pushing the revolutionary wave through its closing phase and transforming rural America in a way the car did in a previous revolution. One thing about a revolution: It creates a lot of opportunity.

Once our goal is stated and our field of action settled, we must prepare ourselves by acquiring the knowledge, polishing the skills, and arranging the material requirements of our task. The most important acquisition is the ability and energy to comunicate our goal to those involved. If this is a network goal, reaching people far away, perhaps in a foreign land, communication must be particularly clear. This demands an understanding of the psychology, goals, and values of others, as well as an ability to discern where they are in the process of moving from an industrial to an information mode.

This ability to communicate is not one we are born with, nor one that we normally learn in school. It is a quality we must strive to acquire, along with the other relevant skills required for the successful pursuit of our goal.

Finally, the moment for venture arrives. Perhaps it means quitting your job, or borrowing money, or signing a lease, or moving to a region more compatible with your goals. In many cases, it will mean helping the shop you are with change course, informationize, globalize, restructure: the entrepreneurial option. Do it. It doesn't matter if you fail, for failure is one of the steps to success. Venture. Make it happen. Act. If there is one thing a revolution teaches, it is that there is no such thing as security, except in your ability to be a growth person, able to dream and plan and share and act.

We are learning to see the economy not as an enemy to be conquered or subdued, nor a mountain to be climbed. It is the life-giving force of civilization. It can integrate our belief, culture, fulfillment, and energies. It is humanizing our planet, and it will humanize the universe. May this force be with you. May you be with this force.

SELECTED BIBLIOGRAPHY

T. S. Ashton's *The Industrial Revolution, 1760–1830,* Oxford University Press (1948); and T. S. Ashton *et al; Capitalism and the Historians: A Defense of the Early Factory System,* University of Chicago Press (1954), edited by F. A. Hayuk.

Postwar British economists reexamine the Industrial Revolution and the origins of the myths of child labor and the oppression of the working classes.

David Baker's *The History of Manned Space Flight,* Crown Publishers, New York (1981).

A highly detailed and fully illustrated account of the history of rocketry and manned space flight. The bravery of the first cosmonauts and astronauts as well as the persistence of the industry's pioneers comes through. Contains logs, project data, comparison tables of Soviet and American spacecraft.

Daniel Bell's *The Coming of Post-Industrial Society, A Venture in Social Forecasting,* Basic Books, New York (1973–76).

This most academic of futurists looks at the factors underlying the transition to an information society, which he sees as based primarily on university research. A classic study with historic antecedents carefully placed in perspective.

Fernand Braudel's *Civilization and Capitalism, Fifteenth to Eighteenth Century.* Vol. 1. *The Structures of Everyday Life* (1979–81); vol. 2, *The Wheels of Commerce* (1979–82); vol. 3, *the Perspective of the World* (1979–84), William Collins Sons & Co., London, and Harper & Row, New York.

The master historian of the West outlines the origins and mechanisms of the commercial economy in this monumental three-volume study. Despite the dates in the title, Braudel takes us back to the first stirrings of the Western economy in the eleventh and twelfth centuries and details the operations of the fairs, markets, and guild shops of the Small-Business Era. At the conclusion, he carefully sets the stage for the Industrial Revolution.

Crane Brinton; *Anatomy of Revolution*, Prentice-Hall, Englewood Cliffs, N.J. (1938, 1952), and Vintage Books (Random House), New York and Toronto (1965).

Armed political revolutions in England, France, America, and Russia are studied, compared, and categorized in this classic study. Arising from many of the same circumstances, they would appear to be an unhappy alternative to economic revolution. Contains an exhaustive annotated bibliography.

Zbigniew Brzezinski's *Between Two Ages, America's Role in the Technotronic Era*, Viking Press, New York (1970).

An early description and analysis of the economic social and political forces tearing our age apart and pulling the new one together by the man who was to become President Carter's senior adviser.

Edward McNall Burns, *Western Civilizations: Their History and Their Culture*, W. W. Norton & Co., New York (1941–80). Eighth Edition.

A good schoolbook history of the West. First written in 1941 and revised and revised, it brings a welcome critical economic bias to the history of the West and the civilizations that led up to it. I kept going back to it.

Thomas Carlyle's *Heroes and Hero Worship and the Heroic in History* (1841). Collins clear type edition, Ca. 1900.

A series of public lectures delivered in 1840 on "greatness" and the evils of democracy and the Enlightenment. This thundering Scotsman helped form the moral fiber and cultural outlook of Britain at the beginning of the railroad age.

Alfred D. Chandler, Jr.'s, *Strategy and Structure: Chapters in the History of the American Industrial Enterprise*, MIT Press (1962); and *The Visible Hand, The Managerial Revolution in American Business*, Harvard University Press, Cambridge, MA (1977).

Superb analysis of the origins and development of the corporation and management during the American Industrial Revolution.

Jan de Vries' *The Economy of Europe in an Age of Crisis*, Cambridge University Press (1976). 1600–1750.

Who better to describe the great Dutch Commercial Revolution than a Dutch historian who happens to teach at Berkeley?

Peter Drucker's *The Age of Discontinuity, Guidelines to Our Changing Society*, Harper Colophon, New York (1968).

Not only the most influential management consultant of our time, but one of our best futurists. Drucker's vision of the transformation to an information economy was the first to appear, and it stands up as useful and insightful reading on structural change after nearly twenty years.

Richard Eells' *Global Corporations: The Emerging System of World Economic Power*, The Free Press (Macmillan), New York (1972, 1976).

Of all the various statements about the conflict between sovereign states and multinational corporations of the early seventies, this book has the wisest and richest vision, and stands up well today. "We live in a revolutionary age comparable with that which ushered in the international system of nation-states at the end of the Middle Ages. Historical perspective is prerequisite to a full understanding of present tensions as compared with those of earlier epochal changes. . . . A revolutionary age brings to the surface conflicts over man's purpose on earth, deep divisions over ends as well as means, sharp conflict over allowable aspirations in the young, and, as an inevitable consequence, profound debate over the meaning of business."

George Gilder's *Wealth and Poverty*, Basic Books, New York (1981); and *The Spirit of Enterprise*, Simon & Schuster, New York (1984).

Gilder is a powerful spokesman for the economic imperative and a warm advocate of the entrepreneurial virtues.

Jean Gimpel's *The Medieval Machine: The Industrial Revolution of the Middle Ages,* Holt Rinehart & Winston, New York (1976); Penguin Books, New York (1976).

A lively account of the Small-Business Age as the West's first Industrial Revolution. Very good on the role of the monasteries in transferring the new technology throughout the West.

Mark Girouard's *The Return to Camelot: Chivalry and the English Gentleman,* Yale University Press, New haven, (1981).

The origins of the Victorian idea of the gentleman are traced back to the age of chivalry in this gorgeous book. Many Victorian institutions, from the playing fields of Eton to the Boy Scouts, helped carry the English gentleman's muscular Christianity to the world.

Richard Goldthwaite, *The Building of Renaissance Florence, An Economic and Social History,* Johns Hopkins University Press, Baltimore (1980).

Braudel taught historians to look for pattern and meaning in the everyday lives of working people. Goldthwaite's accounts of the construction industry and building trades of Florence in the Commercial Revolution help bring this important era to life.

Alex Groner (and the editors of American Heritage and *Business Week), The History of American Business and Industry,* American Heritage Publishing (McGraw-Hill), New York (1972).

An excellent overview of the state of business and industry leading up to and away from the American Industrial Revolution. Contains detailed, lively accounts of the inventors, industrialists, and tycoons who forged the most vigorous economy the world had yet seen.

Patrick Harpur (editor), *The Timetable of Technology,* Marshall Editions Limited, London, and Hearst Books, New York (1982).

Good chronology covering Western technology, year by year from

1900 to 2000 A.D., from a British perspective. Authoritative and handsomely presented.

Christopher Hibbert's *The Rise and Fall of the House of Medici,* Allen Lane, London (1974); Penguin Books, New York (1979).

Biographer Hibbert brings to life this powerful Florentine merchant-banking family, which not only improved the banking system, but used its fortune to usher in the Renaissance.

Stewart Holbrooks's *The Age of the Moguls, The Story of the Robber Barons and the Great Tycoons,* Harmony Books (Crown Publishers), New York (1953).

A highly critical look at the vigorous promoters, industrialists, and financiers of the American Industrial Revolution by a soldier-lumberjack-newspaperman-historian. "The men were as magnificent in their piratical wars as they were pathetic in their dude clothes, trying to eat with a fork, wondering how best to approach a chaise longue. They were a motley crew, yet taken together they fashioned a savage and gaudy age as distinctively purple as that of Imperial Rome, and infinitely more entertaining."

Ivan Ilich's minibooks on our professional institutions: *Celebration of Awareness* (1969), *Deschooling Society* (1970), *Tools for Conviviality* (1973), *Medical Nemesis* (1975), *Disabling Professions* (1977), *Shadow Work* (1981).

Worker priest and radical intellectual, Illich shows how the great institutions and professions of the industrial era have become counterproductive and even deadly. Much better at criticism and paradox than workable alternatives.

Interfutures, *Facing the Future: Mastering the Probable and Managing the Unpredictable,* Organization for Economic Cooperation and Development, Paris (1979).

Occasionally institutions produce valuable studies. This OECD forecast from the end of the seventies paints some illuminating scenarios for world economies to the end of the century.

Herman Kahn's *The Next 200 Years, A Scenario for America and the World* (1976), and *World Economic Development: 1979 and*

Beyond (1979), both published by William Morrow & Co., New York; and *The Coming Boom,* Simon & Schuster, New York (1982).

Herman Kahn ruffled the feathers of the intellectuals because he helped develop the idea of nuclear deterrence and pooh-poohed their fashionable pessimism about our supply of resources and economic future. Forty years of nuclear peace and the continuing discovery of new resources have proved him right. "Over the years I have been variously described as an inhumane and unfeeling warmonger (after *On Thermonuclear War*) as well as a naive and misinformed optimist (after *The Next 200 Years*). My own assessment is that I am a reasonably realistic observer whose imagination and logic often lead to unfamiliar (sometimes apparently outrageous) conclusions and speculations."

Ruth Karen (editor), *Toward the Year 2000: World Business Leaders Speak Out on the Future of Free Enterprise,* William Morrow and Co., New York (1985).

Fascinating collection of statements by European, Japanese, Arab, Indian, and North and South American businessmen on what they think might be done to promote economic growth. Very few PR statements and a lot of good sense from a wide geographical, if narrow, economic perspective.

Thomas Kuhn's *The Structure of Scientific Revolutions,* Chicago University Press (1962, 1970).

Classic analysis of scientific revolutions—how and why they happen, how they spread, and the way the old guard changes its mind. A working manual for those promoting new ideas and structural change.

Steven Levy's *Hackers, Heroes of the Computer Revolution,* Anchor Books (Doubleday & Co.), New York (1984).

An insightful account of the nature, personality, motivation, and methods of the rebellious inventors of the personal computer revolution.

Richard Louw's *America II,* Penguin Books, New York (1983, 1985)

This enterprising and perceptive San Diego journalist trooped across the United States to document the changing life-style, new towns, and privatization trends of a new America.

Norman Macrae's *The 2024 Report: A Concise History of the Future 1974–2024*, Sidgwick & Jackson, London (1984).

The brilliant editor of *The Economist* imagines how the world will be transformed over the next forty years; how America and the Soviets resolve their differences, and the kind of institutions they build together. Among other wonders, Macrae forecasts the depoliticization of government, the withering away of the state, and the internationalization of the tax and social security systems.

Lauro Martines's *Power and Imagination: City-States in Renaissance Italy*, A Borzoi Book from Alfred A. Knopf, New York (1979).

A vivid description of the steps the Italian city-states followed to take charge of the world's political, economic, and intellectual growth from the twelfth to sixteenth centuries.

Yoneji Masuda's *The Information Society*, World Future Society, Washington (1981).

Described by some as the Adam Smith of the Information Revolution, Japanese philosopher and computer specialist Masuda tours the world with his vision of global harmony attained through information technology.

Marshal McLuhan's *The Gutenberg Galaxy*, University of Toronto Press (1962).

A fascinating analysis of the West's transition from a feudal to a commercial outlook at the time of Gutenberg. Probably McLuhan's greatest book.

Jean Monnet's *Memoirs*, Doubleday & Co., New York (1975, 1978).

If any single person changed Europe more than Hitler or Napoleon, it is Jean Monnet, whose life was spent developing the theory and the agreements upon which the Common Market is based. *Memoirs* describes the process in living color.

Jan Morris's *The Venetian Empire: A Sea Voyage,* Faber and Faber, London and Boston (1980).

Venice, half Asian, half Western, and all business, started the West on its path of empire, trade, growth, and artistry. Jan Morris's attractive book helps bring all this to life. Contains a chronology of the Venetian republic to its fall in 1797.

Lewis Mumford's *Technics and Civilization,* Harcourt Brace and World, New York (1934); Harvest Books (Harcourt Brace Jovanovich), New York (1963).

Mumford saw the West in terms of technological eras before others had made the connection. Much of it reads with a freshness that belies its fifty years. Contains a marvelous bibliography, full of spirit (and occasional venom).

John Mundy's *Europe in the High Middle Ages,* Basic Books, New York (1973), 1130–1300.

Professor Mundy describes the arrival and development of the corporate spirit during the Small-Business Revolution in Europe. A magnificent piece of scholarship and synthesis, carefully organized; I kept going back to it.

John Naisbitt's *Megatrends* (1982), and with Patricia Aburdene, *Reinventing the Corporation* (1985), both published by Warner Books, New York.

Naisbitt developed the method of spotting the ebb and flow of trends by measuring the amount of space devoted to them in the press. This was very productive of ideas, but because it lacked perspective and direction, some of the megatrends turned out to be minibusts. "We are living in a time of parenthesis, a time between eras. It is as though we have bracketed off the present from both the past and future, for we are neither here nor there. Those who are willing to handle the ambiguity of this in-between period and to anticipate the new era will be a quantum leap ahead of those who hold on to the past."

Kenichi Ohmae's *Triad Power, The Coming Shape of Global Competition,* The Free Press (Macmillan), New York (1985).

Ohmae is a top business consultant representing McKinsey and

Company in Japan. He sees joint ventures in industrial and high technology leading to a triad of power—Japan, Europe, and North America. Tables chart intercontinental connections in a number of industries.

Mancur Olson's *The Rise and Decline of Nations,* Yale University Press, New Haven (1982).

Olson's theory of the forces of economic decline and awakening in Western history helps explain both the Japanese miracle and the English disease.

Gerard K. O'Neill's *The High Frontier,* Anchor Books (Doubleday & Co.), New York (1976, 1982); and *2081: A Hopeful View of the Human Future,* Simon & Schuster, New York (1981).

This Princeton physics professor has become the leading thinker in the development of space colonies and economies over the next century. We seem to be following the steps if not the timetable of his scenario.

Seymour Papert's *Mindstorms: Children, Computers and Power-ful Ideas,* Basic Books, New York (1980).

This gentle revolutionary is a disciple of developmental psychologist Jean Piaget, as well as a leading computer programming innovator at MIT. His LOGO language has young children playing with advanced mathematical concepts, and is revolutioinizing education. "I see the classroom as an artificial and inefficient learning environment that society has been forced to invent because its informal environments fail in certain essential learning domains, such as writing or grammar or school math. I believe that the computer presence will enable us to so modify the learning environment outside the classrooms that much if not all the knowledge schools presently try to teach with such pain and expense and such limited success will be learned, as the child learns to talk, painlessly, successfully, and without organized instruction. This obviously implies that schools as we know them will have no place in the future."

Karl Polanyi's *The Great Transformation: The Political and Economic Origins of Our Time,* Beacon Press, Boston (1944).

This great-hearted refugee from the Nazis describes the disorder, greed, and misery accompanying economic revolutions through Britain's history, and focuses on the Industrial Revolution.

Denis de Rougemont's *Love in the Western World,* Harper Torchbooks, New York (1940, 1956).

De Rougemont traces our romantic attitudes to love and marriage back to the troubadours of the paradisiacal but ill-fated Provence, one of the High points in Western civilization. "The Albigensian crusade, led by the Abbot of Citeaux at the beginning of the thirteenth century, resulted in the destruction of the towns inhabited by the Cathars, in the burning of their books, the slaughter and burning of the mass of the people who loved them, and the violation of their sanctuaries and supreme High Place, the Castle of Montsegur. The highly refined civilization of which they were the austere and secret spirit was brutally devastated. Nevertheless, to that culture and its fundamental doctrines we still pay tribute. We are its debtors far more than we realize."

Charles A. Reich's *The Greening of America,* Random House, New York (1970).

In the sixties, the revolution of the young in America seemed to be going somewhere, but by the time Reich proclaimed it in the seventies, it was over. A romantic statement of great beauty and charm.

Theodore Roszak's *The Making of a Counterculture,* Doubleday & Co. and Anchor Books, New York (1969); and *Where the Wasteland Ends,* Doubleday & Co. (1972), and Anchor Books (1973).

One age rejects the culture, technology, and economic system of its predecessor. Roszak's is a powerful voice raised against the mechanistic materialism of the Industrial Age.

Jean-Jacques Servan-Schreiber's *The American Challenge* (1967, 1968), Antheneum edition, New York (1979); and *The World Challenge,* Simon & Schuster, New York (1980–81).

Servan-Schreiber is France's great communicator, founder of *L'Express* magazine. His book on the dominance of the American managerial system appeared as the threat was collapsing. *The World Challenge,* in which the new economy is used to awaken the Third World, should enjoy a longer shelf life.

Oswald Spengler's *The Decline of the West* (Vol. 1, 1918; Vol. 2, 1922), first English editions, Alfred A. Knopf, New York, (1926 and 1928).

Nietzschean pessimist Spengler saw the emptiness and materialism of Western culture as a sign of its collapse, an event he foresaw concluded before the end of the present century. He was right, of course; Western industrial society has collapsed. He failed, however, to foresee that an informationized Northern society would arise to take its place.

Paul A. Strassmann's *Payoff, The Transformation of Work in the Electronic Age,* The Free Press (Macmillan), New York (1985).

Xerox's great economist looks at the technology and managerial transformation of our society as an economic revolution, and tries to explain it in quantitative terms. A fascinating and farseeing account of structural change.

Kamekichi Takahashi's *The Rise and Development of Japan's Modern Economy,* Jiji Press, Tokyo (1973).

The Japanese Industrial Revolution that accompanied the Meiji Restoration was carried out by the samurai or warrior class. Takahashi, a distinguished samurai scholar, pays tribute to his ancestors' extraordinary accomplishment.

Alvin Toffler's *Future Shock,* Random House, New York (1970); and *The Third Wave,* William Morrow and Co. New York (1980).

Journalist Alvin Toffler has twice demonstrated an artist's skill at creating images for our time that have grabbed our collective imagination and become cultural symbols. By comparing the present structural upheaval with the Industrial Revolution, he helped us understand the depth of what we are presently undergoing. He has an intuitive sense of the processes of change. "The forces that made mass society have suddenly been thrown into reverse. Nationalism in the high-technology context becomes regionalism instead. The pressures of the melting pot are replaced by the new ethnicity. The media, instead of creating mass culture, demassify it. In turn all these developments parallel the emerging diversity of energy forms and the advance beyond mass production."

Arnold Toynbee's *A Study of History,* Oxford University Press (begun 1920; twelfth volume published 1962; one volume abridgment published 1972).

The lifework of the son of the Victorian economist who first wrote of the Industrial Revolution, this massive study of twenty nine civilizations is a search for patterns that would help us guide our own. A summary volume in 1975 captured the cream of his wisdom and related it to the Asian resurgence. "If the present dominance of the West is followed, as seems likely in the light of comparable past sequences of events, by a unifying and blending of cultures, it is conceivable that Western dynamism might mate with Chinese stability in proportions that would produce a new way of life for all Mankind—a way that would not only permit Mankind's survival but would secure its welfare." Beautifully illustrated. Contains maps and comparative tables of various civilizations.

James Trager's *The People's Chronology: A Year-by-Year Record of Human Events from Prehistory to the Present,* Holt Rinehart & Winston, New York (1979).

Like daily newspapers, chronologies disguise the slow progress of great movements in the rush of simultaneous events. The best of them, however, provide an inclusive overview of world developments—and this is one of the best. Last entries, 1973. Contains an extremely detailed index.

Barbara Tuchman's *A Distant Mirror: The Calamitous Fourteenth Century,* Alfred A. Knopf, New York (1979).

The fourteenth century was "a bad time for humanity," as we struggled to get on with the Commercial Age and the business of making nations. Ms. Tuchman's picture is particularly rich and lively, despite the blackness of its theme. "It was a time of default. Rules crumbled, institutions failed in their functions. Knighthood did not protect; the Church, more worldy than spiritual, did not guide the way to God; the towns, once agents of progress and the commonweal, were absorbed in mutual hostilities and divided by class war. . . . People felt subject to events beyond their control, swept, like flotsam at sea, hither and yon in a universe without reason and purpose. They lived through a period which suffered and struggled without visible advance. They longed for a remedy, a revival of faith, for stability and order that never came."

Sherry Turkle's *The Second Self, Computers and the Human Spirit,* Simon & Schuster, New York (1984).

Before moving to California's Silicon Valley the computer revolution was centered at MIT, where psychologist/sociologist Turkle explored in eloquent detail the way computing transforms our lives and consciousness. "As the computer presence becomes more widespread, relationships between people and computers prefigure changes for our culture as a whole—new forms of intimacy with machines, and a new model of mind as machine."

Martin J. Wiener's *English Culture and the Decline of the Industrial Spirit, 1850–1980,* Cambridge University Press (1981).

A Texas history professor carefully documents the ways the British establishment put their brash industrialists "in their place" and turned off their fabulous growth machine. Gentlemanly values become the English disease if allowed to dominate the economy, and they're still preventing innovation and growth.

J. Patrick Wright, *On a Clear Day You Can See General Motors,* self-published by Wright Enterprises, Grosse Pointe, MI (1979).

Nothing symbolizes the decline of industrialism better than the ascendance of nonindustrialists to the control of General Motors, and the decline of carmakers like John DeLorean. This tale was told by DeLorean to Patrick Wright after his ouster/resignation—and before he thought better of it and tried to have it stopped. "Corporate management . . . must be returned to its traditional function of forming corporate policy and planning the company's future. This . . . would require taking the reins of the corporation out of the hands of the financial managers and putting them into the hands of competent operating executives capable of a broad understanding of the business."

INDEX